MW00380629

SAINT BERNARDS

from the Stoan Perspective

SAINT BERNARDS

from the Stoan Perspective

STAN ZIELINSKI

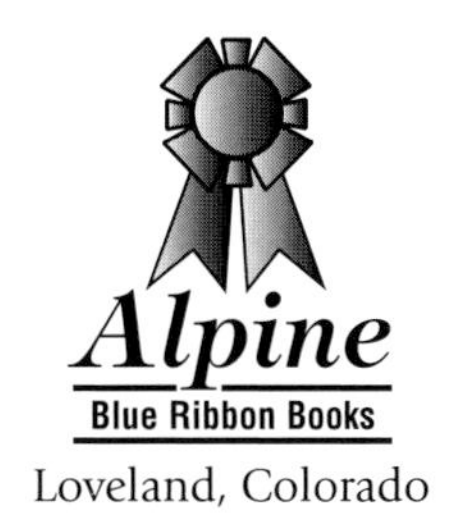

Loveland, Colorado

SAINT BERNARDS FROM THE STOAN PERSPECTIVE

ISBN 1-57779-013-8

Cataloging-in-Publication Data
Zielinski, Stan, 1932-
Saint Bernards from the Stoan perspective / Stan Zielinski. —1st ed.
p. cm.
Includes bibliographical references (p.) and index.
ISBN (invalid) 1-57779-013-8 (hardcover)
1. Saint Bernard dog. I. Title.
SF429.S3Z54 1998
636.73—dc21
98-37919 CIP

This book is available at special quantity discounts for breeders and clubs for promotions, premiums, or educational use. Contact the publisher for details.

Cover Photo: Ch. Lynchcreek's Ace v. Stoan, HOF, POE, at age seven.
Illustrations, pages 13–23: *Noel Gusa*
Cover and Interior Design: *Dianne Nelson, Shadow Canyon Graphics*

First Edition
1 2 3 4 5 6 7 8 9 0

Printed in the United States of America

Contents

Introduction vii
Preface ix
Whatever Happened to Moderation? 1
The Official Standard for the Saint Bernard 7
An Extensive Description of the Saint Bernard 24
The Movement Described in the Standard 35
The Expected Temperament of a Saint Bernard 39
The Skin Game 45
What Size Is the Right Size? 48
No Head, No Saint! 53
Proportions of the Head 56
The Muzzle 60
The Teeth 63
The Flews 66
The Skull 69
The Furrows 73
The Eyes 75
The Ears 79
Markings 83
What Is a Fault? 87
What Makes One Fault More Important Than Another? 90
Taking Care of the Puppies 95
Grading the Litter 111
Guidelines for Buying a Puppy 116
The Rewards and Risks of Inbreeding 125
Choosing a Mate for Your Dog 131
Advice for the Less Experienced Breeder 138
A Short Course on Judging Saint Bernards 145
The Perspective of a Judge Who Also Exhibits 150
Judges Who Fail to Put the Emphasis Where It Belongs 154
The Essence of Breed Type 159
The Three Varieties of Saint Bernards 164
List of Abbreviations Used in This Book 169
Index 173

A TRIBUTE TO BEATRICE KNIGHT

December 7, 1905–June 29, 1997

The Lady of Sanctuary Woods

(Left): Bea Knight with Sanctuary Woods Simply Spiffy, 1973.

(Right): Sanctuary Woods Symphony.

(Right): Bea Knight with Sanctuary Woods Endorsement as her Bernese Mountain Dogs look on.

(Left): Sanctuary Woods Yondo U Ole, who sired many fine dogs and was for a time the most popular stud dog on the West Coast.

Introduction

When my editor asked me why I decided to write this book, I was stumped for an answer. Upon contemplating the question, it came to me that I really didn't have a reason. You can't have a reason for doing something that you didn't do—and I never sat down and decided to write a book. This thing just sort of happened by itself.

All my life I have had the need to write down my thoughts in order to sort through them in my own mind; I just need to see them written out in order to evaluate their worthiness or to see if there is a better way of putting things. From time to time, I found that I had written something that I thought could be shared with others, and I submitted them to our club's newsletter. Because I spent some time as the club's newsletter editor, there was never a question about my writings being accepted. My motive for sharing these written thoughts was to either impress my fellow fanciers or to start an argument. It may be of interest to you to know that I have always been much more successful in starting arguments than in impressing people.

After thirty or so years, I found that I had quite a collection of articles that more or less expressed my philosophy of exhibiting, breeding, and judging Saint Bernards. I also found that most of what I had written when I was much newer to the game no longer expressed my feelings accurately. While rewriting some of my more ancient articles, it occurred to me that if I were to fill in a few holes, the entire collection amounted to a book.

(Left): A representative of Winifred Martin's well-known Prairieaire Kennels, located in Roanoke, Illinois. Pictured is Ch. Prairieaire Rox von Zwing Basko with his owner. Rox was sired by Ch. Basko von Salmegg out of Hilltop's Honey Baby Zwingo.

(Below): Rescue's Hallmark von Rumley, owned by Nancy Hoffman of Elk River, Minnesota. Rumley is trying to entice Sophie (the Clydesdale) and Molly (the goat) into a little playtime. This sort of behavior, as opposed to being in the attack mode, is what one should expect from the Saint Bernard.

No sooner had the thought of a book occurred to me than I excitedly started contacting the big names in the dog-fancy publishing game. This was a discouraging process, because these people had a formula for successful books that did not fit my effort. They pointed out that the big market is the pet-owning public, so that is the audience at which they wanted to aim their books. Unfortunately, all of my writings had been addressed to my peers who, like myself, were somewhat experienced but still in the learning mode.

There were two offers to consider my book if I would rewrite it so that it would appeal more to the novice and the pet owners. It seemed that the world had more of those kinds of books than it really needed, so I decided that it would not be worth my effort to make another.

It was then that my luck turned and I came across a publisher who is in business for some other reason than making a big profit. The existence of such an altruistic business is very fortunate, because there is probably no other way that a book addressed to breeders, exhibitors, and judges can ever be published. You have to wonder how long an enterprise with such a philosophy can stay in business (I have since discovered that Alpine has already been in business for twenty years!), so I must hurry and get this book published before they come to their senses.

This brings me to the question of why would experienced breeders, exhibitors, and/or judges want to read this book. The reason is that, no matter how long you have been involved in dogs, you should *still be in the learning stage.* You will find in this book opinions and advice that come from thirty-plus years of experience. All of you will have your own set of experiences, so this book should simply add to your accumulation. We all learn more from our mistakes than from our successes, and I hope that reading this book will help you spend more of your precious time advancing toward your goals than in learning from negative experiences.

Can reading this book result in producing better dogs? Will you become a more successful exhibitor? Will you become a better judge? The answer is, it's possible! If you can profit from some of the mistakes and successes that are the foundation for this book, then you should be able to avoid some of the pitfalls. If you can learn by reading about the experiences of others, then you may be able to make better choices. Should you, by standing on my shoulders, get a better look down the path you are traveling, then this book will have been worth the time and effort that you and I have both spent on it.

(Below, Left): Ch. Vanity's Regal Touch, owned by Earl and Jamie Johnson of West Oneonta, New York. The dog is working the treadmill of an antique dog-powered butter churn. While this activity is not in the Saint Bernard's usual line of work, you have to believe that the builder of this machine had a Saint Bernard type of dog in mind. It is interesting to note that there was little interest at this auction in this object until the rest of the bidders saw it working; after that, the bidding went out of sight!
(Below, Right): Feeding time at Sanctuary Woods Kennels, circa 1961, with "Granny Bea" (Mrs. Beatrice M. Knight) in the background fixing the food pans. It was a common sight to see forty to fifty Saints at one time come out of the barn together and head for the food pans en masse.

Preface

If you are going to read this book, you should know a little bit about me. I was born on August 7, 1932, and I must admit that I am much older than I want to be. I have been married since 1957 to Joany Mae, the mother of my four offspring. She also shares with me the title of grandparent. I graduated from the University of Washington with a degree in mathematics, which for some reason qualified me to spend more than forty years at the Boeing Company as an aircraft structural engineer.

I have been active in a number of organizations: the Saint Bernard Club of America, the Saint Bernard Club of Puget Sound, and the Puyallup Valley Dog Fanciers. At one time or another, I served as president of each of these clubs. Back in the days when AKC issued licenses for professional handlers, I received one. Since then, I also have been licensed by the AKC to be a dog-show judge.

If I have any claim to fame, it is that I was a student of the world's foremost Saint Bernard authority, Mrs. Beatrice M. Knight. I would like to publicly acknowledge my very large debt to Bea. I am most thankful for the wisdom she shared with us and for the dogs she let us have. Without Bea's influence, Stoan's Saint Bernard Kennels probably would never have come into being, and I never would have written this book.

Now, how did this all come about?

The fall of 1965 found my wife Joan and I leading the "good life." We had a home in the suburbs, four children just starting school, a boat, and two cars. My idea of fun was working in our yard and growing flowers, and my passion was tournament bridge—I dreamed of gaining the title "Life Master."

Oh, those days of tranquility! Gone! All gone! The children all left home. We sold our boat after it went four years without once being put in the water. We now drive a station wagon and a van, neither of which is considered acceptable transportation to nondoggy people with sensitive noses. Our flowers exist under a survival-of-the-fittest philosophy, but even the most fit of plants do not do well under any kind of normal puppy onslaught. I haven't been engaged in a serious bridge game in more than twenty years, because bridge tournaments and doggy events are typically held during the same time frame.

Our transition from "normal" to "doggy" is a rather common but not too pretty story. We had just moved from Seattle to Kent after being without a dog for some time. Our previous dog was a Lab/Airedale mix that was serviced by our local neighborhood dog poisoner, and we decided to not have another dog until we lived in a more suitable situation.

I don't remember who first thought of getting a pure-bred dog, because we both were raised under the philosophy that the pounds were always full of

Beatrice M. Knight at her last dog show. Bea is shown here at the age of eighty-four at the SBCA's 1991 National Specialty show in San Diego. The dog is Sanctuary Woods Uno Itty Chan.

(Above): Annie picking out her late night snack. Owned by Mark and Linda Edwards of Santa Barbara, California.

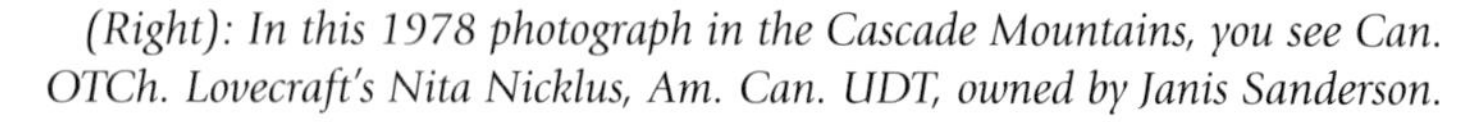

(Right): In this 1978 photograph in the Cascade Mountains, you see Can. OTCh. Lovecraft's Nita Nicklus, Am. Can. UDT, owned by Janis Sanderson.

perfectly wonderful dogs, and they were all free. Somehow, the concept of getting a pure-bred dog appeared in our house like some sort of apparition, and we all knew that family tradition would be abandoned—that we would have a dog paid for with real money.

The decision about the breed was easy to make. I, as head of the house, declared that we would get an Irish Wolfhound, and my child bride expressed the absurd notion that we should get a Great Dane. While I was still pointing out the erroneous nature of her opinion, a small classified ad appeared in the local newspaper: "For sale, Saint Bernard Puppies." This was before the Surgeon General required such advertisements to contain the phrase: "Danger—answering this ad may be detrimental to your lifestyle!"

We went, we saw, we were conquered. I think that the practice of dumping a litter of Saint puppies in the lap of a susceptible family should be classified as unethical. Of course, there was no way that we were going to leave without buying a puppy.

The only problem was, which puppy? When the people told us that the ones with a mask on both sides were classified as "show quality" and cost twenty-five dollars extra, we decided to adopt our extravagant mode and spring for the big bucks. Having made that decision, we eliminated four or five of the litter. At this point, the Lord of Zielinski Manor stated that the puppy would be a male. For some reason, the serfs allowed that decision to stand. This reduced the choice to three puppies, all of which were so cute that there was no way to make a rational decision. The lady selling the puppies then stated that some people liked Saint Bernards to have short noses, so we picked the one with the shortest nose.

We were then informed that we still needed to choose an official name for our puppy. A quick family conference resulted in "Bozo." But our announcement was greeted with a frown. We had forgotten that we were now into the world of pedigrees and registrations and the traditions of the dog people. A pedigree was produced, and we quickly saw that these high-class dogs simply did not have standard dog names. A simple, one-word name just wouldn't do, for all of the dogs in the pedigree had a kennel name as a prefix. Obviously, we needed a kennel name.

I immediately came up with a number of brilliant suggestions, but somehow, they were all vetoed by the rest of the family. They didn't seem to care for names like Whispering Firs, Barker's Inn, or Zielinski Acres. Then Joan suggested that we combine our first names, Stan and Joan, into a new word. The idea was so original and catchy that I couldn't help but agree. Thus, "Stoan" was chosen to grace the registration papers of our new puppy. I look back now and shudder at our naiveté. Since then, we have discovered that our unique scheme is the most common way to create a kennel name. For some reason, that same tasteless thought process occurs with a lot of novices.

Now that we had a fancy kennel prefix, we couldn't name the puppy a simple "Bozo." So the poor little guy was forever saddled with the moniker "Beau Zeau."

This story would have a happy ending except that we had a neighbor who actually entered her dog in a real dog show. Because her dog failed to ever beat another dog in ten or eleven attempts, she didn't think that dog shows were such a big deal. But she did have some entry forms for a local show that she wouldn't be using, and we *did* pay extra to get a "show-quality" dog, so we entered the puppy.

After what seemed to be a very long time, we received a notice that our dog was to be a real show dog. The day of the show finally arrived, and off we went to the magical world of purebred dog exhibiting. That was a very unfortunate day for the Zielinski family, for the very worst possible thing that could happen, happened! Bozo won his class and we were bitten by the show bug.

It seemed like a lot of fun at the time. All those blue ribbons just made you feel good for weeks on end. Once he was awarded a purple ribbon, which we thought was nice but just not as pretty as the blue ones. "Congratulations!" said one of our competitors grudgingly. "You've just won a major."

"Isn't that great?" I replied quizzically. "But what's a major?"

A lot of time and events have gone over the spillway since then, and I now know what a major is. While I still lust after majors, they don't seem to incorporate the same level of excitement as that first one. To shorten up this tale, Bozo finished his championship and became the first of his breed to combine a championship with the UD obedience title.

(Above):
Ch. Sanctuary Woods You Lucky Boy, owned and bred by Beatrice Knight of Sanctuary Woods Kennels, is shown here in a 1964 photograph as a young dog of eighteen months. He was known far and wide as "Bummy" because the name "You Lucky Bum" was rejected by the AKC after he had learned his name. It is difficult to find any dog related to the Sanctuary Woods bloodline that does not have Bummy listed as a forebear more than once.

(Below):
Ch. Sanctuary Woods You Lucky Boy, owned and bred by Beatrice Knight, is shown here in a 1972 photograph as an old dog of nine years. It is interesting to compare the young Bummy with the old Bummy and to note that his quality did not significantly diminish with age. This may explain why this one dog has made such a major contribution to the breed.

Putting titles on a dog seemed to be such great sport that we went out and bought another dog, a female this time, which was to be bred to Bozo. She finished her championship rather easily and got as far as a CDX in the obedience ring. Fortunately, by the time she was old enough to breed, just barely enough wisdom had penetrated our heads to know that Bozo and Mandy were not the best choice for a mating.

Just think—our first two dogs were our first two champions. After that we had to pay our dues. Just as in many fields of endeavor, good judgment is based upon experience, and experience is based upon bad judgment. We went through a long dry spell after our first two dogs. Winning became a much less common occurrence. We learned that poor handling, amateurish grooming, mediocre dogs, and bad judges are a combination that requires a well-known professional handler to convert into wins.

These four negative aspects of dog showing—poor handling, amateurish grooming, mediocre dogs, and bad judges—are what I call "The Four No-No's." We have worked for many years to ameliorate them, and we still work at each one. We considered going the route of hiring a professional to create wins for our dogs, but raising four kids at the time precluded having funds sufficient to do the job. Besides, I've always felt that there are three sports that are a lot of fun for the participants, but I could never understand why anybody would want to watch. Those sports are baseball, sex, and dog shows. If you aren't in the middle of the action, why in the world would you hang around as a spectator?

Over the years we slowly began to realize some semblance of real success based upon our own doings rather than the happenstance of our earlier attainments. Thus encouraged, we established Stoan's Kennel in Kent, Washington, where we have bred a number of champions and obedience title holders. In addition to Saint Bernards, Stoan's Kennel has been the home to a small number of Papillons, Clumber Spaniels, a Borzoi, an American Shorthair cat, and a giant herd of cottontail rabbits.

There have been some high points, and there have been some low points, but our overall involvement in the dog game and in the Saint Bernard fancy is something I would not have missed for all the world. Successes and disappointments seem to have melded into a pleasurable span of years. But our real major accomplishment, the one in which I take the most pride, is that almost all of the dogs we bred turned out to have a Saintly disposition. You see, a dog with a sound mind is something in which Joan and I have always put a great deal of importance.

There you have it! I told you it wasn't a pretty story, but it had to be told. Now you, too, know the derivation of Stoan.

My years of involvement with Saint Bernards have seen many high points that bring fond remembrances. Among these are: showing a bitch to Best-of-Breed at the 1975 National Specialty, being elected to the Board of the Saint Bernard Club of America more than twelve times, knowing many splendid Saint Bernards and being responsible for a few of them, and having an association with the finest people in existence—the Saint Bernard fancy.

Boroniahil Boomerang ready to hit the slopes. Susan Teniswood of Tasmania, Australia, owns Boomer.

Whatever Happened To Moderation?

I had invited Jim, who wanted to add Saint Bernards to his judging license, to come and watch the Saint judging with me, because the judge that day had considerable experience with the breed. It turned out to be the day of the fat dog, and the more pounds any particular dog was packing, the higher was his award. Finally, as the last of the winners waddled over to their place markers, Jim turned to me and asked if there were any Saint Bernard exhibitors who could tell the difference between conditioning a dog for the showring and getting him ready for butchering. "Sure there are!" I replied. "It's just that everyone knows that this judge likes to see dogs with a lot of substance." "It's too bad," responded Jim laughingly, "that somebody doesn't explain to these people the difference between substance and lard. You know, you Saint Bernard people seem to go in for a lot of exaggeration in your dogs."

At first I was offended by Jim's comments, but then I had to admit that his remarks hit pretty close to the mark. Jim's words gave form to something that had been nagging at the back of my mind for a long time. I realized that the hallmark of the Saint Bernard fancy was that almost everyone had the one common goal of "too much."

Not that everyone wants too much of the same feature. Each person seems to have his own pet virtue that he wants to exaggerate. If you just think about it, you will realize that almost every one of the respected Saint Bernard people advocate taking some particular feature or virtue to excess. You would be hard pressed to find a fancier or judge who did not look for a dog that represented some quality carried to an extreme—be it head type, substance (bone), angulation, size, or whatever.

Do we have a problem here? You bet we do! The ancient Greek philosophers made a wonderful case for the path to perfection—called "moderation in all things." This ancient wisdom would have you appreciate the beauty of the "golden mean." Those who have the interest of Saint Bernards at heart need to understand and accept this bit of wisdom. We need to decry the siren call of "too much of a good thing," for at the end of this road lie only bad things for the breed. Let me share some of the reasons I feel this way.

Consider someone, either a breeder or judge, who claims to like a dog with "a lot of bone." This individual is trying to establish that the larger the diameter of the dog's legs, the more correct he considers that dog to be. The extreme of this characteristic, of course, is a dog with legs like those of an elephant.

What is so great about fat legs? Do thick legs enable a dog to function better? The answer, of course, is a resounding "No!" In fact, it should be obvious that extremely fat legs are an encumbrance. The argument has been presented that the words of the Standard calling for legs to be powerful dictate this obsession for fat legs. But that is fallacious, because the tissue that creates these gigantic legs is not muscle tissue. Fat legs are not as strong as more normal legs that are simply well muscled. You will never see elephant legs on any dog athletic enough to perform the breed's historical calling. Well, then, are fat legs prettier to look at? Obviously, some people think so! However, in my definition, pretty legs should be trim, firm, well shaped, and well proportioned.

Any feature taken to an extreme does not contribute to function; in fact, it tends to have only a negative value in this regard. And while beauty lies in the eyes of the beholder, it takes a strange kind of person to think that an exaggeration is beautiful. True beauty must lie closer to what is normal for the function for which the breed was originated. The historical function of the Saint Bernard was

Ch. Belyn's Jesse James v. Twin Oaks finishing his championship under judge Stan Zielinski. Doug and Penny Mahon of Glen Ellen, California, bred Jesse, who is handled here by his owner, Ken Buxton of Loveland, Ohio. The dog's silhouette and proportions were greatly admired though some considered him to be overangulated.

that of a mountain rescue dog. So let's discuss the famous historical functions of the breed and some of the characteristics of the dogs that were valued by the early breeders.

While there is some confusion between the facts and fables concerning the original purposes of the hospice dogs, there cannot be much argument about the aspect of the breed that has attracted the majority of fanciers. There can be little doubt that the dogs were first brought to the hospice to act as guard dogs, except that any large dog would have been satisfactory for that job. If being a guard dog was the major use of those animals, there never would have been a Saint Bernard breed as such. It is the glamour and the glory of rescuing people that has made our breed endure, and it is the ability to perform that function that must be preserved.

I can relate a number of stories that demonstrate that our dogs still retain the instinct to help victims in snowy conditions. One case in particular happened during a Snow Trial of the Saint Bernard Club of Puget Sound. After the trial, a few of us were walking with our dogs away from the main ski area to watch some people sledding. While we stood there at the top of the hill watching, a young lady endeavored to go down a very steep slope, and she crashed and screamed in pain—she had broken her leg. Even though on lead, three of the dogs broke away and ran down that steep slope to her side. The victim saw them coming and cried out to keep them away, because they would jostle her broken leg. The dogs paid no attention to the commands to come back. Two of the dogs lay down gently, one on each side of the victim, and the third dog stood there barking up the hill at all of the people watching. Some of us went for help, and the rest tried to get the dogs to return, but they wouldn't leave or quit barking until the ski patrol arrived to take the victim to the ambulance. A spectator who was watching asked why the dogs behaved so strangely. The answer was, "They're just doing what they were bred to do—they think that that is their job!"

On another occasion, I wanted to see my dogs' reaction to my being covered with snow. I found an overhanging snowbank and pulled it down so that I was covered with a foot or two of snow. To my surprise, two dogs had me uncovered almost before the snow had stopped falling. Over the years, I have heard numerous other Saint Bernard owners relate similar stories about their dogs. The reaction is always the same—utter amazement that these dogs still have the instinct and will to do their historic tasks.

We don't know how the dogs came by these abilities and instincts, and we can only speculate about how they were discovered and exploited when the breed began.

I would imagine that the monks first started taking the dogs with them on their sweeps through the pass to look for lost or fallen travelers as some sort of combination guard and companion. We do know that the early monks soon came to value the dogs for their uncanny ability to sense an impending avalanche—a talent that was much needed and often used. This skill, while sufficient by itself to earn them their keep, was enhanced by the dogs' ability to find people buried under the snow, by their capacity to thrive in the mountainous, snow-covered environment, and by their eagerness to perform the tasks taught to them by those early hospice monks.

It eventually became the practice of the monks to send the dogs out without accompaniment in packs of two or three to make the searches for lost or fallen travelers so that the dogs could lead them back to the hospice if they could travel. If the traveler was down and not able to be aroused, one of the dogs would go back for the monks while the rest tried to arouse the downed traveler by licking and nudging his body. Failing to arouse the victim, the dogs would lie beside him to help keep him warm. By the way, only males were used for this work, because the work was thought to be too arduous for the bitches.

Contemplate the temperament demanded of these dogs. First, they needed to tend to business rather than indulge in squabbles, and they needed to seek out people and try to befriend these strangers. They had to be friendly, gregarious, and people-oriented or they could never perform the jobs that they were asked to accomplish.

Also note that the demand for great size was nonexistent, because the dogs were never asked to perform as draft animals or to physically move the bodies that they found in the snow. They needed the stamina to endure a hard life, but they were not asked to perform feats of strength. Now ask yourself what these functions have to do with the traits sought after by the majority of judges and breeders. The ability to sense impending avalanches, the keen nose for finding the people buried under the snowdrifts, and the eagerness to serve as mountain rescue dogs are *not* traits that are desired by most breeders, and, obviously, no judge can look for them in the showring.

Here is a show champion showing the breed's natural eagerness to work. Ch. Stoan's The Terminator v. Brawe (Arnie), pulling a heavy sledge uphill in the snow at the Saint Bernard Club of Puget Sound's annual Snow Trial.

Excalibur's Distinction, UD, DD. "Dee," owned by Barry and Judy Roland of Ellenwood, Georgia, is in harness in preparation for a Working Dog event. Dee was seven years old at the time of this photo.

Some lip service is given to seeking the physical attributes that would enhance a dog's ability to serve and function in an alpine environment, however. I happen to live relatively close to an area similar to the hospice setting, and I have taken a lot of Saint Bernards to the mountains for a romp in the snow. Let me relate a few observations concerning deep snow, high altitude, and very cold weather as they affect Saint Bernards.

The first time we took our dogs to spend a winter day in the mountains, I was shocked to find that the body type I thought to be the most desirable was absolutely unsuitable for this environment. A wide chest is no asset when plowing through a snowdrift. Short legs, no matter how well angulated, are a disaster in the snow. A too-long back is a hindrance to the rearing/leaping mode that is necessary for successfully traversing deep snow. An exception to this, of course, is the very small and light-boned dog that stays on top of the snow crust. However, once a small dog breaks through the surface crust, he cannot keep up with a large dog. The most surprising discovery was that the very largest males seemed to tire the most quickly from the continual leaping and sinking back into the snow.

To my amazement, the big-chested, heavy-boned, massive dogs that win a lot in the showring were good for only a very short distance in the deep snow. Actually, the body style and proportions of the leaner and racier dogs seem to function best here. Of course, strength, desire, and conditioning play a big part in how any dog handles deep snow and steep terrain—even more than do aspects of the dog's conformation. Nevertheless, the dog's anatomy and some of the ways in which the dog is mechanically assembled can represent a terrible handicap in deep snow and steep terrain.

If you envision this traveling through the snow as an athletic endeavor, you soon come to appreciate the body that is best suited for the performance. Strength is required, but the less mass the dog has to lift over the snow with each leap, the better. Size is important, but too small seems to be as bad as too big—the middle ground is best. Proportions are a factor, because short legs are a big handicap, as is being too long or weak in the back. Both the overangulated and the underangulated dogs tire too quickly. It seems that a moderate dog—that is, one of medium height and medium girth and width, with moderate angulation—is really the one best suited for deep snow in an alpine environment.

Let me note a few additional observations that I made while watching our dogs play in the snow. Feet that are not tight soon pack with snow or ice. The longer and finer the hair, the sooner the dog is back in the car. Ears with very thin leather decrease the dog's willingness to stay out in the cold for long periods of time. Small Saint Bernards dig deeper and faster than big ones (I haven't been able to figure out why, or if it is significant). It takes a real nut to take ten Saint Bernards up to the mountains for a romp in the snow, but it is a fine learning experience.

In my opinion, what is fashionable today tends to be a rather cloddish animal that greatly lacks the attributes sought after by the originators of the breed. I feel that the Saint Bernard should be built more toward a picture of strength and grace than a creature of unwieldy mass and useless bulk.

I find it terribly sad that in today's scenario, technology has removed the Saint Bernard breed from the field of avalanche rescue. When the breed originated, the dogs needed to have a certain amount of mass to keep from freezing, to be of a reasonable size to get up and over very rough terrain, and to be big enough to warm up a downed traveler. Being big was an asset! Today, the dogs have to travel to the scene of the avalanche in a helicopter while sitting on the handler's lap. Great size is now a negative feature, and being the size of a Saint Bernard is prohibitive. The only reason to have a dog at the scene of an avalanche or at any other disaster is for the dog's nose and his intelligence, which can come in a lap-sized package. The long and the short of the situation is that the dogs no longer get themselves to the scene, and once they get there, they only have to locate the victim. Even though the Saint Bernard retains the ability and instincts for the job, the great size of our beloved dogs has put them out of work.

This brings us to the question, "So what?" Since no one employs Saint Bernards to rescue avalanche victims or to dig out snow-covered foot travelers anymore, why not let fashion and fad dictate what is desirable in our breed? The answers are not obvious, but they *are* real. It is important to really understand and accept them.

One problem is that no single breeder can keep up with all of the changes that occur when a philosophy of letting fads dictate correct type is adopted. This year the rage will be some sort of monstrous size. Next year it will be some specific kind of marking that is required to be a winner. The following year will see everybody looking for extreme rear angulation. We end up with a contemporary breed type that is changed for reasons of silly fashion, but less able to perform his original tasks. Over time, the breed changes until it is hardly recognizable by the earlier breeders.

Another problem is that you cannot expect any sort of consistency in the performance of the judges if the breeders are forever changing the dogs. Many judges use the original function of a breed as a guiding principle to lead them to the breed's proper type. If the function is abandoned, so is all hope of correct type being rewarded in the majority of showrings.

Perhaps the most insidious of the problems is the loss of a certain style or sense of elegance that happens when some feature is exaggerated. We all know outstanding successful show dogs that established great winning records by virtue of the fact that they had one particular feature that was noticeable to the point of exaggeration. Indeed, some actually were promoted by advertising, drawing our attention to the very fact that the subject dog had the most wonderful something or another, be it head, bone, angulation, or whatever. While the dog may, in fact, have been a good specimen of the breed, the overaccentuated focal point may have, if we looked at him objectively, thrown him out of balance.

So where does this leave us? If we can agree that we have a problem and that there are certain consequences for ignoring it, then we are left with a need for some course of action. We need a plan, and I would like to suggest one. Each person involved with the breed must make a personal decision as to whether or not the breed is headed in the right direction. If you can accept the concept of the Saint Bernard's original function as being a rescue dog in the hazardous alpine environment, and if you believe that our dogs ought to be able to perform that function, then you cannot like what is fashionable today in the showring. Perhaps it is time for you to make a really concerted effort to seek a little moderation in your breeding, judging, or whatever it is that you do for the breed.

Please remember that the art of appreciating excellence in dogs is knowing how much is enough, and that too much is as bad as too little. One of the most difficult challenges that faces our fancy is the appreciation of the optimum—the beauty of moderation.

Here's the real reason dinosaurs became extinct. These ten-week-old puppies of the Keepsake Kennels are owned by Lynn and Larry Jech of Tolleson, Arizona.

This is a lovely portrait of a seven-year-old dog that has contributed much to the breed. Pictured here is Ch. Lynchcreek's Ace v. Stoan, HOF, POE, who was bred by Candace Blancher of Eatonville, Washington. Ace followed in the footsteps of his sire and of his grandsire by becoming the SBCA's Stud Dog of the Year. Ace also had a marvelous show career and took his turn at being the number-one Saint Bernard in the United States.

The Official Standard for the Saint Bernard

SHORTHAIRED

General

Powerful, proportionately tall figure, strong and muscular in every part, with powerful head and most intelligent expression. In dogs with a dark mask the expression appears more stern, but never ill-natured.

Head

Like the whole body, very powerful and imposing. The massive skull is wide, slightly arched and the sides slope in a gentle curve into the very strongly developed, high cheek bones. Occiput only moderately developed. The supra-orbital ridge is very strongly developed and forms nearly a right angle with the long axis of the head. Deeply imbedded between the eyes and starting at the root of the muzzle, a furrow runs over the whole skull. It is strongly marked in the first half, gradually disappearing toward the base of the occiput. The lines at the sides of the head diverge considerably from the outer corner of the eyes toward the back of the head. The skin of the forehead, above the eyes, forms rather noticeable wrinkles, more or less pronounced, which converge toward the furrow. Especially when the dog is alert or at attention, the wrinkles are more visible without in the least giving the impression of morosity. Too strongly developed wrinkles are not desired. The slope from the skull to the muzzle is sudden and rather steep.

The muzzle is short, does not taper, and the vertical depth at the root of the muzzle must be greater than the length of the muzzle. The bridge of the muzzle is not arched, but straight; in some dogs, occasionally, slightly broken. A rather wide, well-marked, shallow furrow runs from the root of the muzzle over the entire bridge of the muzzle to the nose. The flews of the upper jaw are strongly developed, not sharply cut, but turning in a beautiful curve into the lower edge, and slightly overhanging. The flews of the lower jaw must not be deeply pendant. The teeth should be sound and strong and should meet in either a scissors or an even bite; the scissors bite being preferable. The undershot bite, although sometimes found with good specimens, is not desirable. The overshot bite is a fault. A black roof to the mouth is desirable.

In this November 1996 photograph, Katarina Heiberg is at her home in Norway above the lake with three of her dogs of the Saint Woods Kennels. Left to right, the dogs are my old friend "Per," who is registered as NUCh. DKCh. SUCh. INTUCh. St. Wood's Perfect; his older sister "Mummels," who is registered as NUCh. DKCh. St. Wood's Busybody; and her white-face daughter, St. Wood's Donna. (NUCh. = Norwegian Champion; DKCh. = Danish Champion; SUCh. = Swedish Champion; and INTUCh. = International Champion.)

Nose *(Schwamm)*

Very substantial, broad, with wide open nostrils, and, like the lips, always black.

Ears

Of medium size, rather high set, with very strongly developed burr *(Muschel)* at the base. They stand slightly away from the head at the base, then drop with a sharp bend to the side and cling to the head without a turn. The flap is tender and forms a rounded triangle, slightly elongated toward the point, the front edge lying firmly to the head, whereas the back edge may stand somewhat away from the head, especially when the dog is at attention. Lightly set ears, which at the base immediately cling to the head, give it an oval and too little marked exterior, whereas a strongly developed base gives the skull a squarer, broader and much more expressive appearance.

Eyes

Set more to the front than the sides, are of medium size, dark brown, with intelligent, friendly expression, set moderately deep. The lower eyelids, as a rule, do not close completely and, if that is the case, form an angular wrinkle toward the inner corner of the eye. Eyelids which are too deeply pendant and show conspicuously the lachrymal glands, or a very red, thick haw, and eyes that are too light, are objectionable.

Ch. Siegfried's Hunk von Mardonof was owned by Colonel William Hagel of Siegfried Kennel fame. Hunk was an outstanding producer and is found in the pedigree of many American Saint Bernards.

Neck

Set high, very strong and when alert or at attention is carried erect. Otherwise horizontally or slightly downward. The junction of head and neck is distinctly marked by an indentation. The nape of the neck is very muscular and rounded at the sides which makes the neck appear rather short. The dewlap of throat and neck is well pronounced; too strong development, however, is not desirable.

Ch. Sanctuary Woods Atta Boy, shown in this 1964 photograph, was owned by Beverly Riviera of Southern California. This is an example of a dog that fits the phrase, "Powerful, proportionately tall, strong and muscular in every part."

Ch. San Subira, shown here in a 1964 photograph, was owned and bred by Lillian Buell of Chatsworth, California. This dog was an outstanding producer of many champion offspring, and is found in the pedigrees of many Southern California Saints.

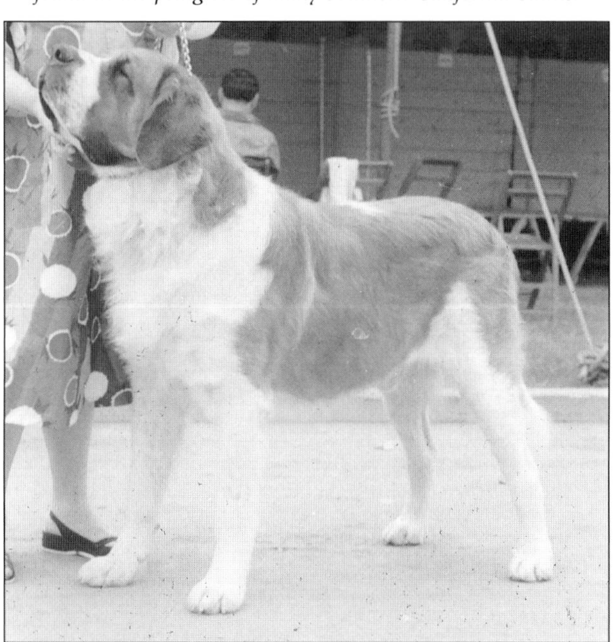

Shoulders

Sloping and broad, very muscular and powerful. The withers are strongly pronounced.

Chest

Very well arched, moderately deep, not reaching below the elbows.

Back

Very broad, perfectly straight as far as the haunches, from there gently sloping to the rump, and merging imperceptibly into the root of the tail.

Hindquarters

Well-developed. Legs very muscular.

Belly

Distinctly set off from the very powerful loin section, only little drawn up.

Tail

Starting broad and powerful directly from the rump is long, very heavy, ending in a powerful tip. In repose it hangs straight down, turning gently upward in the lower third only, which is not considered a fault. In a great many specimens the tail is carried with the end slightly bent and therefore hangs down in the shape of an "*f*". In action all dogs carry the tail more or less turned upward. However it may not be carried too erect or by any means rolled over the back. A slight curling of the tip is sooner admissible.

Upper Arms

Very powerful and extraordinarily muscular.

Lower Leg

Straight, strong.

Hindlegs

Hocks of moderate angulation. Dewclaws are not desired; if present, they must not obstruct gait.

Feet

Broad, with strong toes, moderately closed, and with rather high knuckles. The so-called dewclaws which sometimes occur on the inside of the hind legs are imperfectly developed toes. They are of no use to the dog and are not taken into consideration in judging. They may be removed by surgery.

Ch. Gero Christopher of Skycroft at the Ohio Saint Bernard Club Specialty Show in 1962. This is an example of good proportions in a dog of that era.

Coat

Very dense, shorthaired *(stockhaarig)*, lying smooth, tough, without however feeling rough to the touch. The thighs are slightly bushy. The tail at the root has longer and denser hair which gradually becomes shorter toward the tip. The tail appears bushy, not forming a flag.

Color

White with red or red with white, the red in its various shades; brindle patches with white markings. The colors red and brown-yellow are of entirely equal value. Necessary markings are: white chest, feet and tip of tail, noseband, collar or spot on the nape; the latter and blaze are very desirable. Never of one color or without white. Faulty are all other colors, except the favorite dark shadings on the head (mask) and ears. One distinguishes between mantle dogs and splash-coated dogs.

Height at Shoulder

Of the dog should be 27½ inches minimum, of the bitch 25½ inches. Female animals are of finer and more delicate build.

Considered as Faults

Are all deviations from the Standard, as for instance a swayback and disproportionately long back, hocks too much bent, straight hindquarters, upward growing hair in spaces between the toes, out at elbows, cowhocks and weak pasterns.

LONGHAIRED

The longhaired type completely resembles the shorthaired type except for the coat which is not shorthaired *(stockhaarig)* but of medium length plain to slightly wavy, never rolled or curly and not shaggy either. Usually, on the back, especially from the region of the haunches to the rump, the hair is more wavy, a condition, by the way, that is slightly indicated in the shorthaired dogs. The tail is bushy with dense hair of moderate length. Rolled or curly hair, or a flag tail, is faulty. Face and ears are covered with short and soft hair; longer hair at the base of the ear is permissible. Forelegs only slightly feathered; thighs very bushy.

Approved April 13, 1998, Effective May 31, 1998

Ch. Revilo's Bogart v. Holly, HOF, POE, a dog of excellent type, was bred by William and Marlene Oliver at their Revilo Kennels in Portland, Oregon. He was sired by Ch. Mia Faithful Friend, HOF, POE, out of Ch. Snowland's Holly Christmas, HOF.

GLOSSARY

The following list explains some of the less obvious words and terms used in the Saint Bernard Breed Standard.

blaze: A rather broad and fairly extensive white marking starting at the back of the skull and running down the forehead into the muzzle.

bridge of the muzzle: The upper surface of the muzzle between the skull and the nose.

brindle: A color pattern produced by the presence of darker hairs forming vertical bands and giving a striped effect on a background of tan, brown or yellow.

broken: In this context the reference is to the set of the muzzle on the skull and implies a condition known as "down faced."

burr: The package of inner surface ridges, cartilage and leather thickness that gives the base of the external ear the propensity to stand away from the head.

cheek bones: The bony protuberance below the eye; also known as the zygomatic arch.

cowhocks: An anatomical abnormality in which the hocks are closer together than are the rear feet; either when standing or when in motion.

dewclaws: The first (inner) claw or digit on the pastern, not reaching the ground. On the front pastern the dewclaw is the first metacarpal bone and associated phalanges. On the rear pastern the dewclaw is the first metatarsal bone and associated phalanges. Rear dewclaws are often referred to as wolf's claws or spurs.

dewlap: The pendulous folds of skin under the chin, throat and neck.

even bite: An arrangement of the teeth and mouth in which the lower incisor teeth line up in exact opposition to the upper incisor teeth when the mouth is closed.

"*f*": In the original German version of the standard they used a letter from the German alphabet that has been translated into a lower case letter "f." The German character looks like a rather flattened "S," and that is what was intended here. That is, the intent is to describe a tail in repose that curves downward in a flat shallow curve from its insertion into the rump and then reverses the direction of curvature to curve upward, again in a flat shallow curve.

flag: Long hair on the tail that hangs loosely or limply, such as on the tail of an Irish Setter. Usually such tails fail to have the round bush-like character of a typical Saint Bernard tail.

flap: The portion of the external ear that hangs from the burr.

flews of the lower jaw: The relatively thin lips attached to the lower jaw.

flews of the upper jaw: The fleshy and slightly pendulous lips attached to the upper jaw.

haunches: The muscular development around the haunch bone, which is often called the hip bone. That is, the most forward region of the croup or the pelvic area immediately behind the loin.

haw: A pouching or sagging of the lower eyelid or eyelids resulting in the exposure of the conjunctival (inner) lining of the eyelid.

hindquarters: The part of the dog behind the loin including the haunch, rump, croup and rear limbs, but in many usages the tail is excluded.

hocks: The joints in the hind limbs, located between the lower thighs and the rear pasterns.

lachrymal glands: The tear-producing glands situated at the inner corners of the eyes, one on each side.

loin section: In normal context the loin is that area of the dog between the end of the ribs and the start of the pelvis. In the context of this usage in the Saint Bernard Standard the reference is to the large, prominent, well-developed muscle mass on each side of the spine.

long axis: An axis is a theoretical line in space about which something rotates—in this case the dog's head. The axis here is the one that goes from the back of the skull to the nose.

GLOSSARY (continued)

mantle: Body markings that involve the darker color distributed over the back and sides of the dog similar to a blanket. The color may extend to some extent down the legs and over the shoulders and neck.

mask: Dark shadings on the head that form a mask-like pattern around the eyes.

muschel: A German word that refers to the burr (see above).

nape: The back of the neck.

noseband: A white band encircling the muzzle behind the black nose and ahead of the dark mask.

occiput: The bump located at the back of the skull which forms the forward part of the indentation between the head and the neck. Technically, this is the protuberance of the occipital bone of the skull.

out at elbows: An anatomical abnormality in which the elbows fail to be in close proximity to the chest; either when standing or when in motion.

overshot bite: An arrangement of the teeth and mouth in which the lower incisor teeth are positioned behind the upper incisor teeth and there is a gap between the two sets of incisors when the mouth is closed. This is usually thought of as a lower jaw that failed to grow long enough.

pasterns: In this context the reference is to the front pasterns which are the metacarpus or the region between the carpus (wrist joint) and the digits (foot) below. Similarly, the rear pastern is the metatarsus or the region between the hock joint and the foot below.

root of the muzzle: That portion of the muzzle where it appears to attach to the skull.

rump: The contour of the combined muscle groups covering the upper surface of the pelvis; starting at the end of the loins and blending into the buttocks area behind.

***schwamm*:** A German word that refers to the black fleshy part of the nose.

scissors bite: An arrangement of the teeth and mouth in which the forward surfaces of the lower incisor teeth engage the back surface of the upper incisor teeth when the mouth is closed.

slope from the skull to the muzzle: This is not to be confused with the silhouette of the apparent stop seen in profile. The subject here is the true stop which is the surface of the skull between the two prominent ridges above and in front of the eyes; that is, the floor of the furrow between the eyes.

splash-coated: Body markings that seem to be random islands of the darker color distributed over a white background. Often such dogs appear to be basically white dogs with patches of color.

***stockhaarig*:** A German word meaning shorthaired.

stop: A depression or step down in the topline of the head, situated centrally between the eyes. The junction between the nasal bone and the two frontal bones of the skull.

supraorbital ridge: The bony protuberance above the eye; technically known as the zygomatic process of the frontal bone of the skull.

swayback: A back that sags or is concave to some degree along its length. The actual extent of the sag may vary in depth or position, and may only be evident when the dog is in action.

tender: Not hard, stiff or erect; rather having properties of pliability and softness.

torn mantle: A pattern of body markings which are the mantle type of markings that have additional white patches as if the mantle had tears in it that exposed the white coat underneath.

undershot bite: An arrangement of the teeth and mouth in which the lower incisor teeth are positioned forward and ahead of the upper incisor teeth when the mouth is closed. This is usually thought of as a lower jaw that grew too long.

withers: Technically, the withers are the first through the ninth thoracic vertebrae, with the tips of the spines on the first and second thoracic vertebrae being the highest point on the dog's body.

wry mouth: A type of mouth in which the lower jaw is twisted to one side, placing the upper and lower jaws out of alignment with each other.

THE STANDARD IN PICTURES

The term being depicted here is "PROPORTIONATELY TALL." This term is found in the very first sentence of the Standard, which explains why it is almost universally overlooked.

The correct proportionately tall Saint Bernard.

A dog with a long loin and back. Many breeders and judges fail to recognize this fault for what it is.

A dog that is short on leg. Because short-legged dogs can handle greater angulation, some people admire these incorrect proportions.

THE STANDARD IN PICTURES

The term being depicted here is "THE BRIDGE OF THE MUZZLE IS STRAIGHT."

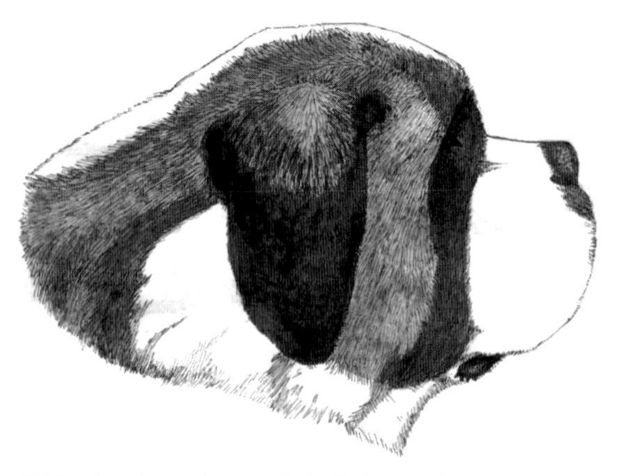

This dog has the straight bridge of the muzzle called for in the Standard.

This dog has a bridge that is dished—a fault in that the bridge of the muzzle fails to be straight.

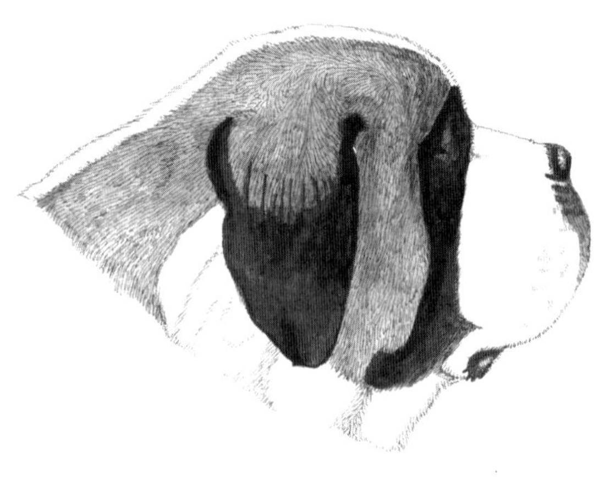

This dog has a muzzle that is down-faced and depicts a broken muzzle that is beyond the "slightly broken" allowed in the Standard.

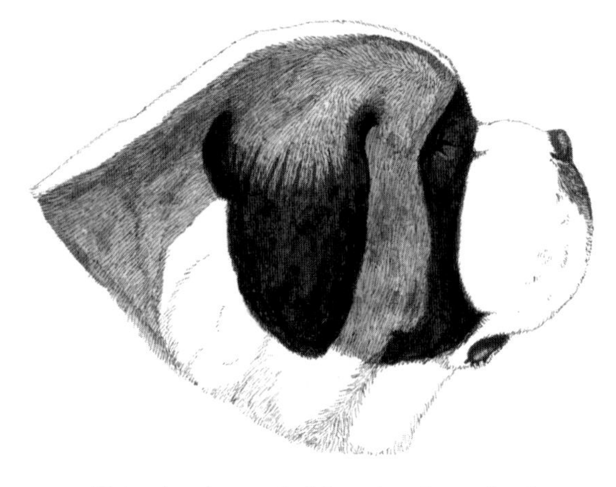

This dog has a bridge that is arched. This fault is not allowed.

This dog has a muzzle with a fold of skin at midlength. This is a fault of excess skin rather than muzzle shape.

THE STANDARD IN PICTURES

The term being depicted here is "THE FLEWS OF THE UPPER JAW ARE STRONGLY DEVELOPED, NOT SHARPLY CUT, BUT TURNING IN A BEAUTIFUL CURVE INTO THE LOWER EDGE, AND SLIGHTLY OVERHANGING."

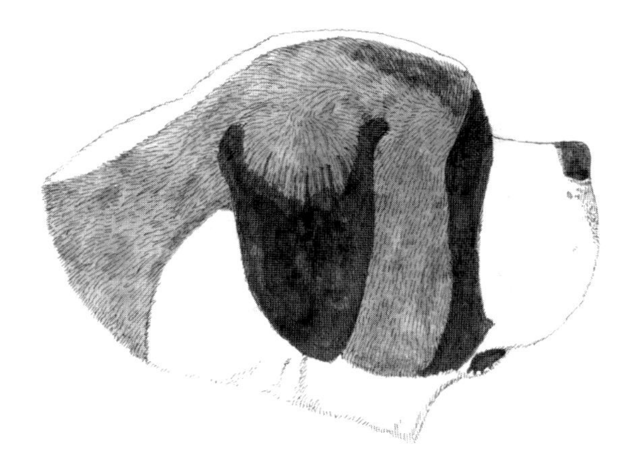

The flews as called for in the Standard; that is, strongly developed, turning in a beautiful curve, and slightly overhanging.

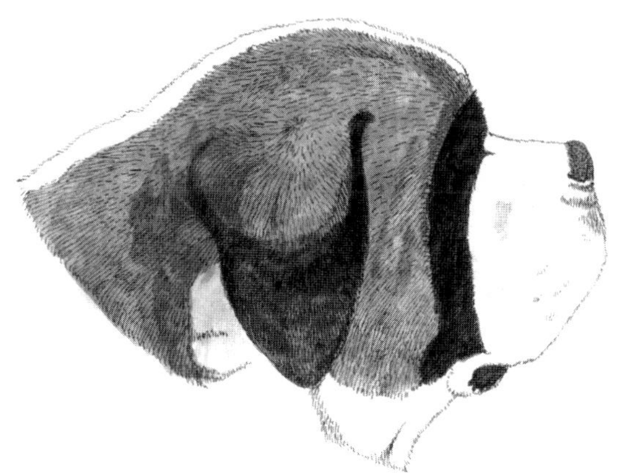

A flew that is sharply cut and hence not a shape allowed by the Standard.

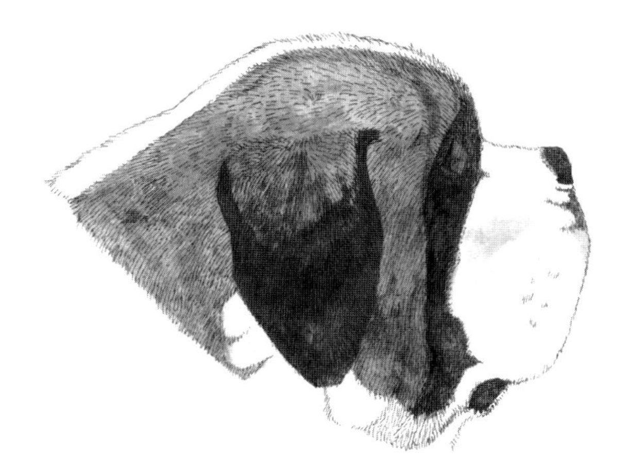

A pendulous flew that greatly exceeds the term "slightly overhanging." This fault is difficult to breed out.

THE STANDARD IN PICTURES

A number of terms concerning the structure surrounding the eyes are depicted in this diagram.

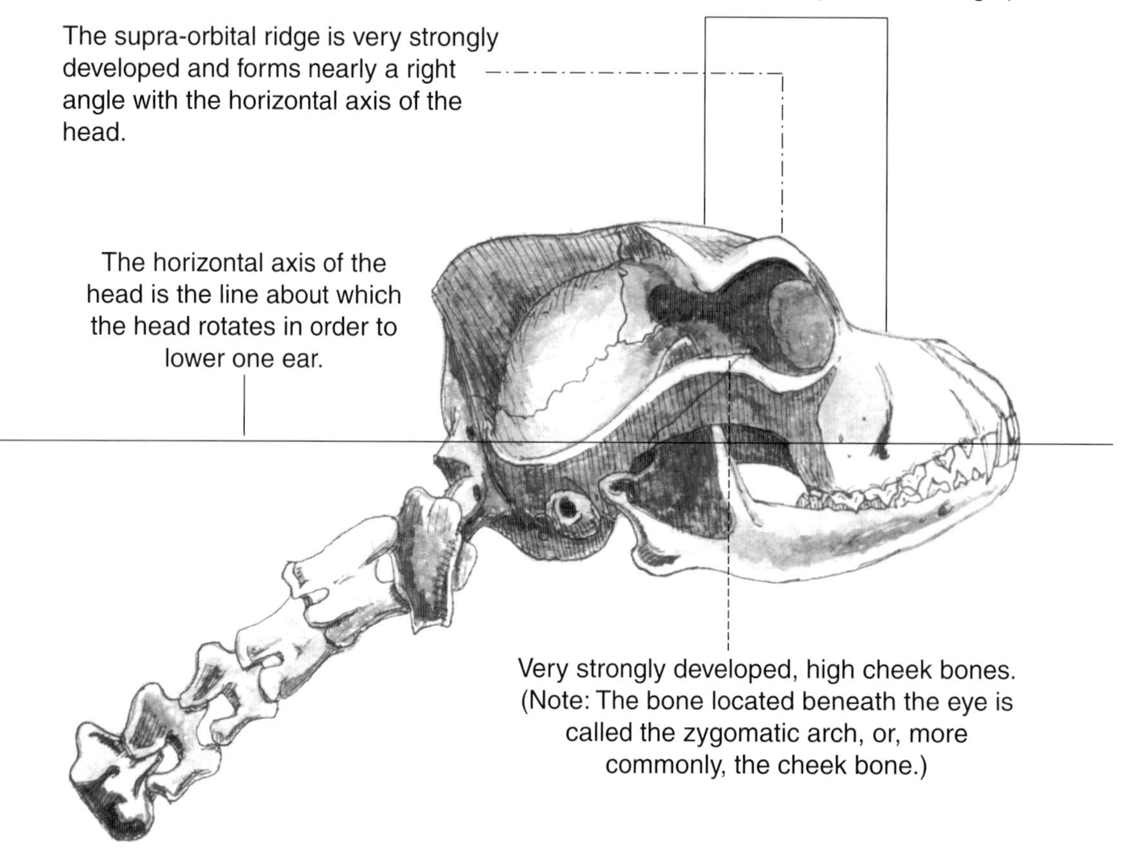

THE STANDARD IN PICTURES

The term being depicted here is "A RATHER WIDE, WELL-MARKED, SHALLOW FURROW RUNS FROM THE ROOT OF MUZZLE OVER THE ENTIRE BRIDGE OF THE MUZZLE TO THE NOSE."

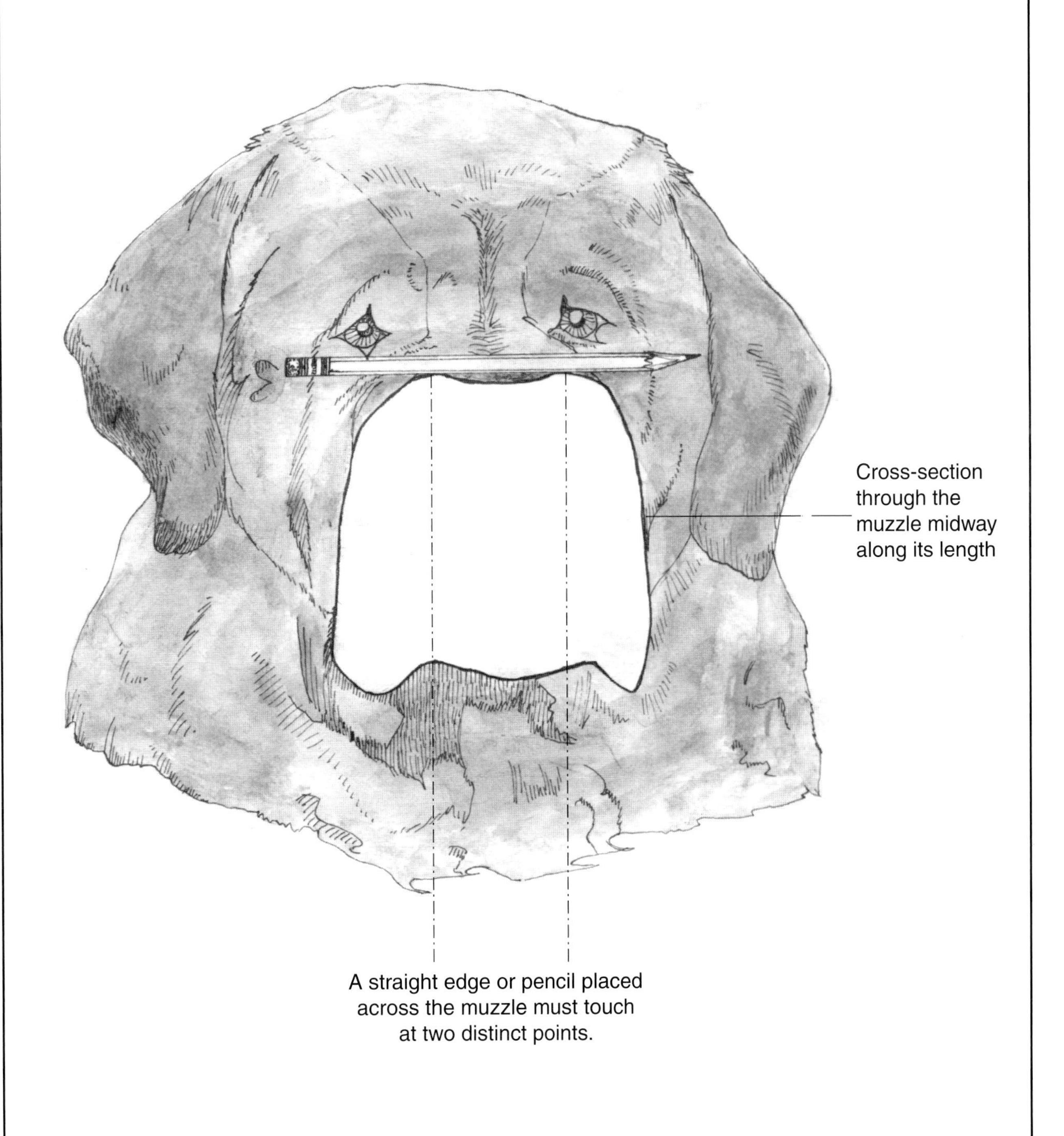

A straight edge or pencil placed across the muzzle must touch at two distinct points.

THE STANDARD IN PICTURES

The term being depicted here is "SHOULDERS (ARE) SLOPING."
You must exercise caution to avoid confusing the size of the shoulder blade with the slope.
You should also note the relationship between the elbow and the brisket.

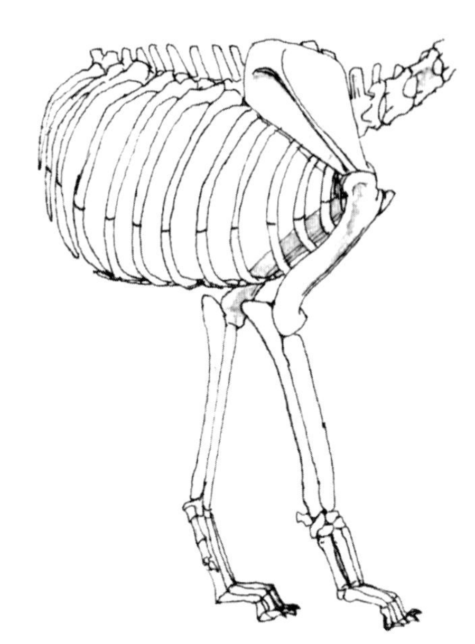

The correct slope of the shoulder blade (scapula)

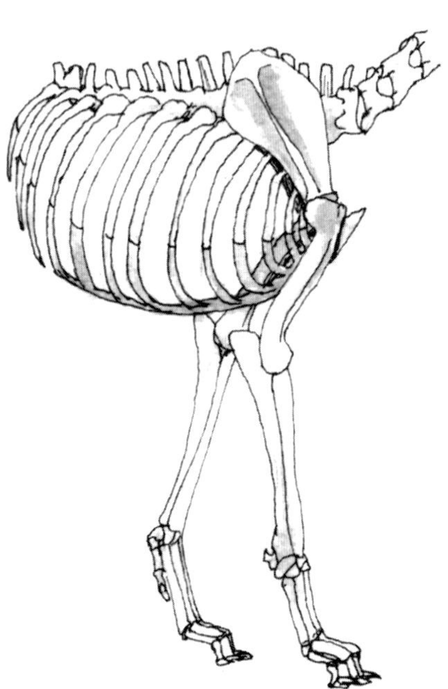

Insufficient slope to the scapula

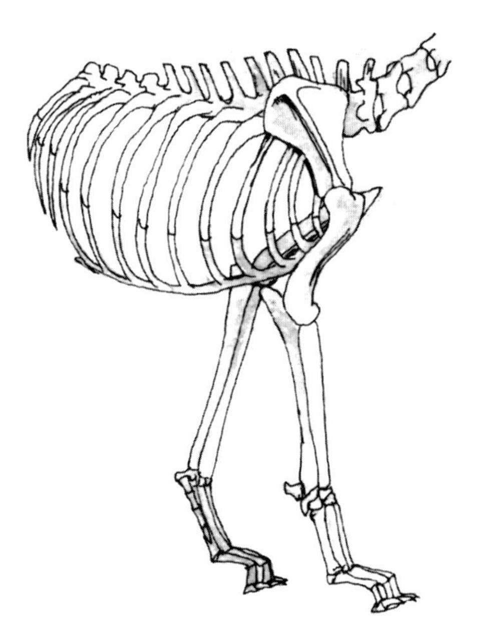

A short scapula and a short upper arm (a common breed problem)

THE STANDARD IN PICTURES

The term being depicted here is "POWERFUL LOIN SECTION."

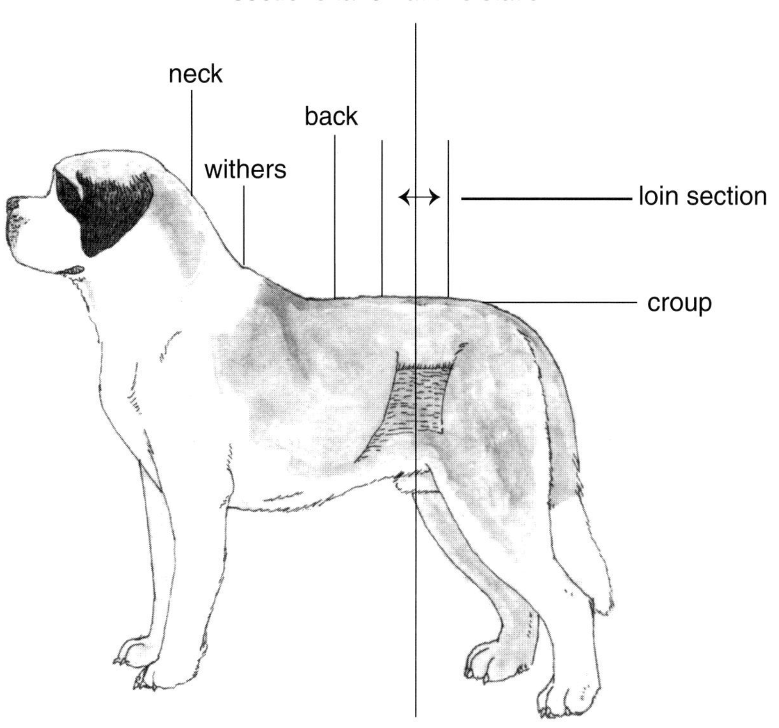

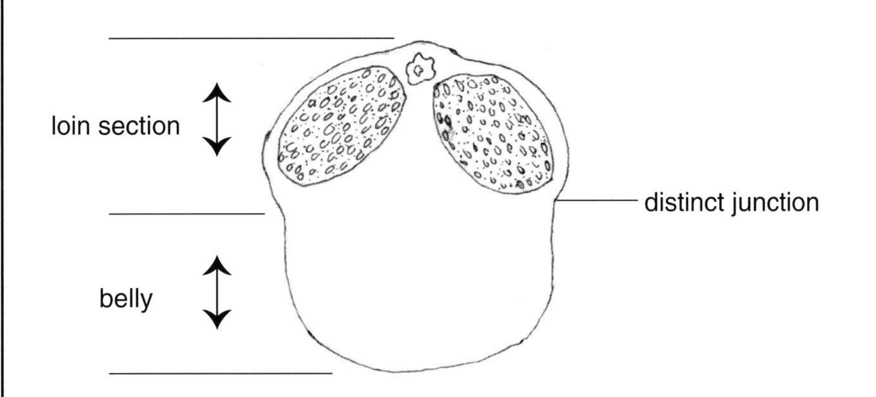

Section through body of a dog with a powerful loin section, which is distinctly set off from the belly.

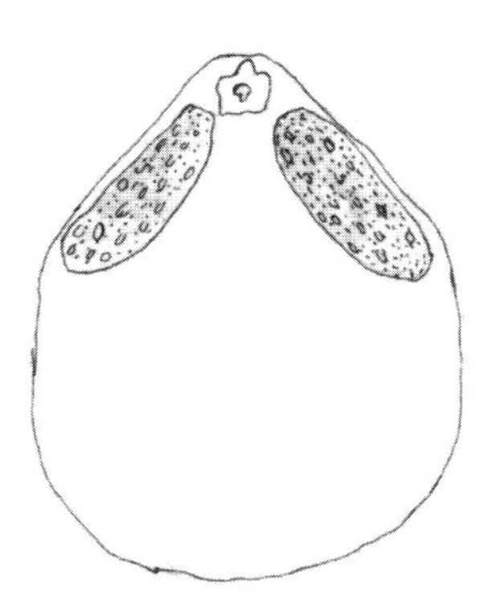

Section through body of a dog with a much less powerful loin section.

THE STANDARD IN PICTURES

The term being depicted here is "HINDQUARTERS WELL-DEVELOPED. LEGS VERY MUSCULAR."

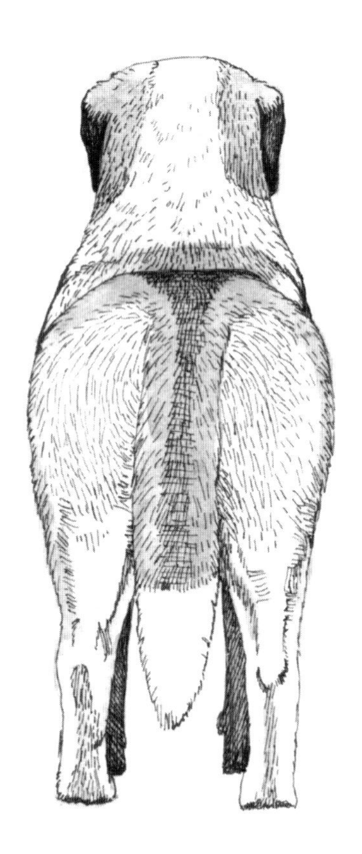

This is the so-called "basketball butt" that is typical of a Saint Bernard with the correct well-developed hindquarters. Even when the dog is out of coat, this shape should be there.

The amount of muscle mass on the thigh that is required to accomplish this shape is usually not achievable by simply adding weight (fat) to the dog—it takes good, thick, muscular hams to get this look.

Some longhaired dogs can approach this appearance by hair dressing and trimming, but a simple laying on of hands will detect the fraud. When evaluating the hindquarters of a Saint Bernard, grasp the upper thigh with both hands. If you can completely encircle the leg with your two hands, the dog lacks sufficient muscle on the rear legs.

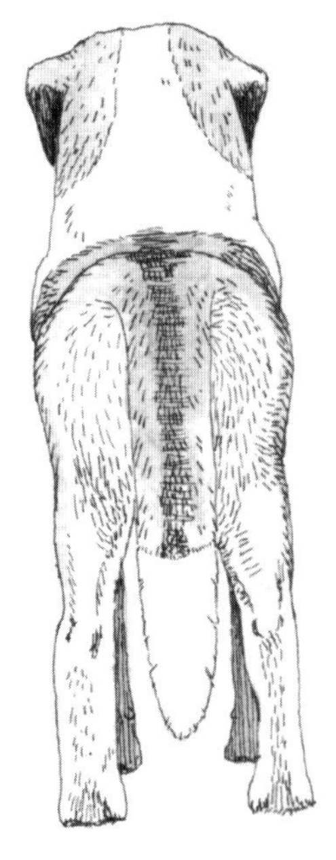

This illustration shows basically the same skeleton lacking the correct amount of muscle mass. The result is the caved-in look that is far too common in the breed.

THE STANDARD IN PICTURES

The term being depicted here is "GENTLY SLOPING TO THE RUMP, AND MERGING IMPERCEPTIBLY INTO THE ROOT OF THE TAIL." In the vernacular of the dog fancy, this portion of the dog's anatomy is called the CROUP and may be thought of as the area above the pelvis.

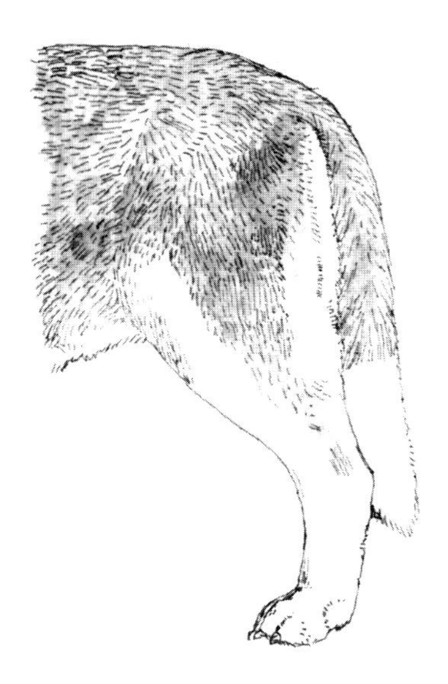

This is a correct croup as described in the Standard.

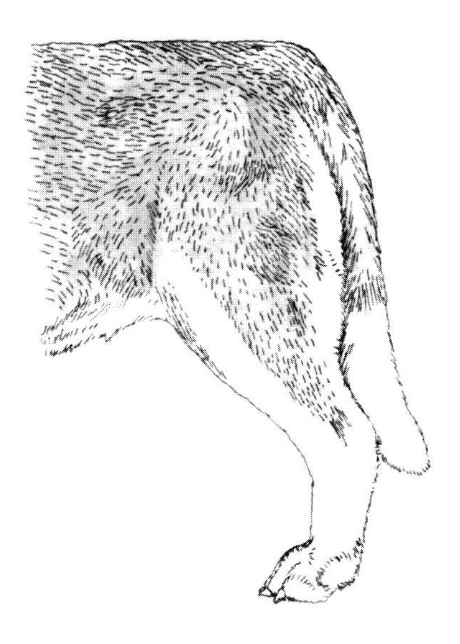

A faulty croup that fails to "slope gently." This is often referred to as a "flat croup."

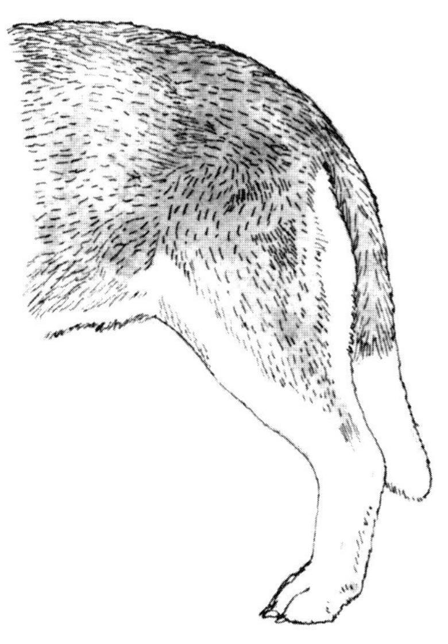

A faulty croup that slopes too much, often referred to as "goose-rumped."

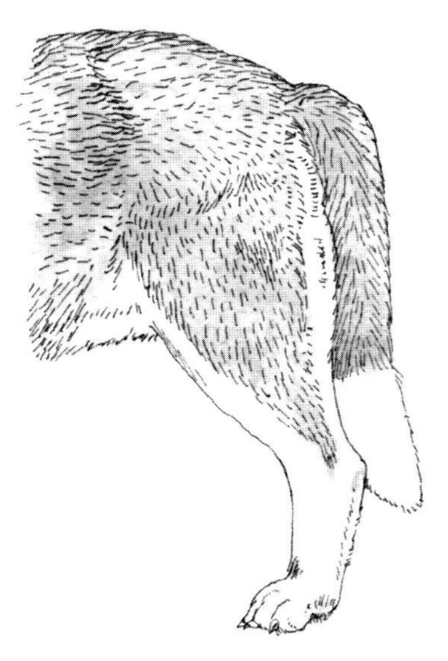

A faulty croup that fails to merge imperceptibly into the root of the tail.

THE STANDARD IN PICTURES

The term being depicted here is "BROAD, WITH STRONG TOES, MODERATELY CLOSED, AND WITH RATHER HIGH KNUCKLES."
The word "broad" in this context should be thought of as a term that gives a sense of proportions. The Standard did not call for a short foot, nor for a long foot, but rather chose to use the term "broad."

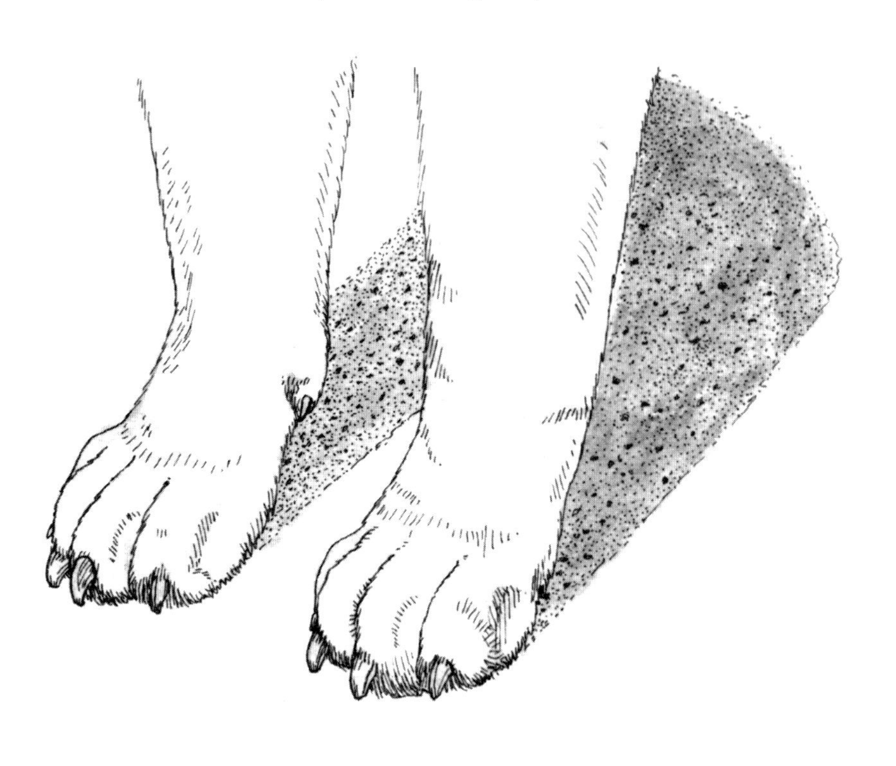

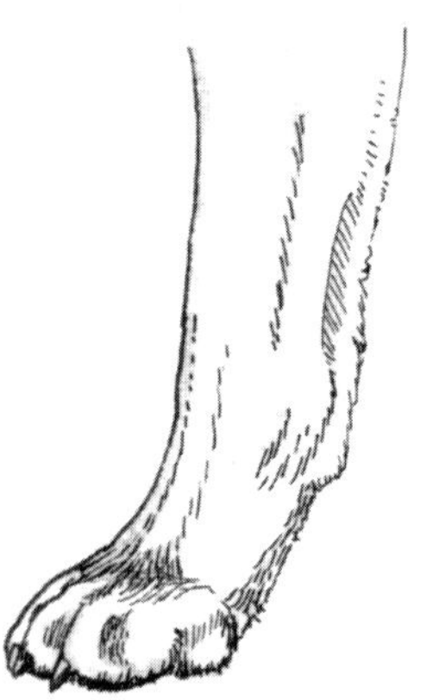

This is a side view of a correct foot.

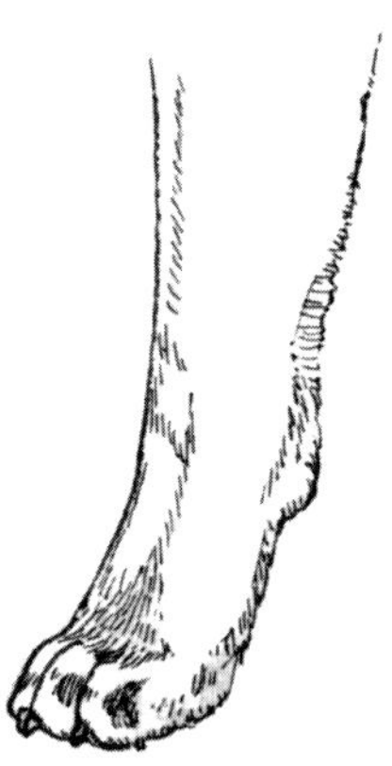

This shape is called a cat foot, and it has toes too short for a Saint Bernard.

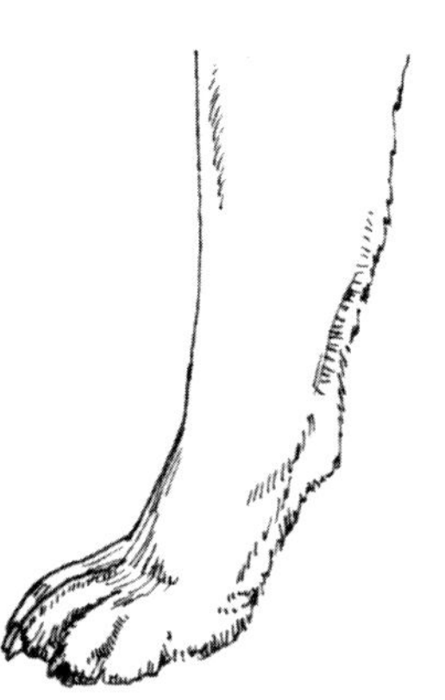

A hare foot, or a foot that has toes that are too long.

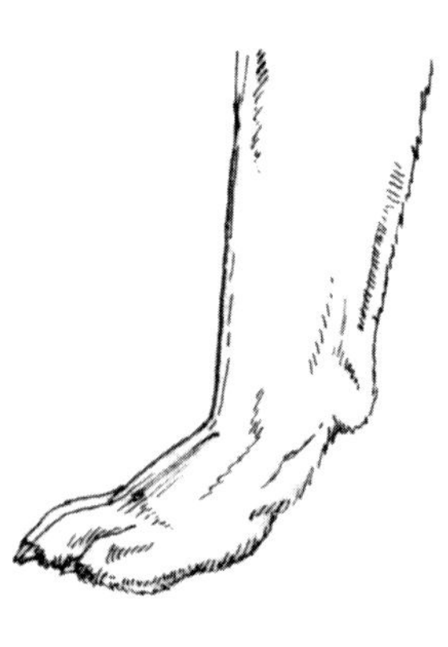

A flat foot that lacks the correct high knuckles.

THE STANDARD IN PICTURES

The term being depicted here is not in the Standard, but the subject is head carriage while the dog is moving at a slow trot.

The upper limit of normal carriage for a Saint Bernard when trotting. A more normal carriage would be with the neck horizontal.

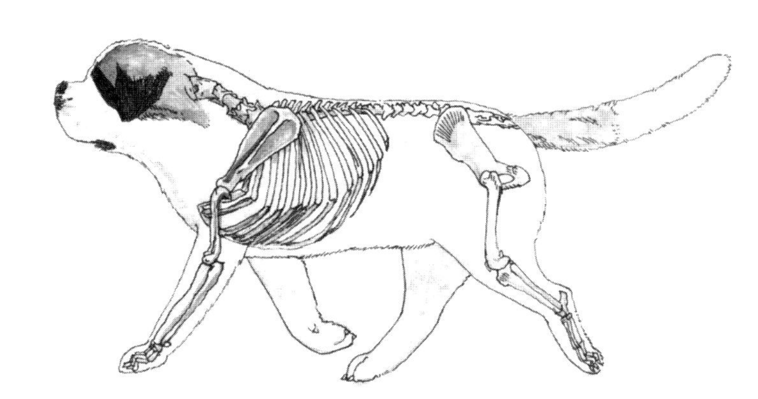

An exaggerated carriage normally achieved only by the handler stringing up the dog as he moves. Some dogs can be trained to move in this stylized manner, but it is not normal.

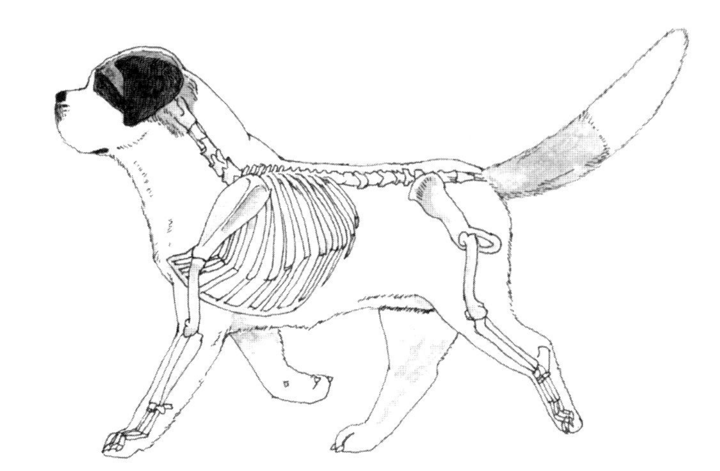

A dog that is running downhill. This carriage indicates that the dog is trying to shift his weight to the front legs, and it usually indicates a lack of soundness.

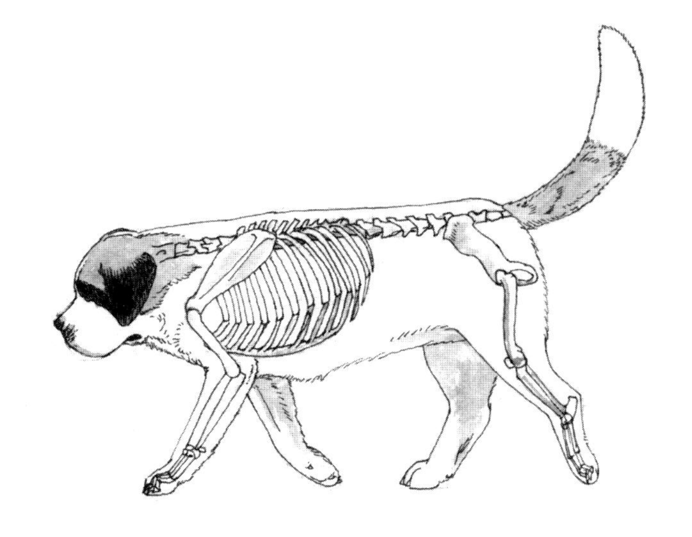

An Extensive Description of the Saint Bernard

PRELUDE

Many texts describe the ideal Saint Bernard, and what follows here is one person's attempt to extend the scope of previous efforts. Before I start, let me state that I like—very much—the current (the version approved in 1998) American Kennel Club (AKC) Standard for the Saint Bernard. Having studied other Standards as a part of becoming licensed to judge those breeds, I have come to appreciate the conciseness and poetry of this particular document. There are a few problems with this edition of the Saint Bernard Standard, but they are not serious enough to warrant a revision. Nevertheless, I would like to touch upon those shortcomings.

Judges who are seeking to become licensed for Saint Bernards have to study our Standard and take a test on the subject. Many of those people complain that there are great gaps in the coverage; that is, some important topics are not mentioned. As an example, the Saint Bernard Standard contains no definitive statements describing either temperament or movement.

Bear in mind that not everybody thinks that our Standard is deficient. One prevailing argument states that any Standard should spell out only those aspects that are not normal for the generic dog, because belaboring the obvious only detracts from the clarity of the description. The other side of the table maintains that if you demand a degree of competence from the people who judge your breed, then you have an obligation to provide a Standard for the breed that is both clear and complete. Both positions have considerable merit, and it is not my intention to join either side. I prefer to share with you something that I found contributed greatly to my own education.

Some years ago, I began to contemplate the process involved in composing a Standard for a breed, and I wondered what went through the minds of the people who wrote our original Standard. I thought to myself, "If I were given the task to write a complete and clear description of the Saint Bernard, would I be up to the job? Could I paint a portrait of the Saint Bernard with a set of words so that breeders, exhibitors, judges, and fanciers in general would understand my vision of the breed? And, if I were to do so, would it be better or worse than what we already have?"

In order to answer some of those questions I tried to write a complete description of the Saint

One expects the family's Saint Bernard to get along with the family's cat, as shown here in this 1989 photograph of Heaven Hi's Golden Opportunity, CD, and Crashcat. Dennis and Jerri Hobbs of Denver, Colorado, owned both.

Am. Can. Ch. Mill Creek's Goodtime Charlie shows off his wonderful saintly disposition as he plays Santa's helper at Sackets Harbor Central School. Charlie is owned and was bred by Shirley Lloyd, owner of Mill Creek Kennels in Sackets Harbor, New York.

Bernard. The following text is the result. This exercise shows the ungainliness of a written description of a Saint Bernard if it even approaches becoming a comprehensive list of virtues and faults.

To compose this description, I used the blank outline supplied by the AKC to all of the parent clubs during the summer of 1987, and I used words from various sources to fill in the blanks. I researched words and phrases used in other Breed Standards, descriptive text from previously published articles, and quotes from people who expressed their thoughts in private conversations. Perhaps I included even a little personal philosophy. The result, to say the least, is interesting.

Remember that this reflects only my personal opinion and private prejudices. It is *not* a substitute for the Standard. I hope that it will not be at odds with the official AKC Standard, but if it is, there is no question that the official Standard takes precedence, and I stand corrected.

While you are reading, think about how you would do it differently. What would you change? I'd like to hear your answer! I am interested in any unclear parts and would welcome your comments on anything that you feel is incorrect.

AN EXTENSIVE DESCRIPTION OF THE SAINT BERNARD

General Appearance

The Saint Bernard is a massive dog, being large in width and height and substance; a dog whose strong, sturdy, and powerful appearance suggests his heritage of service in the harsh alpine environment. His stature and presence should reflect his eagerness and ability to fulfill his ancient task of being sent out in packs of two or three male dogs to seek out and rescue travelers lost in the snowstorms of his native mountain pass—a task that required great soundness in both mind and body.

The soundness of mind is reflected in his intelligent and friendly expression, which should exude a benevolent goodwill toward all with whom he comes in contact. Soundness of body is reflected in the physical features of the dog, for he must be balanced, proportionately tall, robust, athletic, and well put together. The breed ideal is a strong, coordinated athlete without any sign of clumsiness or inefficiency.

Having great strength, a good specimen will display great muscle mass throughout, but the muscle tissue must be hard and firm. Neither soft tissue nor loose skin should be mistaken for proper musculature; there must be very little tendency toward being a wet dog. While being sturdily built with plenty of bone, the dog must be neither clumsy in movement nor cloddy in appearance.

In evaluating the Saint Bernard, his gait, balance, purpose, overall muscle tone and adherence to proper breed type are to be given more emphasis than any of his component parts.

Size, Proportions, Substance

Size. It should be noted that too small dogs generally lack the power and strength and too large dogs the agility and maneuverability desired in a mountain rescue dog. If too small, the dog would find itself under a serious handicap when facing a high snowdrift or other natural obstacle. If too large, the dog would be severely penalized in being required to haul that extra mass and bulk up and over difficult and steep terrain, and in leaping through deep snow he would expend too much energy in trying to move all that weight up and down.

Ideal height for an adult male Saint Bernard is 76 centimeters (30 inches) at the withers; for an adult female, ideal height at the withers is 71 centimeters (28 inches). Good specimens will be within 2.5 centimeters (1 inch) of the ideal height. Less desirable specimens will deviate more than 2.5 centimeters but less than 6.4 centimeters (2½ inches) from the ideal height. Animals deviating more than 6.4 centimeters (2½ inches) from the ideal are extremely faulty and should be given no consideration.

Proportions. A properly built Saint Bernard is nearly square in proportion of body length, as measured from the point of brisket (sternum) to the pin bone (ischium), to height at the withers. Faulty are animals of rectangular proportions, whether due to excessive body length or to shortness of leg. A short loin is of primary importance, but a dog with a slightly longer rib section is acceptable so long as the dog does not have the appearance of being long in body length; that is, if the extra length of body is any more than just barely perceptible, it is faulty. One must penalize an overly short body as severely as an overly long body, for both detract from the dog's ability to perform his legitimate work.

Substance. A Saint Bernard must epitomize the terms massive, powerful, and well boned, yet he must not be coarse or cloddy. It is important that the Saint Bernard be moderately dry with hard, firm muscles. Folds of skin, hanging flesh, and masses of wet or soft tissue are no substitute for real substance. Adult males are more substantial and masculine in appearance and deportment than adult bitches, who are more refined and feminine without weakness or softness. However, doggy bitches and bitchy dogs must both be shunned as not worthy of consideration.

Head

General. It is in the head that the Saint Bernard shows his breed; he shows it in the form of the skull, the muzzle, the eyes, the ears, and that almost indefinable beauty of expression—kindly and benevolent under ordinary circumstances, but full of intelligent concern in difficult situations. To complete the image of an aesthetically correct Saint Bernard, it is essential that the head be relatively large and imposing with the dimensions of length and depth being approximately equal, and with the width greater than the length. The powerful

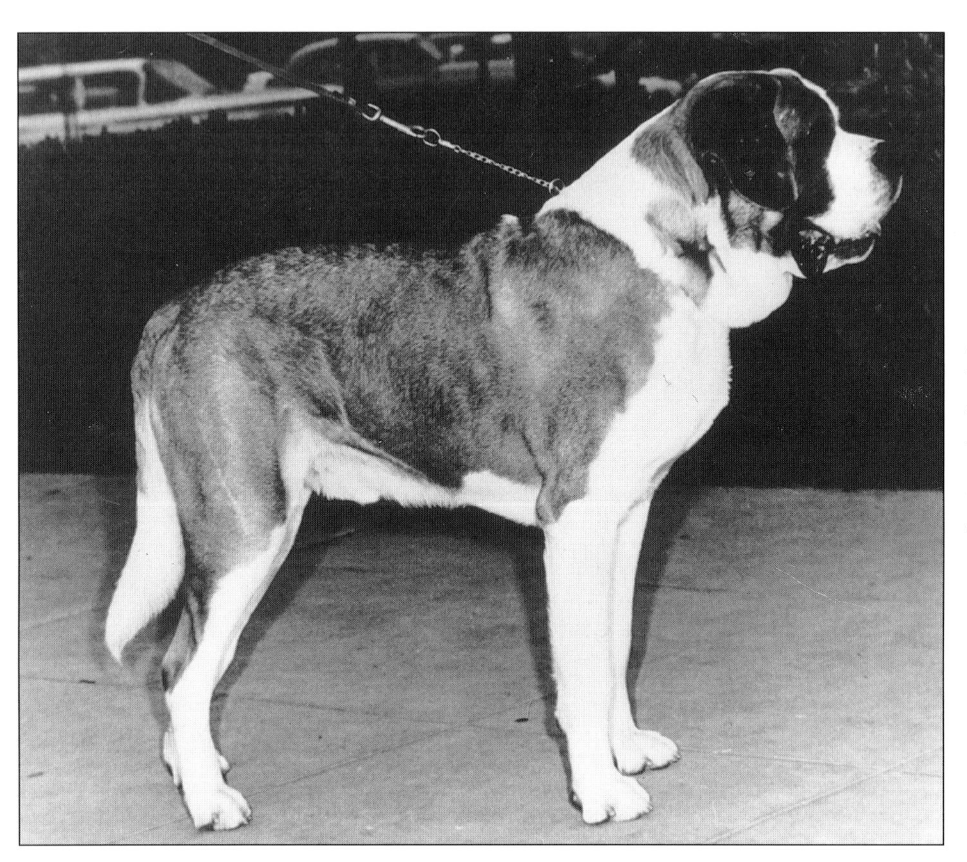

Ch. Sanctuary Woods Better Times, who was owned by Bruce and Fran Gilley, was an all-breed Best in Show Saint from the 1960s. Note his proportionately tall figure with his powerful head and strong neck.

head should give the impression of having been chiseled rather than molded to the proper shape. While there is much more to a Saint Bernard than his head, no dog should be given any consideration if he lacks a proper head.

Expression. The proper Saint Bernard expression must leave the observer with an impression of a kindly and intelligent animal. This feature is normally enhanced by the well-defined dark mask around the eyes. In dogs with a mask that is too extensive, the expression may appear stern or somber, while dogs with too little mask usually have a clownish look about them. The markings on the head are important only to the extent that they affect the expression, and they are not faulty as long as the dog has the look of benevolence and intelligence that is the hallmark of the breed. When the dog is at attention, wrinkles will appear in the skin above the eyes. These wrinkles, along with the properly set ears, greatly enhance the expressiveness of the face. However, these wrinkles must not be so strongly developed that they are evident when the dog is not at attention. Such a dog has a melancholy expression. Therefore, any evidence of excessive skin about the head and neck should be severely penalized.

Ch. Slaton's Piece Of The Action, CD, CGC, HOF, POE, owned by Shirley and Joe Wolf, Marilyn Getz, Barb Salewsky, and Linda Bulicz. He was the top winning Saint Bernard in the United States in both 1995 and 1996. Commonly known as "Sport," he holds the record for Saint Bernards, having won the Best In Show award at twenty-four all-breed shows.

Eye Color. The color of the iris must be dark brown—the darker, the better. Light eyes give the dog a wolflike and staring look that is objectionable. Blue eyes remove the dog from consideration. The haw color is preferably dark in color, since a red, or white, or a black and white haw detracts from the dog's expression.

Eyelids. Eyelids should present a diamond-shaped frame around the eyes caused by an angular fold in each eyelid. That fold is located toward the inner corner of the eye on the upper lid and toward the outer corner on the lower lid. The eyelids should not, however, be so slack that they conspicuously expose the lachrymal glands or the greater part of the inner surface of the eyelid. Evidence of excessive tearing around the eyes indicates a malformation (such as entropion, ectropion, distichiasis, or inward growing eyelashes), which should be penalized.

Eye Placement. Located about even with the top line of the muzzle, the eyes are of medium size. The eyes must be placed more to the front of the skull than to the sides, and, when viewed from above, lines perpendicular to the planes of the eye sockets must intersect behind the occiput. The eyes must be deeply set below the surface of the surrounding bony structure, and any indication of shallow placement should be considered faulty. Bulging, round eyes are an extreme fault.

Ear Color. Saint Bernard ears are usually dark brown at the base, fading into black near the fold. Brown ears, white spots or white patches on the ears, white ears with black spots, or even completely white ears do not detract from the worth of the dog as long as expression is not denigrated.

Ear Placement. The ears are set rather high, and, when the dog is at attention and viewed from the front, the top line of the ears forms an extension of the curved top line of the skull. This gives the skull a much broader and more expressive appearance. Ears protruding above the top line of the skull are set too high and should be penalized. A much more serious fault, however, is that of ears set too low, thus giving the head a houndlike appearance.

Ear Shape and Texture. The base of the ear is very strongly developed and provides the platform that supports the ear leather. At the edge of that platform, the ear drops with a sharp bend to the sides of the skull; and, especially when the dog is at attention, the rear edge of the ear leather stands away from the head while the front edge clings firmly to the side of the head. Ears that do not have a strongly developed base cling closely to the skull, giving it an oval and incorrect appearance. The ear leather, which is soft and flexible but sufficiently thick to withstand lengthy exposure to extremely cold weather, forms a triangle that is slightly elongated toward the rounded point at the bottom.

Ear Size. The ears are of medium size and, when pulled forward, should reach to the inner corner of the eye or just a little beyond. The width of the ear flap, front to back, should be less than the length, top to bottom. Ears that are too large give the dog an incorrect appearance, and ears that are too small detract from the majesty of the head, making it appear out of balance with the rest of the dog.

Skull. The skull is massive, broad, and powerful with a moderately developed occiput. The crown is slightly arched from side to side, and the sides of the head slope in a gentle curve into the very strongly developed, high cheek bones—cheek bones that are so strongly developed, they create a distinct and obvious juncture (bump) at the root of the muzzle. The widest point of the skull is located where the cheekbones (zygomatic arch) join the skull behind the eyes. When viewed from above and starting at a point near the outer corner of the eye, the outline of the head widens toward the back. The slope of the stop is moderate but, because of the very pronounced development of the superciliary ridges, appears in profile to form nearly a right angle with the top line of the muzzle. This configuration results in a very deep furrow, starting at the root of the muzzle, which gradually disappears toward the back of the skull.

Muzzle. The beauty of the head depends upon the harmonious proportion of the muzzle to the skull. The muzzle should always appear powerful, never small, in its relationship to the rest of the head. The muzzle should appear to be a substantial block attached to the front of an even more substantial block.

The muzzle is strongly developed in length, breadth, and depth and does not taper in any direction. The length of the muzzle must be approximately half of the length of the head. It must not be so short that it limits the available space for proper dentition. The depth of the muzzle is greater than its length in the ratio of 11 to 8. One should note that the depth of the muzzle is measured at the base of the muzzle, and from the upper surface of the muzzle to the lower surface of the lower jaw rather than to the lower limits of the flew. The muzzle should be extremely wide, with the width being nearly equal to the length.

Ch. Belyn's Journey v. Exchequer, HOF, owned and bred by Doug and Penny Mahon of Glen Ellen, California, is shown here at the Saint Bernard Club of America's National Specialty Show with his handler, Doug Mahon. Journey was noted for his proportions and his wonderful disposition.

The shape of the muzzle is influenced first through the formation of both jawbones, second through the placement of the teeth, and third through the texture and shape of the lips and flews. Straight in profile, the muzzle appears to be flat on its upper surface. However, a shallow groove is discernible to the touch running along the length of

Ch. Morris' Hawkeye is shown here being awarded Group 1 honors by Judge Dolly Ward. Hawk had the top show record in the United States for two years and was in the top five for two other years. Hawk was bred and owned by Ladd and June Morris, who have now moved away from California to the Pacific Northwest.

the muzzle. Absence of this groove is a very serious fault. Also considered as faults are a Roman nose, lumps on the bridge of the nose, folds of skin on the top and/or sides of the muzzle, or a curved (domed) roof as opposed to the required flat upper muzzle surface.

Planes of the Muzzle and Skull. A line connecting the point of the occiput with the joint between the skull and the nasal bone midway between the eyes is defined as the control line. The upper surface of the muzzle must intersect the control line at least one inch ahead of the stop but no more than ten inches ahead of the stop.

Nose Size, Shape, and Color. The nose should be massive and wide, with the nostrils open and well developed. The nose is completely black. Pink spots or patches on the nose are to be considered faulty but differentiated from a brown nose, which removes the dog from consideration. The profile of the nose often rises above the top line of the muzzle; this condition is not considered a fault as long as it is not too pronounced.

Lips and Mouth. The lips are completely black. An occasional pink spot or break in the pigmentation, while not being desirable, is not very serious as long as it does not detract from the dog's appearance or expression. The tongue and gums are always pink, and the roof of the mouth has a black coloration in many specimens.

Flews. The flews of the upper jaw are strongly developed and slightly overlap the lower jaw to give a square look when viewed from the side. The shape of the flews contributes much to the character of the head; the flews should not be too sharply cut back but rather should turn in a beautiful curve into the lower edge. Gross, hanging, sloppy flews are a terrible detraction from the character of the head; therefore, overly pendulous flews are very undesirable. It is a serious fault for the flews of the upper jaw to hang below the surface of the lower jaw more than 4 centimeters (1.6 inches).

Bite. Acceptable in a Saint Bernard is any bite ranging from a scissors bite, through an even bite, to being undershot by less than one-eighth inch.

Being undershot by more than one-eighth inch is considered faulty. If the dog is so undershot that the teeth are visible when the mouth is closed, he must be removed from any consideration. Any evidence of a wry mouth must also preclude any consideration of the dog. Any overshot bite is a serious fault in a Saint Bernard.

Teeth. The Saint Bernard should have a full compliment of forty-two sound white teeth with 6/6 incisors, 2/2 canines, 8/8 premolars, and 4/6 molars. Missing more than two teeth is a serious discrepancy. The teeth of a Saint Bernard are normally small for so large a dog. The tooth pattern of a Saint Bernard should approximate three sides of a rectangle to provide the proper shape to the muzzle. The incisors should form a nearly straight line across the front of the jaw, the canines should be up front almost on that same line with the upper corner incisors fitting snugly in back of the lower canines on each side, and the premolars and molars should lie on a line more or less directly behind the canines.

Top Line, Neck, and Body

General. Well balanced, powerful, massive, short coupled. Back line strong and level from withers to slightly sloping croup whether standing or moving. Slab-sidedness, narrow chest, lack of depth in brisket, sloping back line, roach or swayback, disproportionately long back, excessive tuck-up, flat croup, or steep croup to be faulted.

Top Line. The junction between the head and the neck is distinctly marked by an indentation. The top line, from the indentation immediately behind the occiput to the root of the tail, must be a smooth, continuously curving line without sudden lumps, bumps, dips, or valleys. The neck silhouette should be slightly arched and should blend cleanly into the withers. The withers should be pronounced with a smooth transition into the back. The back should be straight and level. The very slight arch to the loin should be imperceptible to the eye. The croup should slope gently and imperceptibly into the root of the tail.

Neck. The neck should be rather high set and slightly arched and should blend cleanly into the shoulders. The nape of the neck is sturdy, moderately arched, extremely muscular, and thick. Thus, the neck, while not truly short, appears short because of the strong development and great girth. A neck that gives the illusion of great length is faulty. The dewlap of throat and neck is well pronounced, but too strong development is objectionable. Proper evaluation of the dewlap can only be made with a slack collar and lead.

Body. The body must be massive and powerful, yet have the flexibility required of a dog able to traverse rough mountainous terrain. The depth of the body must be half of the height of the dog at the withers.

Chest, Ribs and Brisket: The brisket extends to the elbows, and, when the dog is viewed from the side, the point of the brisket (sternum) is evident at least one inch forward of the point of the shoulder. When the dog stands freely in a natural stance, the chest between the forelegs must be at least as wide as a man's closed (flat) hand, including the thumb.

The shape and size of the chest are very important! The chest must be as large as possible, yet shaped so that it will not interfere with the dog's legs—neither the front assembly nor the rear one—when the dog is trotting or galloping. The ribs are long and well sprung, but they must not be overly sprung (barrel shaped), as that would force the dog to adopt an inefficient rolling action when moving. The ribs spring well out from the spine and then, in order to allow space for the elbows to move close to the body, flatten at the side in the forward section of the rib cage. They gradually widen toward the rear so that the rib cage becomes oval in cross section toward the rear.

Belly: The belly must be firm but narrow enough to provide room for the stifle and femur to move straight forward when the dog is in motion. The belly should present very little tuck-up, because being herring-gutted detracts seriously from the sense of massiveness required of this breed.

Back: The back must be very broad, perfectly straight and level, and extraordinarily firm whether the dog is standing or moving.

Loin: The loin must be relatively short in length but very broad and powerful, with the loin muscles being very distinctly wider than the belly below. A Saint Bernard lacking these prominent loin muscles fails to display adequate power in a critical location. Such inappropriate construction shows a weakness that is very faulty.

The spinal column of the loin section rises imperceptibly higher than the area of the back. A perceptible arch of loin or sag in the area of the back is a serious fault.

Croup: The profile of the croup slopes slightly; the pelvic bone slopes at a slightly greater angle. The pelvis is wide and blends smoothly into the powerful thighs below; the hip bones are not perceptible to the eye of the observer.

Tail: The tail is well set on, thick and muscular at the base, following the natural line of the croup. Tail bones extend to, but not below, the point of the hock. In repose, the tail hangs either straight down or with a flattened, S-shaped double curve. In action or whenever the dog is alerted, the tail is carried level or with some moderate upward curve; it is never vertical, curled over the back, or hanging straight down. Whether the dog is moving or standing, alert or in repose, the tail is never carried between the legs.

Forequarters

General. Muscular and balanced, well coordinated with hindquarters, and demonstrating a free and graceful movement.

Angulation. The angulation of the front quarters should mirror the moderation of the rear quarters. A lack of adequate angulation (front too straight) or angulation that is excessive (too much layback) are serious faults.

Shoulders. The shoulders must be well muscled but not loaded. Neither a looseness nor a restriction in the shoulders is acceptable.

Shoulder Blades: The shoulder blades should be flat, of medium length, and moderately sloping, with upper tips close together (less than six centimeters) at the withers. The upper tips of the shoulders, if correctly located, will show as a noticeable prominence in the top line of the dog. Small shoulder blades are a fault.

Point of the Shoulder: The point of the shoulder must be behind the point of the brisket, and it should divide that portion of the forequarters lying between the upper point of the scapula and the elbow into two equal segments that lie at two equal, but opposite, slopes.

Upper Arm. The upper arm must be very muscular, with the length of the upper arm being equal to the length of the shoulder blade. Short upper arms are a common fault that must be depreciated.

Elbows. The elbows lie close to the body and, when viewed from the side, appear to lie directly under the upper tips of the shoulder blades and midway between the withers and the ground. In action, the elbows must move freely without any indication of slackness or restriction.

Forelegs. The forelegs are powerful and muscular and, when viewed from the front, are straight with good bone, but not to the point of coarseness.

Pasterns. The pasterns are slightly sloping with no suggestion of weakness. Pasterns that slope at an angle greater than fifteen degrees are too weak to withstand the stresses created by the activities of such a massive animal, while pasterns that slope at an angle less than ten degrees are too straight to perform their shock-absorbing function.

Front Dewclaws. Dewclaws on the front legs should be present, lying close to the leg and being able to function, as closely as possible, as the dog's tool for removing objects from his muzzle and ears.

Front Feet. The front feet are large, compact, round (width equal to length), and well knuckled, with very thick pads. Bad feet, such as flat or splayed feet or those with thin pads or long toes, are a serious handicap to the ability to work in a mountainous alpine environment and should be faulted to the degree that they are present.

Hindquarters

General Appearance. The hindquarters should be very broad, thick, and massive in every part. Great strength should be obvious to the observer; hard, firm muscle should be found here in great abundance. The appearance of weakness or narrowness, the presence of soft, flabby muscles, or a lack of muscle mass in the hindquarter is to be severely penalized.

Rear Angulation. In keeping with the short loin and square body proportions required for correct breed type, the angles formed by the bones of the hindquarter must be moderate in magnitude. The angulation is determined by a number of factors, but the primary one is the length of the bones in the rear assembly. Moderate angulation requires moderate length of the bones in the rear legs. Angulation of the rear end is evaluated with the rear pasterns vertically oriented and positioned so that the center of the foot is directly below the pin bone (ischium). Lack of sufficient angulation shows a weakness that is objectionable. Excessive angulation is not compatible with the efficient gaiting of a proportionately tall dog.

Rear Legs. When viewed from behind, the legs should appear to form a straight, strong column of support for the dog, whether he is moving or standing. Any deviation from this straight column of support, such as cowhocks, moving close behind, spread hocks, or popping hocks, is an indication of weakness that should be strongly penalized.

Upper Thigh. The mass of muscle on the upper thigh of an adult Saint Bernard should be great enough so that it cannot be encircled by both hands of a large man. The upper thigh of an adult bitch, while being of slightly lesser girth than that found in a comparable male, must also be massively muscled. Any specimen that is lacking a most impressive muscle mass here fails to display the powerful construction that is the hallmark of the breed.

Hock Joint. The hock joint should be sound and strong. Popping hocks, hocks that buckle under a load, and sickle or nonarticulating hocks are faults that are not found on a good specimen.

Rear Pasterns. The rear pasterns (metatarsus) should be reasonably short but relatively large in girth.

Rear Dewclaws. Dewclaws on the rear legs are preferably present and lie sufficiently tight to the leg so that they do not interfere with the dog's movement. However, they may be removed by surgery by any owner so enamored by cosmetic fads that he feels thus compelled.

Rear Feet. The rear feet, while almost imperceptibly longer than the front feet, are also large, wide, compact, and well-knuckled with thick pads. As on the front legs, bad feet, such as flat or splayed feet or those with thin pads or long toes, should be faulted to the degree that they are present.

Coat

General. The Saint Bernard is double coated with a dense, thick, close-lying fur. The undercoat is thick, soft, dense, and much shorter than the outer coat. The outer coat is firm and resilient; neither coarse nor silky, it is straight and not wavy, except that an occasional specimen will have a slight indication of waviness over the loin and pelvis. A coat that stands out and away from the body is very faulty, whether this condition is natural or is achieved by fluffing the coat during grooming.

Coat Types. The coat of the Saint Bernard comes in two conditions—shorthaired and longhaired.

The shorthaired coat is short over the entire animal, except that the thighs and the tail appear bushy because they have longer and denser hair. The longer and denser hair at the root of the tail gradually becomes shorter toward the tip. The hair is straight, except that an indication of waviness is occasionally observed over the loin and pelvic areas.

The longhaired type completely resembles the shorthaired type, except that the coat is of medium length, straight to slightly wavy, and never rolled, curly, shaggy, or standing away from the body. Any indications of waviness must be restricted to the loin and pelvic areas. The hair on the ears, neck, back of legs, brisket and lower chest, back of thighs, and tail is especially long but not excessively abundant. The coat should form a ruff around the head and neck, should show feathering of the forelegs and belly, and should give the appearance of very bushy pants around the thighs. Hair on the tail must be bushy, never parted or forming a flag. Excessive hair length, open coats, stand-off coats, or limp, soft coats are very undesirable.

Alterations. It is essential to evaluate the Saint Bernard only in his natural condition. Feet may be trimmed and stray hairs cut away for neatness, but the natural appearance of coat or outline must not be altered by cutting or clipping. The practice of back brushing or blow drying the coat to make it stand away from the body must not be condoned. The amputation of whiskers is undesirable. The practice of adding chalk or other material to the legs to give the appearance of increased girth should bring about the immediate dismissal of the dog from any consideration.

Color And Markings

Color. The Saint Bernard is basically a two-color dog—either a white base with solid-colored patches or a solid base color with white patches. In addition, most specimens have a black mask around the eyes that often extends to the face and ears. Black appearing on other parts of the dog is a minor fault; this faulty black color may appear as a patch, as a border around the base color, or as ticking. Ticking, by the way, may come in other colors such as brown or gray, but ticking is always undesirable because it gives a muddy or dirty look to the dog. The base color may be red in its various shades, brindle, or any shade of brown from a dark walnut color to a pale yellow; all colors in this range are of entirely equal value. No consideration should be given to any solid-colored dog, to one without white, or to any black and white dog.

Markings. Necessary markings are a white chest, white feet and tip of tail, white nose band, white collar, or white spot on the nape of the neck. Considered as highly desirable are the white collar, white muzzle, white blaze between the eyes, white belly and legs, and white on the lower half of the tail. The dark mask around the eyes is greatly favored as an enhancement to the dog's expression, but the partial or complete absence of a mask is not in itself a fault.

Many color patterns have been identified, but they play a rather trivial part in the evaluation of a Saint Bernard. Some of these patterns are:

1. A *mantle coat,* which is a solid blanket of color over the back, sides, and rump;
2. A *torn mantle,* which consists of small patches of white within the mantle of color;
3. A *splash coat,* which is a white dog with colored patches;
4. A *monk's cap,* which is a small circle of color between the ears;
5. *Hospice ears,* which are white ears with black speckles;
6. A *slipped mask,* which is the failure of the black to entirely surround the eye on one or both sides;
7. A *half mask,* which is the absence of black around the eye on one side;
8. A *white face,* which is the absence of black around both of the eyes but the presence or partial presence of black on the ears; and
9. A *sheep's head,* which is a dog that is entirely white forward of the shoulders.

Gait

General. It is not possible to evaluate the gait of a Saint Bernard unless he is moved on a loose lead, because being gaited on a tight lead alters the dog's action and balance so much that the true gait cannot be observed.

When the dog is trotting, his gait is free, smooth, powerful, and well coordinated, showing a moderation in length of stride that is in keeping with his moderate angulation and tall body proportions. When moving, the Saint Bernard should present a picture of dignity and grace combined with massive size, a portrait of strength and power coupled with agility and efficiency.

Single Tracking. When the dog moves at the proper speed, the back foot on each side will set down exactly on the track just vacated by the corresponding front foot. When the dog moves at a trot, the feet converge to the center line beneath him so that the dog single tracks.

Side Gait. As his speed increases, the dog positions his head as far forward as necessary to achieve efficient movement, but never below the horizontal. A dog that "runs downhill" is to be faulted.

When viewed from the side, every joint in each leg must do its full share of work and flexing, especially the hock joint. The back must remain strong, firm, and level at any speed. The observer must depreciate any lack of balance or coordination between the front and rear assemblies.

At any speed, the feet must be lifted efficiently up off the ground, for any Saint Bernard that slides his feet along the ground when moving is unsound. Because his work lies in rough, snow-covered terrain, failure to achieve significant lift of pad would place him at a great disadvantage.

The length of stride must be sufficient to have the rear foot set down on the exact spot just vacated by the front foot on the same side; strides shorter or longer than this indicate inefficient movement, which is a fault. The angle of sweep must be the same for the front and rear assemblies; the pivot point of each leg must lie halfway between the forward reach and the rear reach for that leg.

A prevalent problem within the breed is the rolling gait, which indicates a faulty construction and must be depreciated.

Front and Rear Gaiting. Viewed from any position, legs turn neither in nor out, nor do feet cross or interfere with each other.

When viewed from the front or rear, the front leg and the rear leg on the same side operate in a single plane of action, and any deviation from that plane of action is a serious fault.

Gaiting Faults. Stilted movement, clumsiness, or a lumbering gait are very objectionable. Any undesirable actions, such as paddling, winging, out at the elbows, crabbing, interfering, overreaching, pounding, moving close behind, rolling of the body, weaving, crossing over, short choppy steps, up-and-down movement, hopping, hackneyed motion, running wide, or bicycling, are faults that should be penalized according to the severity of their condition.

Any dog that breaks stride when moving at a steady trot indicates a mechanical problem in his construction, and that problem is a fault relating to proper movement.

Temperament

General. The Saint Bernard must be friendly, reliable, and trustworthy; he must display a disposition that is gentle, loyal, adaptable, and eager to please.

Because the dogs' original task was to travel unsupervised in packs of two or three males through arduous and inclement conditions to rescue lost travelers, it is important that the dogs show no aggressive behavior toward other dogs while in a working situation and that they seek to befriend strangers whenever they are in a normal scenario.

Therefore, any evaluation must focus on the fact that quarrelsomeness or hostility toward other dogs or people in usual and accustomed situations, or an unwarranted show of timidity or nervousness, are not in keeping with the Saint Bernard character.

If you have an appreciation for the breed, such negative actions or any display of uncharacteristic behavior must remove the dog from all consideration. No other aspect of the Saint Bernard is as important as this one!

Nadene Wahnschaffe is shown here being awarded Best Junior Handler at the 1992 National Specialty Show of the Saint Bernard Club of America in Ardmore, Oklahoma, by judge Don Carter. Nadene, who has won this award many times, is shown here with her two-and-one-half-year-old dog Ch. Gulliver van Rijn. This nicely balanced dog shows the correct proportionately tall figure.

The Movement Described in the Standard

Some time ago we were attending a seminar for dog-show judges to learn the finer points of evaluating certain breeds for which we hoped to become licensed. As so often happens, my education was enhanced almost as much from the conversations that occurred during the coffee breaks as from the formal presentations.

During the morning break, a group of judges in one corner seemed to be having a rather heated discussion. As I joined the group, it became obvious that they were engaged in the defamation of German Shepherds. Naturally, I felt morally obliged to add my opinion, and soon the conversation turned from bad-mouthing German Shepherds to picking on Saint Bernards. Because the entire group was licensed to judge Saints, I quickly discovered that trying to categorize their statements as the opinions of the ignorant and uninformed was not an effective tactic.

The position adopted by that bunch was that the Standard for Saint Bernards makes no mention of movement, which explains why breeders think that soundness is not important—which, in turn, is the reason why a "good-moving" Saint Bernard is such a rare animal.

Have you ever thought about what you *should* have said after the opportunity to say it is long past? What I said then to those people was that they had a big problem with their definition of "good" as applied to canine locomotion, and that what might be construed as "good" for a German Shepherd was absolutely wrong for a Saint Bernard. I even had my doubts if it was proper for a German Shepherd. The following represents what I *wish* I had said then instead of the rather ineffectual arguments that occurred to me at the time.

It would have been better to contend that the proper movement of a Saint Bernard is well defined in the official Standard for the breed! Of course, this definition of proper movement is not there in blatant statements that are obvious to the casual reader. Rather, it is buried in the complete and thorough description of the mechanical assembly that is asked to move itself from one location to another.

To illustrate this point, let's examine the words found in the official Standard for the Saint Bernard. The most significant point is the statement in the first paragraph that a Saint Bernard must be proportionately tall. Note that this requirement is in direct opposition to a Saint being proportionately long, and it is not a requirement for maximizing altitude! Being proportionately tall precludes a Saint Bernard from indulging in the great long

Ken Buxton with Twin Oaks Honey Bear, UD, as she clears the broad jump. She is one of the many top obedience dogs of the Twin Oaks Kennels owned by Ken and Donna Buxton of Loveland, Ohio.

strides so admired by most of the purebred dog fancy. Long strides are precluded, because the rear foot will interfere with the front foot sooner if the front leg is attached closer to the back leg. If a dog is not going to take long strides, then he shouldn't be as angulated as the long-stride breeds. And behold—the Saint Bernard Standard says exactly that. The rear assembly is defined as being moderately angulated, and the front shoulder is defined as "sloping," thus avoiding the "well laid back" phrase found in so many other Standards.

Before leaving the subject of stride length, let me caution breeders and judges of Saint Bernards to guard against strides that are either too long or too short, for they are both faults that should be eliminated. What defines the terms "too long" and "too short" when applied to stride length? The answer is that whenever the dog is at a trot, the rear foot must set down exactly on the spot just barely vacated by the corresponding front foot. If the rear foot lands before reaching that location, the stride is too short. If it lands forward of that position, the stride is too long.

This is, perhaps, a good place to address the term "moderate" in defining angulation. Whenever a short-coupled dog has everything functioning as it should, and the rear foot lands exactly on the impression left by the corresponding front foot, that dog has moderate angulation. If the dog overreaches, he is "overangulated"; if he underreaches, he is "too straight."

The details described in the Standard that relate to movement all fit together like pieces of a jigsaw puzzle to make a complete and harmonious picture. For example, the Standard uses the term "short" to describe the neck. This fits nicely with the more upright shoulder blade required to fit the short-coupled body. The ribs are defined as well sprung, which means that there should be as much internal volume as possible without interfering with the articulation of either the front or rear assemblies. This search for maximum volume without interfering with movement is continued in the description of the belly. The belly is asked to be deep but narrower than the loin muscles, in order to preclude interference with stifle action. The legs are defined as being straight, implying that the dog will single track with the legs lying in two converging planes when in motion.

The words "massive," "powerful," and "strong," which are used throughout the Standard, dictate a different kind of action and movement than those that are inherent in lightly constructed animals. A Percheron or Clydesdale can move with a certain

Ch. Stoan's Dudley Do Right Jay-U, Am. Can. CDX, WPS, DD, AGD, CGC, WDCh., is shown here in true weight-pulling form. Dudley is the first dog in the history of the breed to combine an AKC championship title with the SBCA's Working Dog Champion title. Dudley is owned and trained by Lia Greendale of Bend, Oregon.

Ch. D'Aosta Darth Vader, CDX, going Best of Breed at the 1984 Winter Specialty Show of the Saint Bernard Club of South Florida in Miami, Florida. The judge was Herman Peabody, the owner/handler was Cathy Babins, and the trophy presenter was Joan Meadors. As a young dog, he got his first group placement on the same day that he finished his CD. He walked out of the obedience ring straight into the group ring.

beauty and grace, but that movement is distinct from the movement of a Thoroughbred. Likewise, a moose in the wild moves with an awesome sense of power and gracefulness that would be called clumsy and cloddish in a deer.

The terms "perfectly straight" and "very broad," which are used in the description of the back, should give you a mental picture of the rock-solid top line that fits with this kind of movement. Similarly, the slope of the croup influences this movement, and it, too, is clearly described in the Standard. Head and tail carriage also affect movement and are described in considerable detail therein.

The Standard for Saint Bernards is amazingly complete and thorough. However, it is written in a manner that requires you to dig deeply to discover that the descriptions of each and every feature combine to paint a harmonious picture. Furthermore, when all of those pieces are combined, it is clear that only one kind of movement is defined.

If you were to write a paraphrase of the Standard on the subject of movement, you would have to say that it demands a powerful and short-coupled animal that moves smoothly with a sense of strength, massiveness, and grace; one that, when viewed from the side, takes a stride of moderate length (while using proper leg articulation and foot placement); one that single tracks when viewed from the front or rear; and one that never shows any sign of weakness or malfunctioning such as shuffling, lumbering, paddling, pounding, overreaching, underreaching, sickle hocks, popping hocks, cowhocks, elbowing out, rolling, bouncing, whipping top line, or whatever else can be wrong with a dog's gait.

To this I would add my own extrapolation—that is, any Saint Bernard that is so long-bodied and overangulated that he can move like a German Shepherd is one that is as much lacking in type as one with an improper head!

Yes, indeed, that's what I should have said!

Serpentina Trinity Fall is shown here in agility trial training. We are able to see here some of the equipment that a dog must master in order to compete in agility trials: the tunnel, the A-frame, the teeter, and the dog walk (balance beam). Trinity, who is three and one-half years old in this picture, is also a certified therapy dog that regularly visits the patients in a local senior citizens home. Trinity and her owner, Darlene Serpa, live in Clearlake, California.

The Expected Temperament of a Saint Bernard

As I travel throughout the United States and the world, I find a large variation in the temperament of the Saint Bernard. My image of the loving, friendly, benevolent animal that first attracted me to these dogs does not seem to be universally accepted as correct for the breed. This is a source of great concern to me.

I despise seeing a Saint at ringside being held in a viselike grip for fear of the consequences if the dog gets loose and gives vent to his instincts. I see Saints that have to be muzzled before they can be taken to and from the ring. I see Saint Bernards bent on getting into a dog fight the entire time they are in the ring. I see Saint Bernards that hesitate not at all to bite anybody who tries to make them do something other than suiting themselves. In my mind, these are not proper Saint Bernards.

It would be belaboring the obvious to say that Saint breeders and owners should be especially careful about the temperament of their dogs. Clearly, Saints are simply too large to have a dangerous temperament. The question is, "Just what is a dangerous temperament?" I doubt that many will argue with the contention that any indication of viciousness in a Saint Bernard is dangerous. Furthermore, there is usually no distinction made between a dangerous temperament and a vicious one. In our breed, the problem is unfortunately much more extensive than that. My job is to convince you that other traits can be just as unacceptable, and that in a dog the size of a Saint, the term "dangerous" can take on many forms.

The first trait that needs denigrating is shyness or fearfulness. The trouble with having a very big dog that is shy or timid is that he is afraid of every out-of-the-ordinary element in his environment. Such a dog is likely to bite someone—seriously. The overly fearful dog will retreat whenever he has the option, but whenever he feels unable to escape from a frightening situation he will unhesitatingly resort to growling and/or biting. Often, these biting episodes happen when the situation is not truly threatening to the dog but only is perceived as such because of the dog's unstable personality. You often hear stories such as, "He was sleeping on the floor when the four-year-old walked past. He just woke up and attacked the child, and then he seemed ashamed of himself."

According to accepted dog lore, a fearful personality may be other than hereditary in nature. Supposedly, shyness may be something that a dog acquires through some sort of shock or trauma, or the dog may act shy because he was never properly socialized—the so-called kennel personality. It is usually accepted that hereditary shyness is permanent and incurable, that it is sometimes possible to cure, or at least reduce, traumatic fear, and that kennel shyness usually gives way to confidence over time. I, on the other hand, have trouble with the idea of there being different types of timidity,

Ch. Belyn's Grendle v. Exchequer soaking her paw. Grendle was a "Hall of Fame" and "Plateau of Excellence" producer, being the dam of the famous Lynchcreek "A" and "B" litters. Candy Blancher of Eatonville, Washington, owned Grendle.

because I have not been able to find any way to make reliable distinctions between these various categories of shyness. I believe that a basic stable temperament never becomes shy under any circumstance. More often than not, people want to make any excuse other than heredity for their dog's behavior. If you investigate, you will find that almost every condition of shyness in a Saint Bernard is traceable to his ancestors.

"So," you ask, "what's the big deal about shyness? How can shyness be considered as important as viciousness?" It has long been my contention that hereditary shyness and viciousness are simply two sides of the same coin. The nasty dog and the shy one will often come from the same background, and their personalities are simply two different outward expressions of the same genetic flaw in their character—a flaw that cannot be tolerated in a Saint Bernard.

That's enough about shyness. There is another kind of dangerous temperament—the overly boisterous Saint Bernard. This type of personality features an overabundance of exuberance, which I call the "Labrador" personality. While we can all agree that a Saint Bernard with a propensity to bite is dangerous, we may have trouble agreeing that uninhibited and unruly behavior should have the

Ch. Chad's Raleigh with his owner, Carol Terrio, delights the residents of a nursing home in Phoenix, Arizona, with his kind and gentle manner.

Am. Can. Ch. Stoan's Quincy of Cabra, CD, CGC, gathering a crowd of admirers at the International Kennel Club's bench show in Chicago, Illinois. Lyle and Marlys Larson of Edina, Minnesota, owned Quincy.

same label. Let me present my arguments that boisterousness should be identified as dangerous in a dog the size of a Saint Bernard.

This turbulent type of dog shows little interest in what his owner wants in the way of behavior. He shows, however, a keen interest in anything and everything in his environment and feels no compunction about launching an immediate investigation into whatever is foremost in his mind's eye. I usually think of this dog in terms of crash, leap, bang, bash, crunch, lunge, knocking over, or knocking down. This lack of concern about what his master wants is decidedly not what Saint Bernards are about. Nor can you deny that such behavior is dangerous to children, to the elderly, and to anyone who lacks the size and strength to withstand this kind of onslaught. Heads have been fractured, limbs have been broken, and cuts and contusions have ensued from such out-of-control Saint Bernards.

The case for this sort of behavior being genetic is not as clear as it is for the propensity to bite. We often think of this as puppy behavior that was never corrected; that is, learned behavior that was obviously the owner's fault. But, is it? Is it really learned behavior? I think not, and let me tell you why.

The type of temperament that breeders should be seeking is the kind found in dogs that were sent out unattended, in packs of two or three adult males, in terrible weather conditions, and over a treacherous landscape to seek out strangers and render assistance to those in trouble—in short, dogs that are gregarious with strangers, unaggressive toward other dogs and people, intelligent, eager to please, and devoted to their assigned tasks. This is not a description of the self-centered and uncaring behavior characteristic of an overly boisterous animal. Because I believe that breeders can and should breed for the personality characteristics that are supposed to be typical for the breed, then it follows that *not* having those personality characteristics is a genetic flaw in a Saint Bernard.

Heaven Hi's Two Bits Worth shown here in this 1965 photograph giving his young owner, Micah Pentico, a lift. Both are five years old in this picture.

An early spring moment in the Garden of Flowers and Dogs catches the author indulging in an opportunity to sit and visit with some of his Saint Bernards. (He is really trying to protect the flowers from the dogs!) You should expect your dogs to get along with other dogs and to be friendly with people.

Do Saint Bernards dig holes? Here you see Ch. Denoncourt's Barney wondering just why his owner has taken over a hole he has just dug for himself! In the hole is Betty Roberts Nelson, owner of Shagg Bark Kennels in Tolland, Connecticut.

This also holds true for aggressiveness toward other dogs. Many will tell you that they can forgive a male being aggressive toward another male. "Why?" I ask. The breed is not supposed to be like that, so why would anybody want a dog that is forever looking for a fight? Unprovoked dog fights simply are not a proper activity for Saint Bernards.

Two other temperament-related factors should be of concern to the fancy—insanity and intelligence. The concept of intelligence as being important, desirable, and inherited is self-evident and in little need of discussion, but insanity in the Saint Bernard does need our attention. By insanity I am talking about dogs that have a screw loose somewhere—the so-called junkyard dogs that attack anything and everything that moves. These dogs are beyond vicious!

This may be difficult to believe, but there are actually some within the Saint Bernard fancy who admire a "tough, hard" dog. Rottweilers and Pit Bulls are the breeds that usually attract this type of personality. It is our bad luck that it is relatively easy to breed an aggressive personality. In fact, two or three generations are enough to produce a line of these "hounds from hell," even if you start with reasonably sound temperaments in your stock. There are many in the general dog fancy who remember those days, not so long ago, when Saint Bernards were rapidly rising in popularity and attracting breeders of questionable motives or knowledge. In those "good old days," people were afraid, and with good reason, to walk down the aisle where the Saint Bernards were waiting to enter the ring. It behooves us to remember that we are not far from having "insanity" again become a significant feature of our breed. And we don't have to wait for the Saint Bernard to return to those record levels of popularity. Just let some vicious Saint become a big winner and see how long it takes to have lots of vicious puppies growing up to produce the next and succeeding generations.

Now the question must be asked, "What's to be done?" The course of action is clear. If you love Saint Bernards, you must never make or accept any excuse for unacceptable behavior. We have all heard the many reasons offered to explain a dog's bad behavior: "The kids used to tease him through the fence." "His first owner mistreated him." "The breeder didn't spend enough time socializing the litter." "A black dog (fill in any breed here) attacked him when he was young." "When he was a puppy, he was frightened by the sound of the garbage cans dropping from the garbage truck."

One of the greatest dangers associated with a deviant temperament lies with the owners. So often, people rationalize growling, snapping, or even minor biting incidents with these stories, and eventually somebody gets seriously attacked. Making excuses for your dog is the moral equivalent to justifying having a live hand grenade around the house. It may not go off, but who can live with the consequences if it does?

I suggest that no matter what physical or mental trauma the dog has experienced, it must be assumed that any negative behavior is hereditary. There are no allowable excuses! Any Saint that displays negative behavior should be considered to have a genetic fault that requires just as much attention as the faults dealing with poor head type and lack of substance.

Of course, it is not enough to define "undesirable behavior," because it is important to agree on how a Saint Bernard *should* act. In my opinion, the following examples constitute Saintly behavior.

Spike giving Zack a ride. This photo displays the tolerance for abuse by children that one should expect from Saint Bernards. Spike had never seen this child before the boy went into the yard to play with the dog and decided to see if he could use him for a horse substitute.

1. A Saint Bernard should suffer through any imaginable abuse from small toddlers without any display of resentment. Any Saint that will not allow a small child to poke him in the eye or sit straddling his back is not worthy of the name.
2. When the dog has business to which he is supposed to attend, such as being in a showring or walking with his master, the dog should be expected to not challenge other dogs to a fight.
3. A Saint is expected to love and protect his family, not be a source of bumps and bruises. I remember my surprise when I discovered our first Saint's self-imposed duty. He felt that it was his job to stand between my small children and any perceived danger, be it traffic in the street, a passing stranger or dog, or just a loud noise. That is proper Saint Bernard behavior, as opposed to knocking down small children, intentional or not.
4. When a dog is in a nonthreatening situation (and I expect the dog to have and to use good judgment about if and when a situation is threatening), he should wag his tail at every stranger he encounters. You want a Saint eagerly to meet new friends and to just plain like people in general!

There are literally thousands of examples of Saint Bernards behaving appropriately, but these should be enough to give you the picture. Saint

Bernards should have a saintlike disposition, and this is what you should expect—nay, demand!

This brings me back to the course of action that should be followed by responsible members of the fancy. Breeders must select for good temperament. Exhibitors and owners must demand good temperament; they must recognize poor behavior and decry it as being highly objectionable. Judges must never condone any display of deviant behavior; and any such behavior must be penalized as much as any other serious fault.

I want to leave you with these words: Those who care about Saint Bernards must always applaud a Saintly disposition and soundly condemn any behavior that doesn't fit the Saint Bernard ideal—and never make excuses.

In this lovely forest setting, Ch. Lynchcreek's Forbes Elation prepares for Christmas. This photograph was taken in 1996 when Forbes was four years old. Candy Blancher and Sue Allmand bred Forbes, and he is owned by Candy Blancher and Frances Porter of Puyallup, Washington. His sire is Ch. High Chateau's Emir, and his dam is Ch. Belyn's Que Sera.

The Skin Game

This is one of those times when I feel the urge to expound on a subject that has very little interest to most people. I wish to decry the wet Saint Bernard. "So, just what is the problem?" you ask. My answer is, I am concerned with the number of wet dogs that are being promoted as examples of greatness within our breed. Whenever I try to discuss wet dogs with somebody, I am asked, "What are you talking about?" Let me try to explain.

So how do you decide if a dog is dry or wet? Ask yourself whether he more resembles a sack full of wet mush that sloshes as he lumbers along, or is he a superb athlete with muscles of steel and a spring to his step? When you place your hands on that dog, do you feel soft, spongy tissue or hard, firm flesh? If the dog more closely resembles a water balloon than a strong, powerful animal, then he probably can be thought of as "wet." Wet dogs universally have excess skin that seems to sag and flow into ugly wrinkles. They often have poor-fitting ligaments that result in joint slackness as expressed in weak pasterns, loose hocks, or flat feet. Nothing about the dog is tight or firm.

There is a concern that occupies the attention of numerous dog fanciers regarding a material called collagen, which is one of the basic materials used to fabricate animal bodies. A theory exists in some circles that the quality of the collagen in a dog's body determines the wetness or dryness aspect of his anatomy. This theory also claims that collagen quality is an inherited factor and that it determines not only muscle tone, but also the quality of ligaments, connective tissue, bones, organ material, and skin. And, according to this theory, the most obvious evidence of poor collagen quality is excessive skin.

Dad's asleep while his son stands guard. Dad is Ch. Stoan's Adam Mistihil, CD, and junior is Stoan's Gustav Mistihil, both owned by Fran Stephens of Seattle, Washington.

Once you accept this theory, you must follow it to the next logical conclusion, which is that poor connective tissue is the root cause of internal organs not maintaining their proper attachment, thus leading to maladies such as stomach torsion, telescoped bowels, and bowels extruding out through the anus. Further expansion on this theory states that weak, spongy ligaments fail to keep bones in proper alignment, causing problems such as hip dysplasia, elbow dysplasia, rheumatoid arthritis, and popping hocks. The most radical promoters of this theory also claim a connection between poor-quality collagen and various diseases such as heart problems, kidney failure, and susceptibility to certain kinds of bone cancer.

Just think—all of these problems are more likely to happen to a dog that has a little extra skin! Isn't that a scary thought? Personally, I am reserving judgment on this theory until some significant research has been accomplished. On the other hand, I see enough correlation to keep me from disregarding the entire concept. In the meantime, I try to breed a drier dog.

It is not unproven theories alone, however, that make me seek a better-fitting skin for the Saint Bernard. First, wet dogs have a fifty-point head start on the ugly scale—they just are not attractive. Second, and of much more importance, the Standard forbids excess skin:

> "Too strongly developed wrinkles are not desired."
> "The flews of the lower jaw must not be deeply pendant."
> "The dewlap of throat and neck is well pronounced: too strong development, however, is not desirable."

It is clear that the Standard does not want an absolutely dry animal such as the Greyhound or Bull Terrier, but it does indicate that extreme wetness is a fault.

There are also some specific problems. Quite a few Saints have so much skin that their faces seem to be melting—almost to be dripping. Sometimes this same condition can be found on the neck, body, and legs. You get the impression of a size-six dog wearing a size-twelve dog suit. This condition is *not* attractive, and, as just stated, it is defined in the Standard as a decided fault. The Standard allows only a small degree of wetness. Keep in mind that whenever the wrinkles dominate the

(Above): Ch. Shagg-Bark's Buddy, a powerful shorthaired male, being awarded Best of Winners at the 1968 specialty show of the Northern New Jersey Saint Bernard Club. Buddy was handled here by Al Saba for owner Bill Roberts of Connecticut.

(Below): Australian Champion Tremel Distant Saint, owned by Judy Teniswood of Tasmania, Australia, was imported into Australia from England. This dog was the top winning Saint Bernard in Tasmania in 1984, 1985, and 1986.

Cache Retreat Xcerpt of Storm, CD, with Jerri Hobbs, Beth McCarthy, and Doris Fellows, 1985. Each of these people successfully handled the dog to one leg of his CD title for owners Dennis and Jerri Hobbs.

appearance of the head, the fault is very real. If the wrinkles extend to the neck, body, or legs, you are looking at a disaster.

Not that skin is a bad thing. In fact, the skin is very important, because it hides all of the gory stuff that covers the bones! The average dog would be unsightly without his skin. Furthermore, the skin provides a good place for all of the pretty hair to grow. It is only unfortunate that many Saint Bernards have too *much* of this particular good thing, and the reason why this occurs is because having too much skin is not universally recognized as a detriment to the breed.

Some exhibitors do not find this fault as objectionable as I do, because a skillful handler can take too much skin and turn it into an asset. If you can congregate folds of skin where bone ought to be, you can create the illusion of a proper head. A pile of wrinkles over the eyes can fake the presence of a correct supraorbital ridge. A gargantuan fold of skin along each side of the head can make the head seem twice its true width. A great, pendulous flew gives the casual observer the impression of adequate muzzle depth. If you aspire to be an expert fancier of Saint Bernards, you should be able to spot these impostors from sixty feet away. If you don't have this skill, your endeavors—be they breeding, exhibiting, or judging—will be a source of embarrassment.

And then there are people who have a basically good dog, yet choose to breed dogs that have too much skin. I have a suspicion that these folks are trying to achieve more substance—also known as more bone. Of course, they do not really *get* more bone; they end up with the same size bone with more nonmuscle tissue around it. The real problem is that there seems to be a genetic link between increased tissue mass and excess skin—you can't seem to get one without the other. If you want a dog with superior substance, you have to accept superior wetness in the same animal.

The more successful dogs in the ring today have a great amount of bone, yet they have no more muscle mass or bone size than their finer-legged cousins. We breeders (yes, that includes me) seem to have achieved this added mass (tissue) without increasing the amount of muscle or bone on our dogs. Is that good or bad? I think that there is more negative than positive in this situation. For the sake of some empty-headed fad, I believe that we are doing bad things to our beloved Saints. Perhaps it is time for the fancy to rethink its priorities; time to consider a redirection of our goals; time to adopt a new definition of the ideal specimen. I have grave doubts that our present course is in the best interest of the breed or stands any chance of producing a better Saint Bernard.

What Size Is the Right Size?

"What an idiot!" Joan exclaimed angrily as she hung up the telephone. "All this guy wants is a great big dog, and he could care less if it bites somebody or if it dies at the ripe old age of three!" she continued heatedly. This happened some time ago, but I remember it well. It was when we had one of our earliest litters, and we had placed an advertisement in the newspaper in an effort to move the little critters out of the kitchen. For some reason, it seemed that most of the people who called were only concerned about how big the puppies would become. Try as we might, we could not seem to interest them in temperament, soundness, or type.

I was reminded of that event so long ago when I first contemplated putting down my thoughts on "how big" is right for a Saint Bernard, and it made me realize that things are not much different now. There is still that heavy emphasis on giant height, but now I am much more aware that this passion for extreme size is not limited to uninformed puppy buyers. I still hear from every corner, "I want them *big!* Gimme a *big* one!"

"How big?" is the question, but "how come?" must also be answered. Such short questions; you would think they would have short answers, wouldn't you? Unfortunately, the answers are long and complex. My problem in discussing this subject is that I find myself trying to wear two hats at the same time.

My logical hat tells me that the breed was never intended to have its males scale much over the current minimum of twenty-seven and one-half inches. When the breed was in service originally, the body type that was able to survive and function under the rigors of life at the Hospice du Grand Saint Bernard was smaller and much more lightly constructed than the dogs of today. I suspect that the very largest of the males actually used at the Hospice measured less than twenty-eight inches at the withers, and most of them were less than our present-day minimum. If the original "Barry" was to show up at the showring tomorrow, he would probably be directed to the American Foxhound ring.

Sebring's Summer Breeze, WP, WPX, WPS. Summer was the first Saint Bernard to be awarded the Weight Puller Superior title by the Saint Bernard Club of America. She earned this title at the 1988 National Specialty in the weight-pulling event, where she successfully pulled 1,940 pounds, which was 16.4 times her weight. Summer is owned by Carole and Don Dvorak of Benton City, Washington, and was bred by Betty and Jo Benko.

It is sometimes said that we should breed our dogs to maintain their original purpose. Anyone who claims that modern Saint Bernards should represent the ability to perform their historic work would have reason to seek a much smaller and lighter-boned animal than the smallest and slightest of the exhibits in the showring today.

Now I will put on my "I like what I like so don't confuse me with facts" hat. A young lady recently asked me, "Since you don't like big dogs, why did you ever get involved with Saint Bernards in the first place?" My not-too-swift rejoinder was, "Whatever gave you the idea that I don't greatly admire a big Saint?"

(Left): Almshaus Krystal, WP, WPX, WPS, at the age of four years, pulling a huge stack of dog food at the 1989 International Weight Pulling Association trial in Portland, Oregon. Krystal is the Saint Bernard Club of America's highest pointed Saint Bernard in weight pulling with a personal best of 5,020 pounds. She was owned by Ray and Barbara Slish of Kent, Washington, and was bred by Libby Surface.

(Right): Ch. Stoan's Dean Witter of Valinta, owned by Tamiko Van Buskirk of Renton, Washington, and Joan Zielinski of Kent, Washington, is shown here at the Saint Bernard Club of America's 1998 Weight Pull event in St. Louis, Missouri. Dean, who placed second in this event, is shown here pulling a pile of concrete blocks and dog food that weighs just over 3,100 pounds. This picture shows a dog properly using his strength and power to move the load rather than just using his weight and bulk to do the job.

Who can deny that their original attraction to the breed was generated by an admiration of great size? If there is but one factor common to all within the Saint Bernard fancy, it is that we all greatly admire big dogs. If you ask the average man on the street for a one-word synonym for Saint Bernards, that word would be "BIG"; that is the perception with which we all started. So what made some of us change our emphasis? It was only after a period of growth as a true fancier of the breed that my philosophy gave way to an appreciation of the more important aspects of the breed. It does not take too much effort to produce quality animals to pass beyond the "bigger-the-better" mind set. Those with enough experience to know what they are doing and who honestly seek the betterment of the breed do not long subscribe to the siren's call of "big-at-any-cost." This does not mean that concerned and experienced people have lost their desire for an enormous hulk of a dog. It only means that they understand that their desire for size must be tempered with an uncompromising demand for overall quality. Few sights are more terrible than an immense Saint Bernard that is totally devoid of quality.

A misplaced obsession with outsized Saint Bernards is most appalling because, in the final analysis, it is a detriment to breed progress. Any Saint Bernard that just barely exceeds the minimum height is still a very large dog, and his size will not keep him from performing all of the functions desired by the originators of the breed. Yet, there are those among us who seek an animal that is taller by a foot or more. "Why?" I wonder. Could it be that seeking a taller Saint Bernard has nothing to do with the dogs themselves? Perhaps it has more to do with measuring a person's worth by his material possessions, and in America, the trend is towards "the bigger, the better." Just look at the advertisements that permeate so many of the popular canine publications; ad after ad extolling the great height of some dog, as if that was all that was important. It seems to me that they are saying, "My dog is bigger than my competitors' dogs, and therefore my dog is better than theirs, and therefore I am pretty important." I must conclude that the desire for a bigger Saint Bernard most often is not related to what is best for the breed, but rather is just simply a sop for somebody's ego!

I am not trying to make a case for small stature! I only wish to discredit the push for ever greater size. Have you ever wondered what is to be gained by increasing the average height of our dogs? I have, and I only came up with reasons for going the other way. For example, our Saints do not live as long as many of the smaller breeds; and research indicates that increasing the size of our dogs may only shorten their expected lifespan. The time we have with them is so precious, and so short, why would anybody want to shorten it even more?

Then consider the fact that an increase in height has a cubic effect on mass! For example, a 5-percent increase in height results in a 16-percent increase in the amount of blood the kidneys must filter and the heart must pump. A 10-percent increase in altitude results in a 33-percent increase in the load that each joint, ligament, and piece of connective tissue must carry. Adolescent arthritis, hip dysplasia, osteochondritis, bloat, heart problems, kidney failure, cancer, and all other stress-related problems are a heavy price our dogs must pay just for being large. Why, then, would anybody want to place more of a burden on them?

Ch. Engler's Champagne Quint, one of the top stud dogs of the 1970s, was owned by Richard and Dinah Tull of Rockville, Maryland, and was bred by Frank and Doris Engler of Kent, Ohio.

I can't count the number of times I have heard someone say, "If you have two equal dogs then you should choose the bigger one!" I find such thinking wrong. First of all, I have never, ever seen two equal dogs, which means that this statement is erroneous in the first place. You should always choose the better dog, not the bigger one, because this is the path toward betterment of the breed. Secondly, this statement leaves many people with the impression that ever-increasing bigness is a virtue in its own right, and therefore it is some sort of a goal. My task is to convince you that this isn't true. I advocate that there is an optimum size for our breed, and that we should all seek that best size.

I estimate that well over 90 percent of the quality in the adult males of the breed is expressed in dogs that measure between twenty-nine and thirty-one inches at the withers. Almost without exception, well-proportioned males that measure less than twenty-eight inches are much too feminine, which is an unforgivable fault in a stud dog. Short masculine males almost always fail to be well proportioned, which is another kind of fault, and it is one that you can expect in their puppies! In a similar vein, quality seems rare in dogs that rise above thirty-one inches. I have never observed a male dog significantly over thirty-two inches at the shoulder without feeling that he should be neutered in order to serve the best interests of the breed.

If I seem to have slighted the feminine part of the breed, let me fix that now. I bow to the words in the Standard, which clearly define the relationship between male and female Saint Bernards. If you subtract between an inch and a half and two inches from any of my statements about the males of the species, you will have my precise thoughts on what constitute ideal feminine characteristics.

In seeking to better our breed, it is obvious that we should have some sort of agreed-upon standard of perfection. That is, we should all be trying to breed the same type of Saint Bernard. But how can we with the current situation?

While judging, I see very pretty adult male Saints that I estimate measure no more than twenty-five inches at the withers. At the other extreme, I hear claims of thirty-eight-inch males (though such animals are outside of my experience). Supposedly, you could have a ring for adult male Saint Bernards in which there is a twenty-five-inch male and a thirty-eight-inch male being exhibited; could you possibly

Swissong's Marsha Mellow, a very worthy bitch despite her lack of a mask, is being awarded Winners Bitch. Marsha, owned and bred by Don and Carole Dvorak, is being handled by Don Dvorak. This bitch displays the correct proportions and balance one should seek in a Saint Bernard.

say that they are of the same breed? To do so would, of course, be utter nonsense! And yet, that is the position that has been adopted by our fancy.

So, what is the solution? If we want to achieve any pretense at uniformity, we should establish an ideal height and then insist that the dogs all be within one inch of that ideal. Many other breeds have done this with considerable success in achieving breed uniformity. Such a rule would eliminate many worthy animals, so perhaps we could allow a certain degree of faultiness for dogs just outside that range, and disqualify dogs that were outside some other limit. If we were to limit the extreme range to a five-inch span, we would be eliminating almost none of the dogs shown in recent times. This would not be as beneficial to the breed as insisting that the dogs all be within a two-inch range, but it is possibly a change to the perception of correct breed type that would be palatable to exhibitors and breeders.

I therefore propose that, for adult male Saint Bernards, we consider the ideal height at the withers to be thirty inches. Then any dog that measures within one and a half inches of the ideal height (between twenty-eight and one-half inches and thirty-one and one-half inches) would be considered a good specimen of the breed. Logically then, heights just outside this three-inch range by no more than an inch (that is, either between twenty-seven and one-half inches and twenty-eight and one-half inches, or between thirty-one and one-half inches and thirty-two and one-half inches) must be designated as faulty, but allowed. Extending this line of reasoning, heights below twenty-seven and one-half inches and those over thirty-two and one-half inches should be disqualified. Obviously, for female Saint Bernards the height at the withers for every category should be two inches shorter. Table 7.1 clarifies this data.

It is not and never will be possible (or even desirable) to get the official Standard revised to effect such a change. Nor am I absolutely positive that we would want to forever eliminate having larger dogs if it ever became possible to breed such animals and maintain breed quality. I would like to see our fancy put more emphasis on Saint Bernard quality, and move away from the mind set that claims "the bigger the better." What the world really needs is better Saints, not bigger ones.

Having thoroughly discussed altitude with respect to Saint Bernards, we have not exhausted the subject of size until we have looked at the proper weight of our animals. If we accept the words in our Standard, massiveness is a virtue in our dogs, so let's now turn our attention to this well abused topic.

It doesn't matter if your dog is in the upper one percent of the Saint Bernard population with respect to size or weight. If you take him out in public, you will invariably meet someone who has a bigger Saint Bernard at home. People always seem to grossly exaggerate the size of their dogs, and Saint Bernard owners are notorious for their wild claims. For this reason, declarations of any unusually heavy weight must be considered suspect until proven by a believable witness to a certified weighing.

It is generally accepted that the Saint Bernard is the heaviest of all dogs as a breed. About 1988, the *Guinness Book of World Records* listed two English Saint Bernards as being the heaviest weight ever recorded. The first, Brandy, owned by Miss Gwendoline L. White of "Chinnor," Oxfordshire, weighed 259 pounds on February 11, 1966. Another Saint, Westernisles Ross, owned by Jean R. Rankin of Glasgow, Scotland, weighed 256 pounds on April 28, 1966. I would be very surprised if these two dogs were not exceedingly overweight.

TABLE 7.1
PROPOSED CORRECT HEIGHT AT SHOULDERS FOR SAINT BERNARDS

CATEGORY	MALES	FEMALES
Disqualification	Less than 27.5″	Less than 25.5″
Faulty	27.5″ to 28.5″	25.5″ to 26.5″
Good	28.5″ to 30.0″	26.5″ to 28.0″
Perfect	30.0″	28.0″
Good	30.0″ to 31.5″	28.0″ to 29.5″
Faulty	31.5″ to 32.5″	29.5″ to 30.5″
Disqualification	More than 32.5″	More than 30.5″

At the Saint Bernard Club of America National Specialty Show in 1963, eighty-eight Saint Bernards were weighed on certified scales. The heaviest was Ch. Powell's Tristan of Riga, owned by Larry Powell. That dog weighed 217 pounds. Several others weighed in just under 200 pounds; however, most of the adult males ranged between 140 and 195 pounds. The average for the Open Class males was 159 pounds. Adult bitches ranged from 120 pounds to 186 pounds, though the average for the Open Class females was 138 pounds.

The Purdue University School of Veterinary Medicine published in 1996 the measurements taken of adult Saint Bernards used in their bloat study. These were all dogs entered in Saint Bernard specialty shows. They reported the weights of fifty-seven adult females that ranged from a low of 95 pounds to a high of 170 pounds, with an average weight for adult female Saint Bernards of 132.8 pounds. The same report listed the weights of eighty-two adult males; they ranged from a low of 115 pounds to a high of 205 pounds, with an average weight for adult male Saint Bernards of 156 pounds.

At the first "B" match of the Saint Bernard Club of Puget Sound, all of the dogs were weighed. The average weight for adult males was 151 pounds, with a range of 119 to 178 pounds, and the average weight for adult bitches was 132 pounds, with a range of 102 to 172 pounds.

In my limited experience, I have never seen a dog in good weight and good condition that actually weighed more than 185 pounds. I have, however, seen a couple of very fat dogs push a scale to just over 200 pounds. I would expect a fit dog of good substance measuring thirty inches at the shoulders to weigh about 170 pounds.

If you must brag about your dog's weight, this information should help you make your claims reasonable.

So, where does that leave someone who likes great size but is not willing to sacrifice the more important aspects of the breed? This I say to you: Whenever and wherever you can find impressive size and/or imposing massiveness in a Saint Bernard of true quality, go for it! But always remember; quality first, then bigness!

No Head, No Saint!

I have always loved a good argument. It really gives me a sense of accomplishment to get people to angrily wave their arms about and resort to shouting in order to make a point. That's why I want to tell you about what makes a Saint Bernard head so important. I can usually fire up a good debate by stating that an inadequate head on a Saint Bernard makes that dog unusable. Whether we are in the breeding arena or the showring, a poor head is sufficient to remove that animal from all consideration. This is because we all claim that we are trying to produce a perfect Saint Bernard, and one of the features of a perfect Saint Bernard is beauty. Beauty, of course, is in the eyes of the beholder, but the beholder should be greatly influenced by our Standard, which places great importance on a correct head.

I need to make one caveat. Let there be no doubt in anyone's mind that a Saint Bernard is first and foremost a working dog! As such, he must be able to perform his functions as the founders of the breed intended. This applies to both his structure and temperament.

Besides the fact that the Standard says a correct (and, therefore, a beautiful) head is important, common sense insists on the same conclusion. Just as a good-looking girl might have a major shortcoming with respect to her figure and still be considered beautiful, so it is with Saint Bernards. It takes a pretty face to have a pretty animal.

I once read a profound essay that was written many years ago by someone who obviously loved the breed. I was told that this article was first taken from a very old, now defunct, publication. According to one estimate, it was originally written in 1922. Unfortunately, the name of the author was lost in the process of copying from one newsletter to the next. It is likely that the text has seen some revision since that original publication. Nevertheless, it shows that the important aspects of our breed have continued to be a concern over a period of time. This is what that unknown author had to say:

Ch. Stoan's Lorraine of Verb being awarded BOS in Sweepstakes at the SBCA's 1982 National Specialty Show by the noted breeder Beatrice Knight of Sanctuary Woods Kennel. While this picture was being taken, Mrs. Knight remarked that she would have preferred better head type, but that this bitch's construction, muscle tone, and athletic movement were more than adequate compensation. She continued by remarking that she wished people would put as much emphasis on sound bodies and good temperament as they did on just making the dogs pretty.

To both my new friends and adversaries of long standing I must bear the thoughts in my mind about the controversy that confronts the people of our breed.

How can it be possible to judge, efficiently and intelligently, a Saint Bernard dog if the head is neglected? It is in the head that the Saint Bernard shows up his breed; in the form of the skull, the eyes, the ears, and in that almost indefinable beauty of expression—kindly and benevolent when he looks at his people, but full of intelligent concern if danger threatens his master, his home.

Could anyone admire a dog with a well constructed body but with an ugly head? This is an impossibility, and any judge doing this misses the point altogether. He will never know the real emotion of finding in front of him the breath taking beauty of a real Saint!

The broad massive shape of the skull; the finely chiseled junction between the muzzle and the head; the strong, square muzzle with its flat, broad roof; the deep furrow between the eyes; the deep set eyes above the strong flaring cheeks; the well turned flew which displays no tendency of excess; these are the important features of the Saint Bernard head. The ensemble is finished off by the black nose, lips and palate—no intermediate color of pigmentation should be displayed; no pink or brown.

The whole head is made alive by the alert, glowing with good will, look in the dark diamond shaped eyes; eyes that are set distinctly to the front of the skull and never to the side!

But even with the perfect head and eyes, the picture would not be complete without the well placed ears—set rather well up on the skull so that the attentive ears combine with the crown to form a pleasing, broad, expansive curve; V-shaped, rounded at the tips, medium to large in size, heavy in texture and carried with the back edge set well away from the head.

So I appeal to all; please, no unpigmented noses, no dirty speckles on the face or muzzle, no staring light eyes, no wet sloppy lower lips or deeply pendulous flews, no Roman noses (as found in the Great Pyrenees dogs) nor round-topped muzzles (as found in the Newfoundland dogs), no long nor tapered muzzles, no narrow skulls, no shallow stops, no indistinct cheek bones, no heads of unimpressive size! Great care must be given to all of these things; indeed the maintenance of type is difficult to ensure, but a good and severe judgment, without consideration for personal preferences, will greatly benefit the breed.

One last word of advice to judges and breeders; never allow the form of the head to become lost, nor the expression in the eyes of the true Saint Bernard. Once lost, they are most difficult to regain; much more difficult than features of the body or limbs. You may, perhaps, manage to breed a very nice dog, but would anybody know of what breed?

Anon

Ch. Cache Retreat Academy being awarded Best of Opposite Sex at the 1996 National Specialty Show of the Saint Bernard Club of America in Frederick, Maryland. The judge is O. M. Capodice and the handler is Pam Hathaway. Academy's breeder is Ivan Palmblad, who has established his Cache Retreat kennel in northern Utah.

Ch. Revilo's Quincy, CGC, at the age of two and one-half years being awarded Best of Breed and Best in Specialty Show at the SBCA's 1997 National Specialty Show. The handler is Joe Wolf, the breeder is Jane Baird, the judge is Joan Zielinski, and the owners are Bill and Diana Oliver of Beaverton, Oregon. Quincy is a large, sound, and massive dog of good proportions with an excellent head.

There is one big problem that needs mention. You can easily take a lot of correct features, put them together, and end up with a result that is less than attractive. Overall beauty is still more important in defining a Saint head than any number of individually attractive features. Remember that aspects of proportions, balance, and fit must *never* be neglected.

The subject of heads has no bounds. Many words have been written on this topic, and I recommend that you seek out other opinions and reach your own conclusions about what is right in a Saint head, and what is important.

(Right): Ch. Sweetholm's Heartbreak Kid, CGC, HOF, POE, with his handler and co-owner, Melissa Diaz-Getty, a few hours after going Best of Breed at the SBCA's 1995 National Specialty. Heartbreaker is also co-owned by Elizabeth Surface of Maple Valley, Washington, and bred by Marilyn Murphy of Sumner, Washington. His sire was Ch. Stoan's Jupiter v. Oxbow, HOF, and his dam was Cache Retreat U R My Sunshine, WDCh., CDX, DD, WPS, HOF.

Am. Can. Ch. Stoan's Quincy of Cabra, CD, CGC, practicing for more advanced obedience work, 1996. Lyle and Marlys Larson of Edina, Minnesota, own Quincy.

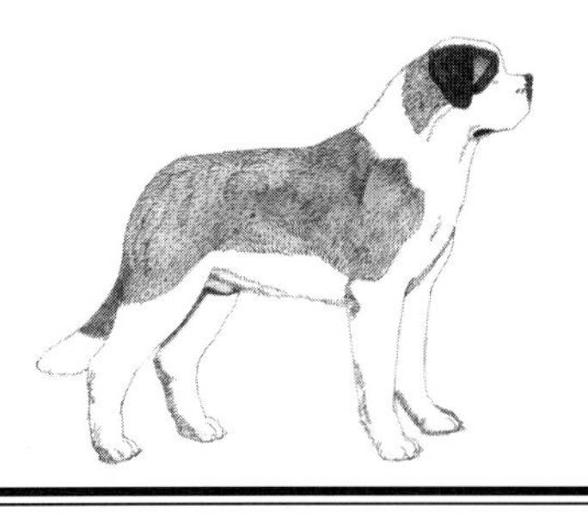

Proportions of the Head

Beauty has been described as all components correct and in proper relationship to the whole. Could there be anything more important to having a beautiful head than having the correct proportions to all of the major features? I don't think so! I am going to relate what I think are the proper proportions of a beautiful Saint Bernard head. However, be aware that others have different criteria for their concept of a good head. In fact, this is the one subject that will generate a heated discussion faster than any other. It's a topic that commands the passions of almost everyone in the fancy.

Many years ago, during a discussion of head proportions, a famous East Coast breeder embarrassed me greatly by asking me what ratios I considered to be necessary for the ideal head. In my usual style, I shot off my mouth before I considered what I was talking about. I then sat down and drew a head profile that fit my specifications and found that such a head was grotesque. You might try doing this when you get the chance. I guarantee that it will be educational. Over the intervening years, I have asked a number of people to define their ideal proportions of a Saint's head, and then to block out a head that fits those proportions. The results have been entertaining and have made me realize that Saint fanciers have a great range in their opinion of a good head. Some of these views appear to relate to particular bloodlines, while others draw upon different factors, such as the type of head found on their own dog or something they have read or been told.

Sanctuary Woods Bodacious, 1964, at Sanctuary Woods Kennels in Drain, Oregon; owned and bred by Beatrice M. Knight. Note the powerful head and excellent balance of this dog.

I attribute this great divergence of opinion to a shortfall in our Standard, in which head proportions have been underdescribed. To illustrate my point, I gleaned the Standard to pick out all of the phrases that have any relationship to head proportions. The following excerpts seem to be the only statements appropriate to this subject.

> "GENERAL—. . . with powerful head . . ."
> "HEAD—Like the whole body, very powerful and imposing."
> "The massive skull is wide . . . ."
> "The supra-orbital ridge is very strongly developed . . . ."
> "The lines at the side of the head diverge considerably from the corner of the eyes toward the back of the head."
> "The muzzle is short, does not taper, and the vertical depth at the root of the muzzle must be greater than the length of the muzzle."
> "A rather wide, well-marked, shallow furrow runs from the root of the muzzle over the entire bridge of the muzzle to the nose."

That's it—and some of these phrases were included only because they imply head proportions.

The Standard asks for a head that is large in comparison to the normal head-to-body proportions found in most dog breeds. In addition, there is a requirement for the head to be wide, but there is no mention of the head being long or deep. I must conclude, then, that the Standard asks for the head to be big for the size of the dog, and proportionately wide!

Let me interject a word of warning. I do not see within our Standard any implication that the bigger the head, the better. The weight of the head is an encumbrance to the dog; it needs to be as minimal as possible within the bounds leveled by the Standard. Just as an overly large head would hinder the dog's athletic abilities, common sense dictates that we want the smallest head that fits the terms "massive" and "imposing."

Let's discuss how to determine head width. Because a correctly shaped skull, when viewed from above, tapers in width, it is necessary to define the point of application for determining the width dimension. The feature that best lends itself to being measured is the widest point of the skull, which is the point on the side of the head where the aft portion of the cheek bone (zygomatic arch) joins the main portion of the skull. This point is just behind the eye and just under the forward edge of the ear flap. If you feel the dog's head, this point is easily discerned. (Please note that these statements about the location of the widest point of the skull apply only to a correctly formed head!)

Next we need a definition of head length. I define the length of the skull as the horizontal distance between the "apparent stop" (which is the apparent intersection of the supraorbital ridge with the top line of the muzzle when the head is viewed in profile) and the back of the occiput. This may sound confusing, but if you look at a Saint Bernard head in profile and try to decide between which points you will measure the length, you will pick these same two points.

Finally, we must define the depth of the head. The most useful dimension is the distance from the top of the skull to the back corner of the lower jaw, which you can find by feeling the dog's lower jawbone until you locate a spot just below and behind the eye that feels like a corner.

Ch. Belyn's Quartermaster, HOF, POE, was owned and bred by Doug and Penny Mahon of Glen Ellen, California, and is pictured here being handled by Don Osborn to a Group Placement. The attribute that you should note here is a very good balance of head to body proportions.

Ch. Cache Retreat Academy at the age of two and one-half years, being awarded Best of Opposite Sex at the Saint Bernard Club of America's 1997 National Specialty Show. This was the second consecutive BOS award at the National Specialty for Academy. The handler is Pam Hathaway, the breeder and owner is Ivan Palmblad of Providence, Utah, and the judge is Joan Zielinski. Academy is a very pretty, rough bitch with outstanding substance and an excellent head, who went on to win the Best of Breed award at the 1998 National Specialty Show.

Because the Standard fails to give us enough information about the correct size of a good head, I am going to render my opinion. I ask that you distinguish between the words found herein that are simply an opinion and those that represent real or implied requirements of the Standard.

Assume that we are talking about a thirty-inch male. In my opinion, the correct size skull should see the following measurements: (1) seven inches in length; (2) seven inches in depth; and (3) eight inches in width. And I would not allow much leeway for males other than thirty inches at the withers. In fact, I would allow no perceptible change in these dimensions for any dog within one and one-half inches of the assumed height. Even in a head of a different size, I would ask to see the same ratio of 1:1:1.15 for the length-to-depth-to-width proportions.

When you are dealing with the females, however, not only is there the basic difference in size to consider, but also the fact that they are supposed to be feminine and more refined. I would allow about one-half inch less in each dimension for an optimum-sized female (twenty-eight inches at the withers). This means that I should look for a head that is six and one-half inches long, six and one-half inches deep, and seven and one-half inches wide. Now it is *your* job to measure nine or ten heads that you think are of good type and the right size and see if you arrive at a different overall size or a different set of proportions.

The size and proportions of a correct muzzle also need to be determined, as well as the amount of rise to the skull above the muzzle top line. Fortunately, the Standard gives us considerably more direction on the subject of muzzles than it does about skulls.

The first phrase that is applicable reads: "The supra-orbital ridge is very strongly developed . . . ." To me, such a bone formation requires that there be a considerable amount of rise to the skull above the muzzle. The question it fails to answer is, "How high?" This will be discussed later.

The next statement on the subject of the muzzle is definitive: "The muzzle is short, does not taper, and the vertical depth at the root of the muzzle must be greater than the length of the muzzle." The Standard leaves to us the job of defining the words "short" and "greater" as used here. Let's postpone this subject, too, until we have considered the last piece of the Standard that applies to this subject. This is the requirement that "a rather wide, well-marked, shallow furrow runs from the root of the muzzle over the entire bridge of the muzzle to the nose." This implies that a relatively wide muzzle is required to support the rather wide furrow on its top side. We must yet discuss the term "wide."

Because the Standard leaves much of this topic undefined, I offer you my opinion—what appeals to my personal sense of beauty. I like to see the muzzle one-half the length of the head. I like a muzzle that is about 30 percent deeper than it is long.

It is important that I digress to make a special point. You must *never* confuse the depth of the muzzle with the depth of the flew, for either can be correct or incorrect entirely independent of the other feature. I remember one big-winning Saint that looked pleasing until you saw his face head on. His muzzle was wide but extremely shallow. However, the six inches of flew hanging below the lower jaw made it appear, when viewed from the side, that the muzzle had adequate depth. Don't ever let yourself be misled into thinking that a deep, pendulous flew is the equivalent of a proper muzzle.

Returning to my concept of a correct muzzle, I like to see the width at least equal to the length. Width of muzzle is the one aspect of the Saint Bernard that needs a lot of work. Correct width of muzzle is not very common among the dogs I see being exhibited.

Finally, we must consider the rise of the skull above the top line of the muzzle. It pleases my senses to see the skull rise above the muzzle top line by an amount equal to the length of the muzzle, and maybe just a tiny bit less. Let me put some actual values to these concepts. If the muzzle is one-half the length of the head, it should be three and one-half inches in length, assuming the skull is seven inches long. It immediately follows, then, that the ideal depth of the muzzle is about four and one-half inches, and that the ideal width is three and one-half inches. Again, in a smaller (or bigger) muzzle, I would like it to have the ratio of 1:1.3:1 for its length-to-depth-to-width proportions.

Regarding the important feature of rise to the skull, a three-and-one-half-inch muzzle would fit best on a head that climbs almost three and one-half inches above the muzzle. Too much or too little rise of the skull will quickly ruin a dog's claim to beauty.

It is useful to think of this entire subject in relation to the length of the muzzle. If the length of the muzzle is defined as one unit, then the muzzle should be a block that is 1 unit long, 1.3 units deep, and 1 unit wide. That block should be mounted on a bigger tapered block that is 2 units long, 2 units deep, and 2.3 units wide at its point of measurement (the widest point on the skull). Further, the top of the muzzle should be lower than the top of the skull by almost 1 unit. If a head has all of these ideal proportions, it is a long way down the road toward correct breed type concerning this feature.

There should be some mention of the consequences of incorrect proportions. For example, if the skull length is too short or if the depth is too great, the head will have a bean-pot look that detracts from the dog's nobility. If the skull length is too long or if the skull depth is too shallow, the dog will have a very uncharacteristic, flat-topped appearance that is even less desirable than the bean-pot look.

Another problem that is common in the showring is having a muzzle that is too small in one or more of its dimensions. Such a head is called snipey; it just simply lacks the majesty required for correct breed type. Then there is the really big problem of a nose that is too long. This type of muzzle is almost always found on a dog that has many other features that are incorrect for a Saint Bernard. I may be mistaken, but in my mind there is a direct correlation between a long nose and an overall lack of type.

If you agree with my thoughts here, I am glad. If you have a well-thought-out differing opinion, that, too, is good.

The Muzzle

Is the muzzle an important aspect of breed type in the Saint Bernard? In my youth, there was a well-used advertising phrase that went, "It's what's up front that counts!" In fact, there is nothing that can destroy the sense of proper breed type faster than an inadequate muzzle. The entire head must render an impression of majestic beauty that simply fails to come off when the muzzle is either narrow, malformed, poorly set, snipey, or out of balance.

According to the AKC Standard for the Saint Bernard:

> "The muzzle is short, does not taper, and the vertical depth at the root of the muzzle must be greater than the length of the muzzle."
>
> "The bridge of the muzzle is not arched, but straight; in some dogs, occasionally, slightly broken."
>
> "A rather wide, well-marked, shallow furrow runs from the root of the muzzle over the entire bridge of the muzzle to the nose."
>
> "Nose very substantial, broad, with wide open nostrils, and, like the lips, always black."
>
> "Necessary markings are: white chest, feet and tip of tail, nose band, collar or spot on the nape; the latter and blaze are very desirable."

My plan of attack is to look at each individual phrase in these five sentences, then expand upon them by adding my thoughts and interpretations.

"The Muzzle Is Short"

The length of the muzzle must be approximately one-half the length of the head (stop to occiput). It must not be so short that it limits the available space for proper dentition. It must not be so long that it destroys the balance of the head. Always bear this in mind: Too long noses are very ugly; too short noses are not functional!

"The Muzzle Does Not Taper"

The muzzle is powerfully developed in length, breadth, and depth and does not taper in any direction. The muzzle must appear to be a substantial, square-sided block attached to the front of that even more massive object called the head.

Ch. Bowser Waller, shown in this 1964 photograph, was owned by Betty Roberts Nelson and her Shagg Bark Kennels in Tolland, Connecticut. This dog had an outstanding show career and was the highest ranked Saint Bernard in the country during the time he was campaigned.

"Depth at the Root of the Muzzle Is Greater than the Length"

The Standard only says that the depth of the muzzle is greater than its length, but it is necessary to be more specific than that. While I feel that perfection is found in the ratio of ten units long to thirteen units deep, I would not argue with anybody who preferred another ratio that was close to this one.

Note that the depth of the muzzle is measured at the root of the muzzle, but if the muzzle did not taper, it could just as easily be measured midway along the length of the muzzle. Unfortunately, most Saint Bernard muzzles have a slight taper.

It is extremely important to remember that the depth of the muzzle has nothing to do with the depth of the flew. These are independent features that can be deep or shallow in their own right! The muzzle depth must be measured from the upper surface of the muzzle to the lower surface of the lower jaw, rather than to the lower limits of the flew.

The Missing Requirement

I have always faulted our Standard for failing to discuss the width of the muzzle. I feel that the muzzle should be extremely wide. I like to see the width almost equal to the length. Such a muzzle would be much wider than most! A narrow muzzle is troublesome to look at. I don't think I have ever seen a muzzle that I thought to be too wide!

"The Bridge of the Muzzle Is Not Arched, but Straight"

This statement is about the top line of the muzzle as seen in profile. This requirement prohibits a curved top line on the muzzle. Also considered as faults are a Roman nose, lumps or humps on the bridge of the nose, or folds of skin on the top and/or sides of the muzzle. The so-called dish face, which is found in some otherwise attractive dogs, also should not be tolerated.

"The Muzzle Is in Some Dogs, Occasionally, Slightly Broken"

This is the most diversely interpreted phrase in the Standard. I believe that the term "slightly broken" refers to the set of the muzzle on the skull! Many people in the fancy call this condition "down-faced." The Saint Bernard fancy, however, must refrain using "down-faced," for it means something else to the rest of the dog world.

This "slightly broken" term does not allow the bridge of the muzzle to have a hump in the middle (Roman nose), nor does it allow a lump midway down the length created by a fold of skin. Nor may the muzzle curve upward like a dish. Humps, lumps, and dishes are all bad faults and should be treated as such, but they are covered under the section of our Standard that requires a straight top line to the muzzle. The term "broken" is, obviously, another subject.

Ch. Belyn's Quartermaster, HOF, POE, is visiting across the fence with his friend Katarina Heiberg of Norway. Quartermaster was owned and bred by Doug and Penny Mahon at their Belyn's Kennels in Glen Ellen, California. Quartermaster's classic head, with its broad, flat-topped muzzle, and his friendly, welcoming nature were among his attributes.

Sometimes the condition of "slightly broken" is hard to recognize. What is meant here is that the muzzle is set onto the skull in such a manner that it slopes down away from the skull, while the skull is held in a position such that the eyes look horizontally straight ahead. Skillful handlers in the showring will disguise this condition by tilting the head back until the muzzle is level. Of course, tilting the head does *not* remove the fault.

Because referring to this condition as "downfaced" will not be understood, and because there is great controversy over the term "slightly broken," what is to be done? Fortunately, the dog fancy in Europe has come to the rescue. They use the terms "convergent" and "divergent" when speaking of muzzles. A line connecting the point of the occiput with the joint between the skull and nasal bone (midway between the eyes) is defined as the control line. The control line will normally slope downward as you move forward along its length, and it will normally intersect the top line of the muzzle somewhere along its length. In a "convergent muzzle," the top line of the muzzle and the control line intersect forward of the stop. In a "divergent muzzle," the extension of the muzzle top line and the control line intersect behind the stop.

I feel that a Saint must have a convergent muzzle and, to be acceptable, the upper surface of the muzzle must intersect the control line at least one inch ahead of the stop but no more than ten inches ahead of the stop. I find a broken muzzle to be a severe fault, because it is also to be expected in the offspring. I don't believe that the authors of the Standard intended to sound so lenient with this fault. It is a persistent trait that is hard to breed out of a line and therefore must be considered serious. The top line of the muzzle should be both straight and level. I could accept a slightly broken muzzle on a dog only to the extent that it was just barely perceptible.

"A Rather Wide, Well-Marked, Shallow Furrow Runs from the Root of the Muzzle over the Entire Bridge of the Muzzle to the Nose"

Straight in profile, the muzzle appears to be flat on its upper surface. However, a shallow groove is discernible to the touch running along the length of the muzzle. Absence of this groove is a serious fault! Without the furrow, the entire muzzle has a domed roof down its entire length. Such muzzles are supposed to be found on Newfoundlands but are inappropriate for a correct Saint Bernard. I must warn breeders that dogs with these domed muzzles tend to have offspring with rather faulty muzzles, so this is not a feature to be glossed over lightly.

"Nose Very Substantial, Broad, with Wide Open Nostrils, and, Like the Lips, Always Black"

There is little to add here, for the words are very clear. A big nose is demanded. Obviously, a big muzzle must terminate in a big nose if it is not to appear ridiculous. A requirement for a black nose and for black lips is expressed. A brownish-colored nose or one with pink spots need to be shunned and eliminated from any breeding program. I am a little more tolerant about the color of the lips. To me, pink lips are very unattractive, and pink spots on the lips are objectionable to the extent that they intrude upon the overall appearance of the muzzle.

"Necessary Markings Are: White . . . Nose Band"

Everybody wants a white muzzle. Many people grudgingly accept the extension of face color onto the muzzle. Most of the fancy object to freckles or ticking on the muzzle as a terrible detraction from that which is beautiful. I know no one who accepts an entirely black muzzle. The least acceptable amount of white, according to most of the people with whom I have talked, is a thin stripe down the length of the bridge.

That Which Can Be Inferred

Although the Standard does not mention the correct proportion of muzzle to head, it can easily be concluded that the desirable appearance be substantial and imposing. The beauty of the head depends upon the harmonious proportion of the muzzle to the skull; the muzzle should always appear powerful—never small—in its relationship to the rest of the head. The Standard does not mention the word "beauty" but only describes what is correct. It is people like me who claim that what is correct is also beautiful.

Let me leave you with one final thought. Consider the question, "Are muzzles an important aspect of evaluating Saint Bernards?" I think that we can all agree that they are, because just as most people start their evaluation of a dog at the front, correct breed type starts with the muzzle! By no means does it end there, but if you don't have good breed type at the beginning, many people (and judges) will not look any further.

The Teeth

Conversations about teeth are not heard very often in Saint Bernard circles, yet a good mouth should be as important to breeders and fanciers as it is to the dogs. The last time I tried to get into discuss this subject with a Saint Bernard person, I was accused of being a nut case. If you have this same reaction, please bear with me while I try to convince you that you should be concerned with your dog's mouth.

An adult Saint has forty-two permanent teeth—that is, if he has a full set! In the upper jaw there are twenty teeth—six incisors, two canines (the so-called fangs), eight premolars (four on each side), and four molars (two on each side). In the lower jaw there are twenty-two teeth; these are the same as in the upper jaw except that there are six molars instead of four (three on each side). Puppies, on the other hand, have twenty-eight temporary or deciduous teeth that begin to appear at about two or three weeks of age. These first teeth, or "milk teeth" as they have been called, are sharp. It is very uncommon for puppies to have trouble with teeth during these first eruptions.

At sixteen weeks, the process of losing the baby teeth and replacing them with permanent teeth usually begins. This can be a trauma for the owner of the puppy, but a time of little consequence in the young dog's life. What bothers the owner is that as the teeth loosen, the puppy usually simply swallows them as they break free. I have never heard of any complication arising from this procedure, so I conclude that it is perfectly normal and harmless.

It is important, however, to keep track of what is going on in the puppy's mouth as he grows. Occasionally, a baby tooth will not fall out before the permanent tooth grows in right alongside it. This usually happens with the canine teeth. Whenever this occurs, you should gently extract the puppy tooth. If it won't come out easily, have your veterinarian remove it. The permanent teeth must have room to grow without being crowded by the baby teeth. Saints have enough trouble with malocclusion without letting another factor get into the act.

Now let's turn our attention to the reasons why Saint Bernard fanciers should expend time and energy contemplating their dogs' dentition. The first point to consider concerns the conflicting objectives of breeders. Who could possibly say that they don't care if their dogs have functional teeth? Of course, nobody wants bad mouths, bad teeth, or bad bites. Who wants to look in a dog's mouth and see ugliness? Yet, we admire and seek a short, boxlike muzzle on our animals. This is a conflict—and the source of the problem. The trouble occurs

Ch. Forever Gotcha, a dog of imposing size, substance and proportions, was bred by Sara and Terry Temple of Illinois. He was sired by High Chateau's Faust out of Ch. High Chateau Forever Bliss. This dog was awarded a Selection of Merit by the author at the SBCA's 1987 National Specialty.

Ch. Cache Retreat On A Clear Day being awarded Best of Breed at the 1991 National Specialty Show of the Saint Bernard Club of America, held in San Diego, California. This lovely shorthaired bitch was owned and bred by Ivan Palmblad and Pam Hathaway of Utah. The people in the picture are, left to right, Ivan Palmblad, Judge Marcia Carter, Minnie Horlings, Pam Hathaway, and Ray Horlings (show chairman).

when, in the quest for a short muzzle (as demanded for proper breed type), the objective is achieved by shortening the upper and lower mandibles. Unfortunately, shorter jawbones mean crowded teeth and/or smaller teeth. If you look into the mouth of any Saint that displays good head type, you will find small, crowded teeth. We who breed these dogs must take responsibility for the difficulties we have inflicted on our friends for the sake of fashion.

It is my opinion that breeders should limit their desire for an extremely short muzzle to the point that room for functional teeth is retained. Nor should the people who make the awards in the showring shirk their duty. It is up to the judges to be aware of this problem when they are doing their Saint Bernard assignments so that some more extreme expression of this fad does not overtake our breed.

Now let's move on to the subject of achieving the boxlike shape to the muzzle through tooth placement. In a Saint Bernard with a well-shaped muzzle, the six incisors on each jaw will lie in a very flat curve between the canines—in fact, the canines and incisors should lie in almost a straight line across the front of the mouth. If the muzzle is to be broad, the canines must be extraordinarily wide apart. Within such a muzzle, the four premolars on each side will lie in a nearly straight line directly behind each canine tooth. Then the molars (two in the upper jaw and three in the lower jaw) must lie more or less behind the premolars. When viewed from above, the teeth lie in a pattern like three sides of a rectangle.

This boxlike tooth pattern is a prerequisite to having a correct, nontapering muzzle. What you see when you look at the outer surface of the muzzle are the lips and flews that are positioned by lying flat against the teeth. They are simply a fabric draped across the framework formed by the teeth. If the tooth pattern is narrow or tapered, then the muzzle will have the same characteristics.

These, then, are the components of muzzle beauty as defined by today's Saint breeder. These are our concerns, however, and not the concerns of the dogs. I have never known a Saint Bernard that really cared whether or not he had a short muzzle or if his nose resembled an ice-cream cone. If our priorities are straight, correct breed type will not be our only concern. We will worry just as much or more about the dog's health and his ability to use his mouth.

At a relatively young age, a large percentage of the Saint Bernard population can expect to have worn-out or decayed teeth. Most Saint Bernard teeth are exceedingly small in the first place, which means that very little wear reduces them to the gum line. This is just one more reason to question the eternal quest for "type" that results in abnormally small teeth.

The best strategy is to minimize the amount of idle chewing your dog does over the course of his life. Softer foods seem to be called for. Knock off the knucklebones; use the rawhide toys instead. Whenever you allow your dog to have something to chew, first consider the wear factor it involves. This means that you will need to resort to using toothbrushes and scaling tools, or let your veterinarian do the "icky" job. No matter what you do, however, the fact is that abnormally small teeth are a health hazard that you buy into when you own a Saint Bernard. Any dog can be trained to accept having his teeth brushed and descaled, and that is your responsibility to your dog.

Now I would like to explore some old wives' tales regarding bites and teeth. *"An undershot bite is not functional for cutting the umbilical chord."* This is utter nonsense, because the bitch uses her premolars and molars to cut the cord. *"An overshot or undershot bite cannot pick up or hold objects very well."* I know a man whose bulldog could retrieve a dime from a tile floor. I never saw any dog walk past an object that he wanted to have in his mouth because he couldn't pick it up. *"A guard dog needs a good bite to be efficient at his task."* Such statements can only be made by people who have never been bitten by an undershot dog. The dog game is rampant with these sort of truisms that just don't stand up under scrutiny.

I want to leave you with this thought: A good mouth is the result of the jawbone shape, size, and substance combined with the quality and placement of the teeth. A good mouth is important because the components have a large effect on correct breed type, the dog's health, and the psychological well-being of the dog. Be assured that Saint Bernards in general need to have good mouths!

Osage's Duchess of Scandia at the age of two years, eight months, being awarded Winners Bitch at the Saint Bernard Club of America's 1997 National Specialty Show. The breeders are Sara Sykora and Donna Buxton, and the owners are Paul and Julie Boorsma of Cologne, Minnesota. Duchess has excellent size and substance and a very nice head.

The Flews

After a dog show one Sunday afternoon, a group of Saint Bernard exhibitors met in a restaurant to discuss which dog should have won. The conversation soon became a three-sided debate about correct flews. "How can there be this much controversy on the subject of flews?" I was asked by one of my skeptical friends. "That's an easy question!" I replied. "The flews can vary so greatly in shape and texture that the whole character of the dog is affected. Some people have simplistically claimed that the significant difference between the major bloodlines is just the size and shape of the flews. While I don't agree with that premise, I must admit that there is an element of truth there. After all, the flews are the finishing touch to the muzzle—the fabric draped over the underlying framework. If the muzzle of your dog has perfectly lovely bone structure and gorgeous dentition, he may still fail to be beautiful if he has ugly flews."

There are three sentences in the Saint Bernard Standard that touch on this subject.

(1) "The flews of the upper jaw are strongly developed, not sharply cut, but turning in a beautiful curve into the lower edge, and slightly overhanging."

(2) "The flews of the lower jaw must not be deeply pendant."

(3) "Nose . . . , like the lips, always black."

These three sentences cover four topics in the description of a correct flew:

From the Land of Down Under come these three fine fellows. They are Actongold St. Clement (twelve months), his sire, Australian Ch. Tremble Distant Saint (an import from the United Kingdom), and Actongold Monterosa (litter brother to St. Clement). They are owned by Susan Teniswood (on left) and Judy Teniswood (on right) of Tasmania, Australia.

A: The required quality or substance of the upper flews;

B: The correct shape or profile of the upper flew;

C: The allowed overhang; that is, the amount of lip allowed to be swinging in the breeze; and

D: The required color along the edges of the flews.

Ch. Zimbo v. Burestubli with handler Al Saba and the respected judge Arthur Hesser, a lifelong historian and fancier of the Saint Bernard breed. Zimbo was a good longhaired male of the 1960s era and was the Best of Breed dog at the SBCA's 1966 National Specialty.

TOPIC A: THE REQUIRED QUALITY OR SUBSTANCE

Let's examine the exact meanings of the words, "The flews of the upper jaw are strongly developed." This phrase dictates that the flews have a great amount of substance and that they must be thick and meaty with a firm texture. This could lead to the conclusion that strongly developed flews do not flutter with every movement of the head or with every breath the dog takes. In my opinion, to qualify as being "strongly developed," the flews of the upper jaw must each be a slab of good, firm meat, each of which is almost one-half inch thick. Obviously, this is the item that gives that last little bit of width to the overall muzzle—a width that is so important to the dog with correct breed type.

TOPIC B: THE CORRECT SHAPE OR PROFILE

Next, let's consider the phrase, ". . . not sharply cut, but turning in a beautiful curve into the lower edge." The flews, even when of the right size (that is, when they are not overly pendulous), can still be a source of problems because of their shape. The shape of the flews imparts the final element of beauty to the muzzle, and it must be right. The flews must have the beautiful curve required by the Standard.

The curve of the flew should be easy to describe, but it is not. All I can say is that a beautiful curve is a beautiful curve, and there is no mistaking it. I have heard this curve described as the quarter arc of a true circle, but I don't find this to be precise. It is close, but not truly accurate. To me, the term "beautiful curve" seemed nebulous, and I was troubled by the apparent ambiguity that it represented in our Standard. So I sat down and drew a profile of a Saint Bernard head and took the eraser to it time and time again until I had a profile that pleased me. I then tried to find another shape to the flew that I could accept. There were none! I recommend this procedure for all who wish to establish in their own minds an independent evaluation of the correct shape of this curve.

In the real world, there is only one problem with the shape of otherwise correct flews (that is, on the ones that do not lack substance or that do not droop too far). In an unattractive flew, the flew may cut back too quickly—the "sharply cut" look that is prohibited in the Standard. It almost looks like the designer was trying to take a shortcut between the front of the muzzle and the back of the flew. This sort of shape exposes the front of the lower jaw, and the overall effect is one of non-beautifulness. (Where does it say that I can't make up my own words?) This problem tends to recur in the dog's offspring and grandchildren (or grand-puppies, since I'm inventing words) and hence should be given serious thought.

TOPIC C: THE ALLOWED OVERHANG

This deals with the two phrases from the Standard: (1) "The flews of the upper jaw are . . . slightly overhanging" and (2) "The flews of the lower jaw must not be deeply pendant." There seems to be considerable misinformation or intentional disregard of the Standard expressed in the dogs seen in today's showrings. Many dogs that have a "lot of lip" are being exhibited. I believe that people rationalize overly pendulous flews by claiming that the Standard calls for a deep muzzle. The problem with this "non-logic" is that the depth of the muzzle has nothing to do with the depth of the flew! In a proper muzzle and flew there will not be a lot of difference. However, whenever there is a significant disparity between the depth of the muzzle and the depth of the flew, then one item or both are terribly faulty. Your status as a Saint Bernard expert depends upon your ability to recognize and evaluate these kinds of significant faults.

So, just what is correct? The answer is rather subjective. I like to see the upper flew overhang by about an inch. To me, the term "slightly overhanging" starts to stretch my imagination beyond that point. I don't understand how anyone can justify more overhang than this. There are reasonable limits on how far you can go with your personal opinion and still claim compliance with the Standard. Similarly, the term "deeply pendant" gains real meaning to me when the dog has a big wet lower lip exposed all of the time, when the neck and chest are stained by the dog's own saliva, and when the dog drools constantly. Whenever puppy buyers ask you for a "dry mouth," they are really asking for a puppy that will grow up to *not* have deeply pendant flews.

TOPIC D: THE REQUIRED COLOR ALONG THE EDGES

The Standard says that the lips are always black. If you surveyed today's show dogs, you would find that the lips are mostly black most of the time. I don't recall ever seeing a dog whose lips were some solid color other than black or dark chocolate. The usual feature encountered is pink spots or segments on the lips. Much too often you see a mouth with lips that are mostly pink. I have the impression that there are far more dogs with pink spots on their lips than dogs with solid black lips. An interesting sidelight is that there seems to be a correlation between the quantity of pink on the lips and the lack of black pigmentation on the roof of the mouth.

Does this preponderance of pink-spotted lips within the Saint Bernard population make it acceptable? Of course not! The Standard says that it is wrong, and that makes it so! However, in my judging and in breedings, I have always had much more important concerns when making my evaluations. I look forward to the day when the color of some Saint Bernard's lips is his most significant problem.

Belyn's Bacchus at the age of two years being awarded Best of Winners and Winners Dog at the Saint Bernard Club of America's 1997 National Specialty Show. The handler is Doug Mahon, the breeder is Penny Mahon, the judge is Joan Zielinski, and the owners are Doug and Penny Mahon of Glen Ellen, California. Bacchus is an excellent smooth male of very good size, proportions, and breed type.

The Skull

The Saint Bernard breed depends significantly upon the head to express correct breed type. Of all the features of the head, the skull is the source of most of whatever is right or wrong with any particular dog's head. The skull determines the size and shape of the head, the placement and set of the eyes, and, to some degree, the ear set.

A search through the Standard finds the following words that are applicable to the skull.

(1) "GENERAL—. . . with powerful head"

(2) "HEAD—Like the whole body, very powerful and imposing. The massive skull is wide, slightly arched and the sides slope in a gentle curve into very strongly developed, high cheek bones. Occiput only moderately developed."

(3) "The supra-orbital ridge is very strongly developed and forms nearly a right angle with the long axis of the head. Deeply imbedded between the eyes and starting at the root of the muzzle, a furrow runs over the whole skull. It is strongly marked in the first half, gradually disappearing towards the base of the occiput. The lines at the sides of the head diverge considerably from the outer corner of the eyes toward the back of the head. The slope from the skull to the muzzle is sudden and rather steep."

(4) "EYES—Set more to the front than the sides . . ."

Ch. Sanctuary Woods Prefix v. Banz at fourteen months of age is shown in this 1964 photograph at the Middle Atlantic Saint Bernard Club Show in Philadelphia. Prefix is being handled by Herman Peabody under Judge Arthur Hesser for owner Merc Cresap.

The Standard commands the skull to be extraordinarily big and relatively wide in order to maintain proper head proportions. The skull must have very pronounced bones above and below the eyes; the eyebrow bones (supraorbital ridge) and the cheek bones (zygomatic arch) must be impressive in their prominence. If these bones are not well developed, the shape of the head is wrong and the eyes cannot be more to the front than to the side, as required by our Standard. If the cheekbones do not flare out from the root of the muzzle, then the dog fails to meet the Standard-imposed requirement that the lines of the head must diverge considerably toward the back of the head. Whenever you have this condition, breed type fails to be present.

Next, consider what the Standard says about the stop, because the stop is not what it appears to be. Many people think that the stop of a Saint Bernard should approximate a right angle with the muzzle. Not so!

The Standard makes two statements that some people misinterpret. The first is, "The supra-orbital ridge is very strongly developed and forms a nearly right angle with the long axis of the head." The second is, "The slope from the skull to the muzzle is sudden and rather steep." A shallow interpretation of these two statements could identify a contradiction. That's because so many people erroneously think that both statements are discussing the same part of the dog's anatomy.

It is important to define some terms used here—first, the long axis of the head. An axis is a center of rotation. A dog's head can rotate in any direction, so, for the sake of convenience, there are three mutually perpendicular axes. In the airplane business those three axes are called pitch, roll, and yaw. Yaw is rotation about a vertical axis; roll and pitch are rotation about horizontal axes. One of these horizontal axes is parallel to the long center line of the dog's body (the roll axis), and the other (the pitch axis) is positioned across the dog's body.

It is obvious that the Saint Bernard Standard, in discussing the long axis of the head, is referring to its roll axis. It is also obvious that the authors of the Standard are discussing what can be seen in a side view of the dog's profile when they ask for the supraorbital ridge to form a nearly right angle with the long (roll) axis of the head. I suspect that the people who wrote the Standard thought about asking for the supraorbital ridge to be (in profile) almost perpendicular to the top line of the muzzle, but they were afraid that too many dogs had muzzles that were not parallel to the long axis of the head.

International Ch. Bernegarden's Ragtime, owned and bred by Britt Marit Halvorson of Belgium, shown here at the age of two and one-half years. This dog has had one of the most successful show careers in Europe with many all-breed Best in Shows and Best in Specialty Shows to his credit. As this book goes to press, Ragtime has the following titles: Norwegian Champion, Swedish Champion, Danish Champion, Belgium Champion, Netherlands Champion, Luxembourg Champion, European Champion, and International Champion. In addition, Ragtime has completed his AKC Championship in the United States.

This montage shows three views of the same good head of a long-haired bitch. The purpose of these pictures is to depict a correct skull. Note the shape of the top of the skull in the side and front views and the way in which the sides of the skull diverge toward the back in the view looking down on the top of the head. Note also that the eyes are placed more to the front than to the side, which is primarily the result of both the supraorbital ridges and the cheek bones being well developed. The very well-pronounced furrow starting at the base of the muzzle and disappearing toward the occiput is also in evidence here.

Now it is time to contemplate the phrase, "The slope from the skull to the muzzle is sudden and rather steep." There is indeed a slope from the skull to the muzzle, but many people are unaware of such a slope because it is not visible in profile. It is, rather, between the supraorbital ridges; it is, in fact, the floor of the valley between the two ridges.

With regard to the top of the skull, the Standard states that the "massive skull is wide, slightly arched . . . ." If you picture the top skull as being a rather smooth, flattish bone such as found in humans, you have the wrong idea. The top of the skull is not bone, except for a high ridge running right down the center of the skull—a ridge that is similar to the crest on the ancient Roman helmets. This ridge is about one inch high and protrudes out of the top of the skull.

But wait a minute! The Standard says that there is a furrow running down the center of the skull, not a *ridge*! How can this be? What happens in a correct type of Saint Bernard is that there are two masses of muscle on top of the head that are attached to that ridge of bone. Those slabs of muscle are so thick that they protrude above the ridge. This means that the ridge of bone is the bottom of the furrow between the two masses of muscle on either side. Therefore, the shape of the dog's top skull is determined not only by the size and shape of the skull, but also by the amount of muscle that fills the space above the bone. This is the feature that makes some dogs change the shape of their skull and relocate their ears as they mature and gain muscle mass, and again as they grow old and lose that mass of muscle.

Now I want to discuss the words from the Standard that say, "The lines at the sides of the head diverge considerably from the outer corner of the eyes toward the back of the head." Basically, this is just a requirement for the head to get bigger as you move toward the rear. This is what you see when looking straight down on top of the dog's head. When viewed from above, the outline of the head widens toward the back.

There is a distinction between the widest point on the skull, which is a hard, bony spot, and the widest point on the head. The widest point of the skull is located where the cheek bones (zygomatic arch) join the skull behind the eyes. (If the widest point of the skull is on the aft part of the lower jaw, the head is very faulty.) Why, then, does the head appear to get larger behind the widest point of the skull? This is because you are looking at skin, muscle, ligaments, and other soft tissue connecting the skull to the extremely powerful and thick neck behind.

Negative aspects to watch out for include a proportionately small skull and a proportionately narrow skull. Skulls that have improper shapes (such as round heads—those without the flattened arch between the ears—and smooth heads—those without the prominent supraorbital ridges and highly developed cheek bones) should offend you. These are all features that are very hard to correct in future generations.

It is important to discuss Saint Bernard skulls, because a correct head has more to do with overall Saint Bernard breed type than any other single feature. Most of the problems with a head depend upon features of the skull. The skull must be right in so many ways or the dog fails to be beautiful; he fails to have correct breed type.

Ch. Chad's Katarina, HOF, POE, is shown here by Carol Terrio, who, along with her husband Jack Terrio, is the owner and breeder. Note the excellent size and substance of this bitch.

Ch. Stoan's Dean Witter of Valinta with his owner, Tamiko Van Buskirk of Renton, Washington, at the Saint Bernard Club of Puget Sound's 1997 Weight Pull and Harness Match event. Dean, who won this event, is shown here pulling a load of concrete blocks that is just a few bricks short of 3,000 pounds.

The Furrows

When spring embraces the land, farmers break out their plows and start to turn over the winter-ravaged ground. What a grand feeling is the sight of that first furrow! It gives the plowman the feeling that God is in His heaven and all is right with this planet. There is a warm, comfortable elation that comes with the sight of a good furrow being turned in the dark spring earth.

But it is not farmers alone who appreciate a well-formed furrow! Those who are connoisseurs of correct breed type in a Saint Bernard must also experience a quickened pulse at the sight of a good and proper furrow. There are grooves in the head and muzzle of a correct Saint Bernard that are very important. A Saint Bernard without proper furrows has a great shortcoming in breed type; a Saint Bernard lacking furrows fails to have a good head. Further, while just having good furrows is not sufficient to have a proper head, I almost never see a good set of furrows on a head that is other than beautiful.

Two furrows are under discussion here—the one on the forehead and the one along the top of the muzzle. I'll start with the furrow on the forehead. Not a furrow, but a canyon must lie between the eyes. You should be able to place a finger between the dog's eyes and then lay a straightedge across the eyebrows without touching the finger in the furrow below. This furrow is created not by a depression in the skull, but rather from the magnificent protrusion of the bony ridges above the eyes—the so-called supraorbital ridge that defines both the apparent stop and the furrow.

Of no less importance is the furrow running down the length of the muzzle. Without this furrow, the muzzle is just plain faulty! This furrow is

A proud moment for Ch. Slaton's Harlow Jean v. Smalley, CD, HOF, POE, at the age of ten years as she is awarded first place in the Brood Bitch class at the SBCA's 1995 National Specialty Show in Tennessee. This was the third time that Jean, owned by Shirley and Joe Wolf and Linda Bulicz, received this award at the National Specialty. Jean holds the Saint Bernard record for producing champions, having produced twenty-five AKC champions. Pictured with Jean are her two offspring, who also did very well at this show; her son, Ch. Slaton's Piece Of The Action, was awarded Selection of Merit, and her daughter, Ch. Slaton's Juno v. Majewski, was awarded Best of Opposite Sex from the Veterans Bitch class.

(Above): Ch. Matterhorn's Lucille is co-owned by Mike Gardner and her breeder, Nancy Sanders. Lucille was sired by an SBCA National Specialty BOB winner, Ch. Opdyke's Lancaster, and is out of Matterhorn's White Linen. Lucille shows that true quality can be found in a Saint Bernard with imperfect facial markings.

often overlooked, because even on a proper muzzle it is hard to see. It is supposed to be a rather shallow and wide furrow. In fact, it will appear to be a flat plane on top of the muzzle because the hair growing there will fill in the furrow. Although this furrow may be camouflaged to the eye, it cannot hide from the fingers. Touch a proper muzzle and you will easily discover the magic furrow that gives the muzzle the squared-off look that is essential for proper type.

Again, please note that the furrow is not so much a depression in the top of the muzzle as it is a valley lying between the two bony, tubelike ridges over the nasal passages. Without the furrow, the entire muzzle has a domed roof down its entire length. Such muzzles remind me of a Quonset hut, and Saint Bernards are not supposed to have Quonset huts for muzzles! Dogs with these domed muzzles tend to have offspring with rather snipey or tapered muzzles; therefore, this is not a feature to be taken lightly.

There are two places in the Standard that describe the furrows:

(1) ". . . Deeply imbedded between the eyes and starting at the root of the muzzle, a furrow runs over the whole skull. It is strongly marked in the first half, gradually disappearing toward the base of the occiput."

(2) ". . . A rather wide, well-marked, shallow furrow runs from the root of the muzzle over the entire bridge of the muzzle to the nose."

I think that the unwritten part of this message is that furrows are absolutely essential! The old saying, "No head, no Saint Bernard!" could be expanded to, "No furrows, no head!" A proper Saint Bernard head cannot be achieved without furrows. They are a prerequisite to proper head type.

(Left): Ch. Almshaus Double The Pleasure, HOF (aka Doug), being awarded an all-breed group placement. Doug is co-owned by his breeder, Elizabeth Surface, and his handler, Melissa Diaz-Getty. Doug follows in the footsteps of his famous father, Ch. Sweetholm's Heartbreak Kid, CGC, HOF, POE, and has the following accomplishments to his credit: Number-One Saint Bernard for 1997—All Aystems; thirty all-breed group placings; seven all-breed Group 1 placings; and twelve Best in Specialty Show/Best of Breed awards at regional Saint Bernard specialties.

The Eyes

Any discussion on the subject of eyes must deal with three major and distinct topics: (1) the visible components of the eyeball, (2) the location and setting of the eye, and (3) the flaps of tissue (eyelids, third eyelids, and haws) that surround the eye. It is uncommon to think of these items separately, but each must be correct in its own right or the overall character of the eyes is wrong.

The Standard has only one quality that enters into the evaluation of the eyeball, and that is the color of the iris. The Standard calls for dark eyes, and that is what we must have. A medium brown is the minimum degree of darkness that is acceptable. Anything lighter than that gives the dog a startled appearance, and that look is a fault. Care must be taken, however, in judging the quality of eye color. If the eye is deeply recessed in a very dark mask, it will appear to be a dark eye no matter what color it is. To make a true evaluation of any Saint's eye color, the head must be tilted so that the light shines directly on the iris. If you encounter a blue eye during an evaluation of a Saint Bernard, stop right there. A blue eye is a genetic fault that is to be avoided at all cost.

Just as having the eyes deeply recessed enhances the appearance of the dog, having eyes that protrude detracts greatly from the image of a good head. Bulging eyeballs are unattractive and are a fault that is readily transmitted to the dog's offspring.

The effect on eye color is only one of the reasons why the location and setting of the eyes is one of the most important features of a Saint's head. When something is not right about a Saint's head, you are probably dealing with the depth of the eye socket and/or the amount of development of the bones above and below the eye. Breeders need to be sure just which part of the skull is faulty when they are planning a mating.

This photograph, taken in the mid-1960s, depicts Powell's Erik von Echo with his owner/breeder/handler Laurence Powell at one of the specialty shows of the Northern New Jersey Saint Bernard Club. Mr. Powell was one of the primary breeders on the East Coast for several decades, and his stock is found in the pedigrees of many dogs currently being exhibited.

The eyes must be more to the front of the skull than to the side. This is undoubtedly the one feature that most differentiates the good skulls from the bad ones. Eye placement is a function of the supraorbital ridge (the eyebrow ridge) and of the cheek bones (the zygomatic arch) being correct. If they are correct, the whole head is right almost without exception. When both of these bones are strongly pronounced, the eyes are in the right place, the deep furrow between the eyes is present, the top skull is the right shape, and the sides of the skull diverge as called for by the Standard.

The eyes should be level with the bridge of the muzzle. There must be enough spacing between the eyes to make them proportional to the width of the muzzle and skull. If the eyes are not in the right place, the dog has a strangeness to his expression that is really hard to define. The eyes are the focal point of the dog's expression; therefore, when the eyes are not right, the animal cannot have a proper expression. You may occasionally hear descriptions of dogs with strange eyes—terms such as walleyed, cross-eyed, beady-eyed, wild-eyed, bug-eyed, staring, mean-looking, startled, or headlight eyes. Usually, such a dog has some basic fault with his eye color and/or with the basic structure of his head. A fault in the placement of the eye, a fault in the set of the eye, or a fault in the shape of the skull around the eye can ruin a dog's expression just as surely as can bright yellow eyes. This is why correct eyes are so important to correct breed type in a Saint Bernard.

The expression of the Saint Bernard is also a function of the haws (inner surfaces of the eyelids or the conjunctiva), the eyelids, and the third eyelids (membrana nictitans). If the eyelids droop excessively, the dog has a sluggish, dull-witted, sad expression. This sense of sadness exuded by a Bloodhound or a Basset is a fault in the Saint Bernard. This problem has a strong correlation to having excess skin on the rest of the head and, indeed, on the rest of the dog.

If the eyelids turn inward, or the dog has an extra row of eyelashes inside his eyelid, he will tend to have inflamed eyes combined with a noticeable amount of weeping around the eyes. In

Ch. Emir of Highpoint being shown at the 1975 Mt. Pocono Kennel Club show by owner Mickey Alpert under Specialty Judge Merc Cresap. Emir was one of the more successful dogs campaigned during the early and mid-1970s.

this sense, problems like runny eyes, inflamed eyes, mattery eyes, swollen eyelids, and/or a blue cast over the eyeball, while not being faults in their own right, are indications that a serious problem is present—one that might well be a concern to the breeder and a source of trauma for the dog. Caution is required here, however. The problem may simply be a bit of foreign matter trapped behind the eyelid and not a genetic fault at all! At any rate, if it makes your eyes water to look into the eyes of a dog, there is something wrong. If you are going to evaluate this sort of situation, you must learn to distinguish between the various causes of the conditions you observe. It would be well to seek expert help whenever you are in doubt, for this is a difficult task at best, even for knowledgeable people.

No subject of eyes would be complete without discussing both the haws and the third eyelids. Haws are the inner surfaces of the eyelids and are technically called the conjunctiva. The third eyelid is the membrane (membrana nictitans) visible at the inner corner of the eye and covers the eye whenever the eye becomes diseased and sinks back into the socket.

Haws are either pink or red. A red haw may be nothing more than an inflamed haw and, hence, an indication that something is wrong. The turning in of the eyelid is known as entropion, and the wrinkles in the eyelids required by the Standard are a controlled, entropion-like condition. It is possible that the entire eyelid structure sags so far that what should be inside is hanging outside, where it is exposed to the elements. No matter—that much haw exposure is a fault!

Third eyelids come in three colors—white, black, and pinto.

A white third eyelid is very noticeable and tends to give the dog a clownish expression. While this may not technically be a fault, it is certainly not an asset. A third eyelid is sometimes black and white (pinto). This condition is best described as disconcerting to see. Again, I would hesitate to call this condition a fault, but it is obviously less attractive than a black third eyelid.

A black third eyelid (which is really a deep chocolate brown) tends to blend in with the black mask, the black eyelids, and the dark eye. The overall effect is to add to the desired expression, and it is pleasing to look upon. All other third eyelid colors tend to detract from the dog, because they lessen the quality of the expression.

It has been said that the eyes are the windows to the soul, and so it is with the Saint Bernard. Is there anybody so unfeeling that they are not moved when looking into the eyes of one of these gentle giants? Such experiences are what make people become fanciers of the breed.

Ch. Sweetholm's Heartbreak Kid, CGC, HOF, POE (aka Heartbreaker), is shown here at the Saint Bernard Club of America's 1994 National Specialty Show being awarded Select by Judge Ivan Palmblad. Heartbreaker, who was awarded Best of Breed at the subsequent 1995 National Specialty Show, was co-owned by Elizabeth Surface and his handler, Melissa Diaz-Getty. Heartbreaker has to his credits: 1996 SBCA's Stud Dog of the Year; forty all-breed group placements; 149 all-breed Best of Breed awards; twenty-eight Best in Specialty Show/Best of Breed awards at regional Saint Bernard specialties; and two all-breed Best in Show awards.

Agility trials are fast paced and are filled with high drama. This picture shows Joast Postma and his famous dog, Am. Can. Ch. Benbaron's Abraham von Yondo, TT, Am. Can. CD, competing at top speed in an official agility trial. Abraham and his owners, Pat and Joast Postma, resided at the Kennebank Kennels in Nova Scotia, Canada.

The Ears

The subject of ears should be of special interest to fanciers of the breed. Let me start by describing the uses your dog finds for his ears. Obviously, he uses his ears for listening! But what you may not realize is that all dogs use their ears to signal their mood and feelings. The ears denote one set of emotions or another depending upon their position and shape. Ears are to a dog what some facial expressions are to humans.

When you deal with people, you observe their facial expression to obtain a clue about their emotions. You look at the position of the lips, the eyelids, and the eyebrows. You notice if the wrinkles on the forehead are horizontal or vertical. This is what is meant by expression. Now dogs cannot frown, smile, scowl, laugh, or weep. In fact, dogs have a very limited ability to control facial expression. But this is not a problem! Dogs also display expression, just in different ways. Some of these methods are head position, the fur on his neck and shoulders, the eyes and eyelids, any skin wrinkles, the position of the flews (is he snarling or not?), the tail position (and motion), general body language, and the ears. And of all these factors, the ears probably have as much or more effect on a dog's expression than any other element.

When a dog's ears come up, it usually means that the dog thinks that the situation is positive, or he anticipates something pleasant. The dog may think that he is going for a car ride or a walk. He might just be happy to be on the receiving end of human conversation. The dog may be alerted to a noise outside the home or the sight of someone he knows approaching the yard. The sight, sound, or smell of good things will always get the ears in a perked mode. When the ears are up and at attention, you know that the dog is really focused on whatever is in front of his eyes—be it food, a bitch in season, or just something interesting.

When the ears just hang in a neutral position, you know that the dog is just hanging out with nothing in particular on his mind. This is often the sign of a bored dog or one that is thinking of taking a nap. Indifference to the immediate surroundings is signaled by ears held in a neutral position.

Laid-back ears signal that the dog finds the current situation unpleasant or negative. If the dog is distressed, the first thing he does is pull back his ears tight against his head. Laid-back ears are the dog's way to display emotions such as aggression, fear, submission, uncertainty, and sometimes simple concern.

So—why should Saint Bernard fanciers be concerned about their dogs' ears? The answer is probably obvious. You want to relate to your dog, so you want to recognize his moods. You want your dog to be pretty, so you want correct ears. And finally, you want your dog to win awards. This brings me to the subject of dog shows.

When a dog is exhibited, the handler wants his dog to have an expression that denotes a keen interest—an intelligent awareness of the present surroundings. This requires that the handler get the dog's ears up and "at attention." When the dog has a good set of ears and a good temperament, it is easiest to stand back and let him observe the proceedings and, whenever he gets bored, wave a morsel of food in front of him. When even the food fails to dispel his boredom, the handler can always pull up on the collar in a manner that forces the ears into the desired position. This is called plan "B." The importance of plan "B" is that a very similar maneuver will allow a faulty set of ears to simulate a correct set. In this maneuver, the handler pulls up the collar in the same manner, then grabs great handfuls of loose skin from the neck, pulls them through the collar, and traps them along with the ears just ahead of the collar.

Australian and New Zealand Ch. Stiniyasu Itchy Feet, bred and owned by John and Matina Butcher of New South Wales, Australia, is shown here at the age of twelve months in this lovely setting with Matina Butcher.

This wonderful procedure makes the head appear to be much wider and makes the ears look like they are set just where they ought to be.

Just a short side note: If you judge Saint Bernards, never evaluate ears and/or head width when the handler has the collar pulled up behind the ears. Make the handler drop the collar at least once during the proceedings so that you can see the real dog.

To understand correct and faulty ears, it is necessary to discuss technical aspects, including size, shape, texture, and placement. Seldom are size and shape a concern to the fancy, probably because they are not much of a problem within our breed. In all my years in the game, I have seen two dogs whose ears struck me as being too small and one dog whose ears were too rounded—not much of a problem in my way of thinking.

However, there are a number of Saint Bernards with faulty ears—that is, Saints whose ears are not located in the right place or whose ears do not hang properly because they lack substance. These kinds of ears just hang like wet tissue paper clinging to the side of a rock. Less often seen are dogs whose ears stick straight out from the sides of their head like a pair of airplane wings. All such dogs have severe faults in the ear department. These sorts of ears take away from the overall elegance of the dog. Ears are to the head what the flews are to the muzzle—the finishing touch! An otherwise good head becomes unappealing when topped off with faulty ears. A good-looking head is not possible without correct ears.

It is difficult to define the ears that are required for a good head, because the complex descriptions found in the Standard sometimes require a little help to comprehend. For example, the term "burr" is used in the Standard to discuss ears. Picture a Saint Bernard ear. You will notice that the base seems determined to have the ear stand erect, but part way up, the ear seems to have a change of

Ch. Sanctuary Woods Going My Way going Best of Breed at the Golden Gate Kennel Club show under Judge Merc Cresap. Going, who was bred by Beatrice Knight and owned by Al and Beverly Holt of San Diego, California, was also awarded Best of Breed at the SBCA's 1970 National Specialty Show.

mind and simply folds over and hangs there from the part standing erect. The "burr" refers to those characteristics of cartilage and ear geometry in the lower part of the ear that give it the tendency to stand erect. This propensity is partly due to the ridges inside the ear, partly to the thickness and shape of the ear, and partly to the quality of the cartilage within the ear. The burr is mostly important because it determines the point at which the ear bends over and changes direction—I call this the fold line.

When you view a good Saint Bernard head from the front while the dog has his ears "pricked" at attention, the fold line must line up with the top line of the skull. When it does this, and the Standard declares that it must, the apparent width of the head is enhanced. The effects of having the fold line either below or above the top line of the skull are subtle but very negative on the overall picture. One extreme is when the ears seem to be too successful in their attempt to stand erect. The opposite condition is when the ears have no more body or character than a wet dishrag.

I do not see a big problem with the too-erect type of ear within the breed. It doesn't seem to happen all that often. On the other hand, dogs with ears that lack burr are often the wet ones that lack proper form and substance elsewhere on their body. Some breeders have set this fault in their dogs, which is too bad. These faults are very difficult to breed out of a line.

Often, the ear set is confused with a fault of the burr. If the fold line is above the top line of the skull, it might be because the ears are set too high, or it might be because the burr is overdeveloped and the ears do not fold over soon enough. The distinction between a low ear set and a lack of proper burr is relatively easy to discern. When the ears simply droop because of insufficient burr, there is no fold line to speak of. If the fold line is below the top line of the skull, it is almost always because the ears are set down on the side of the skull. It doesn't matter which condition you have on your dog—both are extreme faults

The worst thing that can happen to a Saint Bernard's ears is to have both problems on the same dog. When you encounter a Saint with a low ear set *and* a lack of proper burr, you are looking at conformation that is correct for a Bloodhound but inappropriate for a Saint Bernard.

If you are judging dogs, the difference between a bad ear set and a faulty burr is not too important—wrong is wrong, and why doesn't matter. If you are breeding dogs, however, you should make this distinction, because you may be looking for entirely different mates depending upon which fault you are trying to correct.

Other aspects of good ears are well defined in the Standard. The flap that hangs down from the burr must have its front edge against the dog's head and its back edge well away from the head. If you were to look down from the top at the hanging flaps of the ears, they would appear to lie at an angle of about forty-five degrees to the dog's center line.

In my opinion, the ear should reach at least to the inner corner of the dog's eye, but it should not be so long that it reaches the end of the muzzle. I make an exception here for puppies—good-quality puppies often look like they are wearing their daddy's ears.

The Standard says that the ear flap should be tender, and I have been at a loss to explain that term for many years. I think that the ear should be relatively thick—thick enough to give the impression that the ear will not quickly freeze when exposed to extremely cold weather. A proper ear with the correct thickness will feel soft and resilient—about like the eraser on the end of a pencil. I have long suspected that this is what the authors of the Standard meant when they used the term "tender." It seems that very thin ears cannot be tender.

So as you can see, the ears are an essential part of the dog's expression. If you want to communicate with your dog, you must understand his emotions. Further, in the showring, you cannot evaluate your dog's expression unless his ears are in the "at attention" position. The ears are also an essential ingredient of breed type. If you were to put the ears of a German Shepherd or Bloodhound on a Saint Bernard, you would utterly destroy his claim to breed type. And then there is the matter of aesthetics. The ears must be correct for the dog to have a beautiful head. If you take pleasure in seeing a good Saint Bernard, you must love and appreciate correct ears.

Markings

Markings, especially those found on the head, are the cosmetic aspects of the Saint Bernard that I refer to as the "paint job." Some people find the color patterns on the head to be very important, while others don't place much value on them. Perhaps there is another aspect to this phenomenon, and that is knowing what is correct. An uneducated novice can easily recognize pretty markings, but it takes some depth of knowledge to understand what it really takes to be a good Saint Bernard. However that might be, I confess that whenever I hear anybody expounding upon the importance of facial markings on a Saint Bernard, my imagination immediately paints the word "Novice" across his forehead.

Here comes the surprising part! It doesn't matter that I find markings to be less important than some other features of a Saint Bernard, because I still have a lot to say about what constitutes pretty markings, what is acceptable, and what is not attractive.

The only really important part about markings is their effect upon the dog's expression. The Standard requires that the Saint Bernard have an intelligent expression, and it is my opinion that it is mandatory that the dog's expression also instill a feeling of friendliness in the mind of the observer. If you look into the face of a Saint Bernard and have any doubts about that dog's benevolence, then you are looking at a dog with a very faulty expression. A Saint Bernard must give the impression that he is an extremely friendly dog or else the term "beautiful" does not apply.

Let's start with a description of what many people consider to be beautiful and desirable, and then we can discuss deviations from that model. A common term for a dog with a well-marked head is that he has a "painted" face. In a painted face, the white predominates over a crisp, clearly defined mask. On the very front part of the muzzle, just barely beyond the limits of the nose, is a small black patch, which makes the nose seem more substantial; otherwise, the muzzle is snowy white. The white of the muzzle runs up between the eyes, creating a wide blaze, and across the top of the head, where it connects to the white collar covering the dog's neck.

The final winners at the SBCA's 1987 National Specialty. On the left is Am. Can. Ch. Benbaron's Yondo von Gizer being awarded Best of Breed for the second year in a row, and on the right is Ch. Forever Moxie, who was awarded Best of Opposite Sex, Best of Winners, and Winners Bitch at this show to complete her championship. The people, from left to right, are Vic Dingus, president of the SBCA; Brian Beninger, Yondo's owner and breeder; Stan Zielinski, judge; and Sara Temple, Moxie's owner and breeder.

The white of the muzzle also extends back along the side of the head under the eye and ear and connects to the white throat and neck of the dog. In effect, two islands of color are created, surrounding, on each side, the dog's eye and ear. Each island of color consists of a black patch around the eye and a black ear, which, in turn, are each surrounded by a sea of reddish-brown. These islands of color do not extend forward enough to touch the lips of the dog. The colors are clear and, indeed, look like they were painted on.

This is the optimum in facial markings—a standard, so to speak, from which deviations from perfection arise. Of course, most Saints don't have perfect markings. For example, a "self-colored" face is one in which the island of color around the ear and eye seems to extend forward and/or down across the dog's face in an unattractive manner. The spread of color is usually black or very dark and is most apparent when it creeps forward onto the muzzle. A lesser expression of this phenomenon is a large black spot or patch on the side of the muzzle. The extreme of a self-colored dog is one in which the black color seems to cover the majority of the head and muzzle—the so-called "black-faced" dog. This sort of marking tends to appear in the offspring to an equal or greater extent than in the parents. It seems to be difficult to eliminate from a strain.

If self-colored and black-faced represent too much color, then the opposite extreme is that of too little color. The smallest degree of too little color would be the so-called "slipped mask." A slipped mask occurs when the mask on one side is much smaller than the other side; often such a mask just barely has a rim around the eye or else does not entirely surround the eye on the one side. The next degree of too little color is the "monocle mask," where the island of color on one or both sides seems to shrink until it becomes two separate islands, one around the eye and one around the ear. Then follows the more extreme degree of too little color—the "half mask." A half mask is, as the name implies, a dog with the mask missing on one side so that the island of color misses the eye altogether. Often, a half mask will be missing some or all of the color from the ear on the same side as the missing mask. Following the half mask is the type of marking where the mask is missing from both eyes. This is called the "white face." This phenomenon

Ch. Zelda von Bliss of Bliss Farms Kennel, a longhaired female, being awarded Best of Opposite Sex at the 1968 Specialty Show of the Northern New Jersey Saint Bernard Club. The judge is the late Alfred Moulton, and the owner/handler is Robert Wilson, who now lives in Texas.

Ch. Belyn's Victoria being awarded Best of Breed by Judge Alane Gomez. Victoria is being handled by Lynn Jech for owners Becky Allan and Penny Mahon. Victoria was bred at the Belyn's Kennels in Glen Ellen, California, by Doug and Penny Mahon. She exemplifies very good breed type in spite of her less-than-perfect facial markings.

carried to the extreme is the dog with no color on his head or ears, which is known far and wide as a "sheep's head."

When dogs with too little marking are bred, it seems that, as long as the lips and eyes are rimmed with black, they have much less trouble producing well-marked puppies than the dogs with too much color.

One other kind of marking is ticking or freckles on the face and/or muzzle. I personally find this unattractive. The Standard does not discuss this subject. I assume that this silence is because the authors could not agree on the subject. There are many in the fancy who think that ticking is highly objectionable.

Now we get to the controversial part. Be aware that you cannot find my opinion anywhere in the Saint Bernard Standard. Nevertheless, the following is my list of head markings in descending order of desirability:

1. the painted face
2. the monocle mask
3. the self-colored face
4. the slipped mask
5. the half-mask
6. the white face (no mask with black ears)
7. the sheep's head
8. the black face
9. freckles or ticking

If you were to make small changes to the above order, I wouldn't argue. You might move the black face much higher in the order, but I have a problem with that because of the trouble involved in reducing the extent of coloring in succeeding generations.

Another topic to consider is special markings. There are two types of these markings that have names but that have very little to do with the beauty of the dog. The first is the "monk's cap." A monk's cap is a small circle of brown on top of the head located in the extension of the wide white blaze running up between the eyes and over the head. The next is the "hospice ear," which is either completely or partially white. Very often a hospice ear will be covered with brown speckles. Some people find a monk's cap to be desirable and the hospice ear to be undesirable. Personally, I am completely indifferent to the absence *or* presence of either the monk's cap or hospice ear. To my way of thinking, neither type of marking has the slightest effect upon the dog's expression; hence, it is a trivial concern.

The last point about external color that causes some concern is the color of the nose and lips. The Standard asks that both be black! Because a brown nose is a genetic fault, it cannot be found on a worthy specimen. Pink spots on either the nose or lips, however, can be tolerated if, and only if, they are

The author, Stan Zielinski, makes his awards at the seventh Chiba All Saint Bernard Club Specialty Show held under the auspices of the Japan Kennel Club on May 4, 1994 in Sawara City, which is near Tokyo. The Best of Opposite Sex bitch was Japanese Ch. Starlight Davie, owned and bred by Hirofumi Shimabe. The Best of Breed dog, Japanese Ch. Starlight Danke, was bred by Hirofumi Shimabe and owned by Mieko Sato.

Ch. Stoan's Umeko of Jaz, whose strengths were her proportions, soundness, and head construction. Her major shortcoming was facial markings that gave her the stern expression that is denigrated in the Standard for the Saint Bernard.

Ch. Sanctuary Woods Gulliver, shown here in this 1965 photograph taken at the Sanctuary Woods Kennel near Drain, Oregon. Gulliver was not only a great producer in his own right, but he was the sire and grandsire of many other great producers.

small and unobtrusive. Whenever the the pink lips are what you first notice about a Saint Bernard, you are looking at a dog with a serious fault! You are looking at a dog that will probably have puppies with overly pink lips.

Then there are the markings on the body—a truly unimportant topic. The "mantle coat" is a dog whose blanket of color covers his back and sides like a cape that has been draped over his back. The extreme of this type of marking is a solid color over the entire dog with just a few white hairs in the spots where white is required—not an attractive condition in my opinion. A "torn mantle" is just like the mantle coat except it has splashes of white, ranging from a little to a lot, distributed in the basic body color. It looks like tears in the mantle letting the white show through. The "splash coat" is simply a coat with so much white that the basic body color seems to be spots of color on a white dog. The extreme in my experience is a dog that is solid white except for three patches of color—one around each eye and one around the base of the tail.

At one time, the color of the legs was a source of contention within the Saint Bernard fancy. Originally, the Saint Bernard Standard called for white legs below the elbow and stifle joint. After a lot of argument and hard feelings, the Standard was eventually changed to allow Saint Bernards to have color down to their feet. While I would never denigrate an animal with dark legs, either in my judging or when selecting a breeding match-up, I have always found white legs to be more pleasing to behold.

One last word of caution. I don't want to leave you with the impression that we should always belittle the importance of markings to a Saint Bernard. Markings are the frosting on the cake, the finish on a new car, the final touch that completes a beautiful picture. While the markings must be considered much less important than features such as size, shape, substance, soundness, temperament, and proportions, they certainly play a significant part in establishing any dog's plateau of beauty.

What Is a Fault?

A fault is a deviation from the standard of perfection as described in the AKC Standard for Saint Bernards. Because nobody has ever seen a dog that meets every aspect of the Standard, you must assume that every dog has his share of faults. Yet the showrings are full of good dogs with virtues that are far more significant and numerous than their faults. The judge's job is to find the dog in the class before him that most closely meets the Standard. So where is the problem?

Have you ever stood quietly outside the ring and listened to the opposing factions describe the same dog? The first group will decry that animal as being an awful specimen that is nothing but a collection of odious faults with only a sprinkling of acceptable attributes. Meanwhile, the other bunch will glowingly conclude that the same dog is a compendium of virtues enhanced by an occasional minor flaw—the sort of deviation from perfection that only adds character to a thing of beauty. Is one party wrong and the other right? Perhaps not, because it would be pretty hard to argue with scientific precision against either position.

This muddle is given birth by the subjective nature of faults and by the fact that the discerning of faults seems not to be a truly objective process. Not only does beauty lie in the eyes of the beholder, so also does the state of having faults. From a rather shallow perspective, it appears that a truly objective evaluation of any particular dog or group of dogs is almost impossible to obtain.

You may well ask, "How can this be, when we are only asking of the experts that those features and functions which deviate from the official Standard be identified and evaluated? Can this be so hard to do?" The answer appears to be, "Yes!"

Three separate elements are at work here to cause all of this confusion. They are:

1. The so-called experts' knowledge, ethics, reasoning ability, and freedom from kennel chauvinism.
2. The method of determining the relative importance of various faults.
3. The clarity of the written Standard.

The first item—the degree of expertise found in the experts—is a trivial subject. As long as you think logically while talking to all of the experts and look skeptically upon all the bits of wisdom you are told, you will be able to deal adequately with the problem.

The second item—the relative importance of one specific fault in comparison to another—is the subject of the next chapter and will not be covered here.

The third item—the clarity of the Standard—must be discussed in depth. That is because our Standard, like all written Standards, is highly subject to various interpretations. The obvious solution would be to simply to fix the Standard so that it is clear. As I will explain, this simply will not work.

The problem with any written Standard is that each is the output of a committee, and any such committee effort must result in a series of compromises. Those areas of any Standard where the committee members had unresolvable differing opinions are always obvious. They are the places containing the most vague language. Less obvious, perhaps, are the topics that were considered to be so well understood that they were not worth mentioning. These are the subjects that are just plain missing. Certainly, vague language and assumptions of the obvious do not lead to the exactness and clarity that we would like to see.

Let's contemplate the Standard-writing process for a moment. Consider, for example, a right front

Ch. Snowsage Lisa being handled by her breeder, Sue Peterson, at the SBCA's 1986 National Specialty Show in St. Louis, Missouri. At this show, Judge Joan Zielinski gave Lisa the Best of Opposite Sex award and gave her daughter, Snowsage Rapscallion, the Best of Winners award.

Ch. Stoan's Absolut of Cara is an example of a properly balanced shorthaired bitch. Note here that she is just short of being overangulated; her angulation, both front and rear, are nearly at the limit of acceptability.

foot. You would think that a majority of fanciers could agree upon an ideal right front foot—one that is free of faults and in no need of improvement. Given that agreement, we could then proceed to write a standard of perfection for a "right front foot." Such a foot might be symmetrical (the same size and shape as the left one) and harmoniously sized to fit nicely on the end of the leg to which it is attached.

As soon as we begin to discuss the height, length, and breadth of that foot, however, we get into a controversy. The question becomes, "What is correct—your concept of a well-proportioned foot, or mine?" Could we not also argue about foot shape, or about the proper thickness of pad? I'll bet I could even get into a heated discussion on the correct color of toenails! I have heard people say that white toenails are better than dark ones, and I am sure that others feel that it simply does not matter.

You can see how complicated this gets even though we are only talking about a right front foot. It would get much worse if you were to try to agree on some truly complex part of the dog, such as the head or rear assembly. It is clear that committees and clarity are simply not compatible. That is the reason why forming a new committee to clarify the Standard would be a lost cause.

This, however, does not mean that the problem is unresolvable. We can sneak up on this dilemma from another direction. It is my opinion that if you really study the Standard, dismember it down to its smallest components, and then put it back together one piece at a time, you will gain the insight required to see through the fog inherent to all Standards.

You have to add some wording to the Standard that is only implied but that is required to make the pieces fit together. You have to contemplate the fuzzy text to understand the two sides that were compromised over a particular issue. You have to surrender some of your pet concepts and preconceived notions—and that can be a real trauma. Nevertheless, I strongly recommend that you take the trouble to do it. I promise that there is a complete Saint Bernard described in our official Standard—you just have to look for it carefully.

Why is it important to gain this knowledge? Remember that a fault is a deviation from the Standard. Therefore, you can never truly deal with a fault without first gaining a thorough knowledge of what a perfect Saint Bernard should be.

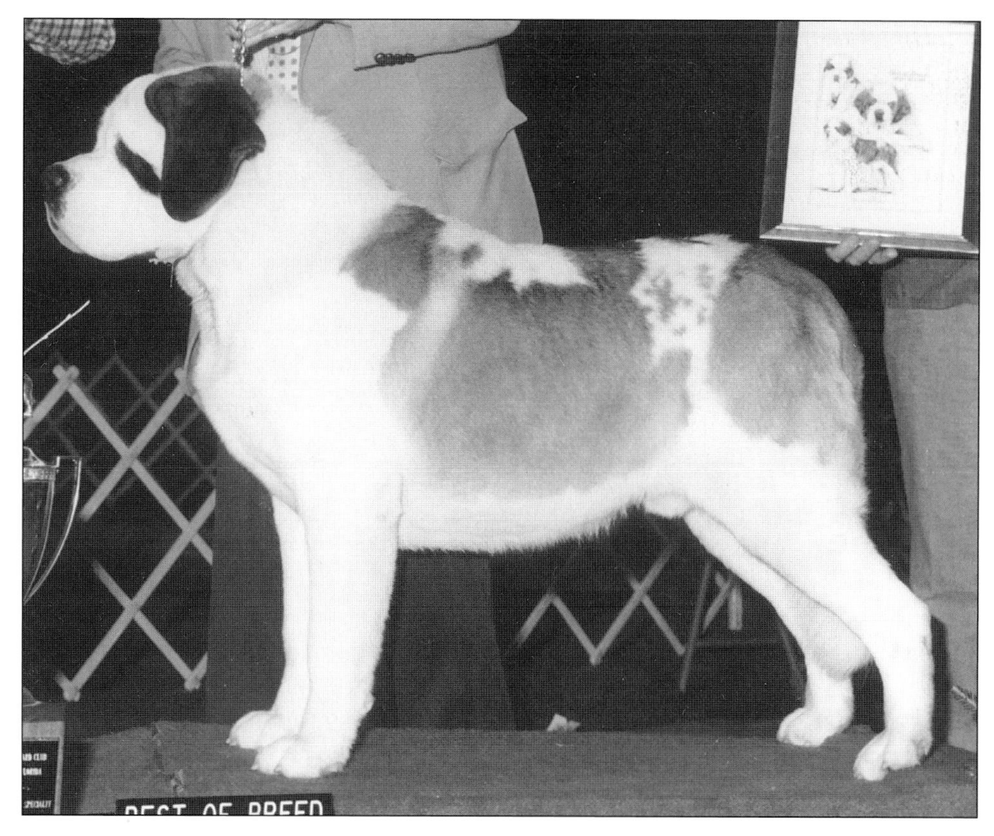

Shown here is Ch. Stoan's Vector of Jona, who finished his championship at thirteen months. Because Vector had many sterling qualities, he was chosen to sire quite a few litters in spite of his rectangular proportions. It is unfortunate that his proportions can be found in many of his offspring and grandchildren. When one breeds to a dog with an obvious fault, one should ensure that the bitch does not share the problem, and this concern should be exercised in the next generation with equal diligence.

What Makes One Fault More Important Than Another?

Is it possible to say that one particular fault is more important than another? Is there a scheme to compare the relative importance of the various faults with which Saint Bernards are afflicted? Listening to the talk around any ringside would soon convince you that some sort of scheme had already been established. Whenever the experts gather after the judging, you can hear the remarks of the disgruntled. "How could he put up that cripple? Doesn't he know a Saint Bernard is supposed to be a working dog?" "How could he award Best of Breed to that ugly-headed thing when it doesn't even look like a Saint Bernard?" "My God! Is that judge so blind she can't see that dippy top line?" "Did you see that idiot give points to that awful gay tail? Obviously, he's never read the Standard!" Whenever someone makes a remark like this, he is really implying that the particular fault being singled out is so important as to outweigh all other considerations. The question you should be asking is, "What makes one fault more important than another?"

The most popular method used to assign relative importance to the various faults among Saint Bernards is based upon a philosophy that I must classify as kennel blind. Dog owners seem to be saying that any fault on *your* dog is critical and very serious, while any fault on *their* dog is trivial and unimportant. We should demand a more rational method.

The obvious formula is to group faults into categories and then assign a value to those categories. For example, most people first do an intuitive evaluation of faults. For those of us to whom this plan has real appeal, it is obvious that certain faults are more significant than others. Unfortunately, I've found that not everybody's intuition leads them to the same conclusion. Still, there are also some positive aspects to this thought process. Let me develop such a scheme and then discuss its shortcomings and virtues.

When I first contemplated this subject, I thought that one way of classifying faults would be to weigh the consequence of each particular fault—that is, having any particular fault should have a negative impact upon some specific aspect of the dog. I like to think that there are three categories in which we can group the various features of the Saint Bernard. I call them "Current Function," "Past Function," and "Aesthetic Function."

1. Current function: The use we have for our dogs today and in the immediate future. Some of these uses are in competitions (such as weight-pulling contests or carting events) and achieving awards (such as in Obedience trials or dog shows).
2. Past function: Serving as a search-and-rescue dog in a very cold alpine environment. In other words, serving the purpose for which the breed was established.
3. Aesthetic function: Serving as a source of pleasure or well-being. Some of the uses in this area are as a pet, companion, decoration, and/or status symbol. This is sometimes called the "Objet d'Art Function!"

Now, are we ready to say that one specific fault is more important than another? I am afraid not! My conclusion is that, having labeled any given fault as to its impact on some aspect of our animals, we are still stuck with a purely subjective evaluation of its relative importance. That is, it seems that it is only a matter of opinion whether an unsound dog is worse than an ugly one. Obviously, this scheme needs some help if it is going to be of any use to us. We need a method of further evaluating some of the faults that we find in our dogs.

Fortunately, there is a way of classifying faults that tends to be a bit more objective! To wit, we must determine just how hard each particular fault

Mont Blanc's Foreign Exchange, owned by Dennis and Jerri Hobbs, is successfully completing a pull of 2,770 pounds at the January 1997 Weight Pull held in conjunction with the National Western Stock Show in Denver, Colorado.

is to eliminate—not in the dog under consideration, but in his offspring or in the offspring of his offspring! In other words, we must determine the genetic aspect of the fault. I propose that we consider a fault to be significant in proportion to the degree of difficulty involved with eliminating that fault in the next and succeeding generations. In this light, I have defined the following categories.

1. Trivial: Not generic in nature. A fault that you would not expect to find in the dog's offspring, such as a scar, a torn ear, or a lack of grooming.
2. Minor: Assuming that reasonable breeding practices are followed, the fault will disappear in the next generation and never be seen again—for example, ticking on the face and legs.
3. Difficult: With strict adherence to proper breeding practices and severe culling, and with a little luck, the fault will show up with a reasonably low rate of incidence in future generations—for example, eyelids with entropion.
4. Very Serious: With concentrated effort, it will take three or more generations to correct and eternal vigilance to keep corrected—for example, a very faulty head type.
5. Forbidding: A fault that does not behave in accordance with the laws of genetic inheritance and/or your life span is too short to be able to deal with a problem so complex—for example, hip dysplasia.

In an effort to make sense out of this, Table 23-1 has been prepared. In it you will find a number of faults that have been distributed throughout the fifteen categories. (The five genetic categories of Trivial, Minor, Difficult, Very Serious, and Forbidding each have the three functional classes of Current Function, Past Function, and Aesthetic Function.) This distribution is based upon research into the very little literature that has been published, upon observations of the Saint Bernard world, and upon my experiences as a breeder of Saint Bernards.

Bergundtal Yakima Chief, shown here at the age of twenty-two months, participating joyfully in the Saint Bernard Club of Puget Sound's 1997 Winter Snow Trial. Chief displays here the kind of athleticism one should expect in a mountain rescue dog. Chief is owned by Lyn and Carlos Bradburn of Everett, Washington, and is co-owned with his breeders, Winston and Trudy Vitous of Marysville, Washington.

It is important for you to understand the perspective of the person who created this table. As a breeder, I can't help but put a lot of importance on the genetic aspect of faults. As an exhibitor, I put considerable emphasis on faults that keep my dog from winning. As a fancier of Saint Bernards, I truly love a thing of beauty—it just makes my heart go pitty-pat. As a judge, I feel obliged to place the most weight with the breeder's position. After you have absorbed this material, you should be prepared to look at any dog and find fault with him. This ability is invaluable when discussing other peoples' dogs or when trying to pass yourself off as an expert.

Ch. Chad's Night in White Satin being awarded Winners Bitch by Judge Joan Zielinski and being handled by her breeder/owner, Carol Terrio of Chandler, Arizona. This is a quality longhaired bitch that demonstrates the term "splash coat" used in the Standard to describe body markings.

TABLE 23-1
SAINT BERNARD FAULTS

Category	Type 1 Faults (Trivial)	Type 2 Faults (Minor)	Type 3 Faults (Difficult)	Type 4 Faults (Very Serious)	Type 5 Faults (Forbidding)
CLASS A Faults (Interferes with aesthetic functions)	scars hot spots foreign substance on coat	light eyes light 3rd eyelids black-and-white 3rd eyelids red haw drooping eyelids dish-faced Roman nose down-faced ticking mismarked head mismarked body/legs cutback flew pink on nose brown nose blue eye	missing teeth scrambled teeth undershot jaw ears too large ears too small ears too low ears too high ears too thin ears too rounded at point dishrag ears flying ears white head gay tail malproportion of head to body malproportion of skull to muzzle cloddishness wetness (spongy tissue, loose skin) pink on lips or around eyes	excessive face wrinkles too pendant flews too much dewlap skull undersized malformed top skull malformed supraorbital ridge malformed cheek bones malformed upper mandible malformed lower mandible overshot jaw lack of substance lack of virtue	sarcoptic mange

TABLE 23-1
SAINT BERNARD FAULTS (continued)

Category	Type 1 Faults (Trivial)	Type 2 Faults (Minor)	Type 3 Faults (Difficult)	Type 4 Faults (Very Serious)	Type 5 Faults (Forbidding)
CLASS B Faults (Interferes with past functions)	illness	flat croup	herring gut	barrel-chested	epilepsy
	seasonally out of coat	goose-rumped	too dry	slab-sided	arthritis
	temporary lameness	swaybacked	entropion	small shoulder blade	cancer
		roach-backed	bull-shouldered	small upper arm	early heart failure
		too wet	unsound limbs	general lack of muscle mass	
		long/flowing coat	weak pasterns	poor muscle tone	
			flat feet	weak loin	
			long feet	small ham (weak thigh)	
			long back	thin neck	
			long loin		
			long neck		
			short legs		
CLASS C Faults (Interferes with current functions)	unwashed (dirty)	overly boisterous	cowhocked	viciousness	hip dysplasia
	untrained	dull-witted	out-at-elbows	timidity	
	poorly groomed	doggy bitch	French-footed	propensity to bloat	
		long legbones	humped tail set	underangulated front assembly	
			overangulated front	underangulated rear assembly	
			overangulated rear		
			bitchy dog		
			malproportion of height to length		

Taking Care of the Puppies

At our house, taking care of puppies is an eighteen-week process—the nine weeks before they are born, plus the nine weeks after they are born. In other words, the work starts at the conception of the litter and lasts until the puppies are placed in their new homes at nine weeks of age.

One caveat before I begin: I don't advocate that our way is the best of all possible methods. Many successful breeders approach this topic with a different philosophy. I don't know if their schemes are better or worse than ours—I can only tell you what works well for us.

Four aspects of our puppy-care program are described in this chapter. First, we try to ensure that the puppies are born strong. Second, we try to guarantee that the puppies stay healthy. Third, we make certain that the puppies are properly socialized. And fourth, we do what we can to ensure that each of the puppies goes to a good home.

ENSURING THAT THE PUPPIES ARE BORN STRONG

The probability of your having considerable trouble in producing a litter of puppies is greatly increased if the puppies are weak and underdeveloped when they are born. If you want to undertake the job of producing a litter, try to ensure that the puppies are born strong. The very first thing you must do is make sure that the bitch you are mating is a good, strong, healthy bitch with her head on straight. If the bitch has health problems, is in poor condition, or has a screw loose in her head, the odds against your retaining your sanity or ending up with viable puppies are rather long.

Your next concern is keeping the bitch healthy while she is carrying the litter. Do not allow her to become wet, chilled, dirty/unsanitary, stressed, or sick. You must furnish her with a clean, dry, warm kennel during this period. She will need clean, sanitary water and an adequate supply of good-quality food. She needs to be in a situation where she will not fret, which usually means that she will need to be close to her family. This is no time to let her visit with strange dogs that may be carrying some strange germ or virus. This *is* the time to have her checked by a veterinarian.

It is not unusual for a bitch to develop a reproductive-tract infection shortly after being bred. Look for signs of fever or a discharge from the vulva. At the first sign of a problem, get her to a veterinarian and make sure that the vet understands that she is in whelp. The treatment must be tailored for a pregnant bitch. Whenever we have a bitch that we plan to breed, it is our practice to have our veterinarian prescribe preventive antibiotics, starting with the first of her season and lasting until she is completely out of season. We believe that this results in more litters, bigger litters, and healthier puppies.

When the puppies are ready to be born, you will experience one of two situations—a *normal* whelping or a *not-so-normal* whelping. Because the first situation is much more pleasant, let's discuss it first.

Most people use a whelping box as the site for the birth. The primary features of a good whelping box are that it is clean, warm, and comfortable. Special emphasis needs to be placed upon the word "comfortable." The bitch must feel that this is the place she wants to be while she has her puppies—not just physically comfortable, but mentally comfortable also. In the wild, dogs used to whelp their puppies in a hollowed-out spot, usually in a den. The more acceptable whelping boxes have a denlike quality—a small room with her spot in a corner, not much light or noise, and no unnecessary people or other animals. Your bitch will not appreciate spectators—a trusted helper maybe, but no spectators.

Many people make a box out of plywood that measures about four feet by five feet with two-foot-high sides. In one of the sides an entrance is cut so that the wall is only about six inches high at that point. Most people install a pig rail all around the whelping box to keep the mother from smashing puppies. This is simply a rail (usually a two-by-four on edge) nailed to the side of the box so that a puppy-size cavity is formed all around the bottom of the box. While the bitch is whelping and all during the time she is nursing her puppies, the usual practice is to line the bottom of the whelping box with paper or carpeting.

We haven't used a wooden whelping box for a number of years. We prefer a child's six-foot-diameter plastic wading pool. We achieve the denlike quality by pushing the plastic pool partially under a countertop. The plastic pools are light and flexible enough to be easily handled, moved, and stored. Cleaning is a snap, because the plastic material can be hosed down and dried with little effort. When the puppies get between the mother and the side of the whelping box, the sides simply move away instead of crushing the puppy. If you hit the stores early in the fall, you will be surprised just how cheap these pools can be. We think that they make the ideal whelping box.

It is easier to start the bitch sleeping in the whelping box three or four days before the puppies are due. Sometimes it is difficult to convince her to have her puppies in the whelping box when the first time she sees it is just as she starts into labor. Such a scenario tends to make her think negatively about the place. If the bitch doesn't like the whelping box, she usually won't stay in it and often will try to move the puppies to her idea of a better place.

How do you know when it is time to whelp the puppies? The most important criterion is to know exactly when she was bred and identify the sixty-third day after that. If she was bred more than once, this can be difficult. One good sign is that the bitch's temperature will drop about twelve to fifteen hours before she goes into labor. We start taking temperature readings the day before the earliest possible due day and repeat them at about twelve-hour intervals. You are looking for a three-degree drop in temperature; that is, to something below 99°F. Once we see that drop in temperature, we insist that the puppies be out of the bitch within thirty hours; they either must exit naturally or we insist on a caesarean section!

It is important to know about disposal of the placenta (afterbirth) and tying off of the umbilical cord. In the wild, the bitch takes care of these tasks. She eats the placentas and cuts the umbilical cords with her teeth so that each cord is crushed and does not bleed significantly. It is our practice to let the bitch do as much as she wants; we just stand by to tidy up whatever she fails to do. I am told that the placenta contains a hormone that starts the milk flowing; therefore, the bitch should eat at least one. Most people find this abominable, to say the least. All I know is that you will usually upset the bitch if you try to keep her from eating the afterbirth, and I have never seen any ill effects from this practice. We keep on hand clean, warm water, cleaning rags, towels, plastic disposal bags, sharp scissors, and small strips of cloth (shoestring size) for tying off the umbilicals if they won't stop bleeding. We usually only need the towels to dry each puppy after the bitch has cleaned it.

Be sure to count the placentas! You must be certain that you saw a placenta exit the bitch for every puppy that came out. If there is any doubt, see your vet. The bitch will develop a life-threatening infection if any placenta remains inside. It is a good idea to take the bitch to the veterinarian the day after whelping. The veterinarian will check the bitch's general health and try to determine whether or not she has any unborn puppies or retained placentas still inside. The veterinarian will, undoubtedly, give her a shot of oxytocin (the so-called "pit shot") to clean out her uterus.

So much for the normal whelpings, which usually pose little problem. Even breech births are typically handled by the bitch. Your primary concern is to recognize when there is a problem. Unless you have some experience, you will probably not be able to recognize when your bitch is straining to have a puppy without any result. Nor will you know that progress has stopped and it is time to get to the veterinarian. Because bitches are so stoic, you will have a difficult time identifying that you have a problem. I recommend that you have someone with adequate experience help you through your first couple of whelpings. If there is a problem, you will almost invariably end up having a caesarean section performed on your bitch. The difference is, if you do it in time, you will save the puppies. If you wait too long, the puppies will all be dead—and sometimes the bitch won't survive the operation if she has been in labor too long.

Your veterinarian may give you bad advice in these situations. I don't know why this happens; I can only report what has happened to us and to most of the breeders we know. Almost without exception, veterinarians want to wait too long before performing a caesarean section. I don't know how you will solve the problem, but we have trained our veterinarian to just do the section without arguing when we see a complication. This has allowed us to save a lot of puppies that otherwise would have been lost. I recommend that you insist that the puppies get out of the bitch immediately at the first sign of trouble.

Now we have some puppies on the ground. Our task is to get them off to a good start. A good start means that they are cleaned and dried immediately—a task that the bitch usually handles but one that you must perform if she doesn't.

KEEPING THE PUPPIES HEALTHY

From a breeder's point of view, a puppy's life is divided into three stages. Stage one is the newly born phase and covers age zero to age five or six days. Stage two is the nursing stage and covers from age one week to five weeks. Stage three is the postweaning stage and covers from five weeks of age until the puppies go to their permanent home when they are nine weeks old.

A wagon full of future champions! These puppies, left to right, became Ch. Lynchcreek's Anthony, Ch. Lynchcreek's Amelia Bearhart, Ch. Lynchcreek's Albrecht v. Stoan, and Ch. Lynchcreek's Ace v. Stoan. Their sire was Ch. Stoan's Nicholas of Klafa, HOF, POE, and their dam was Ch. Belyn's Grendle v. Exchequer, HOF, POE.

Stage One: The Newly Born

The newly born stage is a critical one, and it lasts for five to seven days. The puppies that are not going to make it usually die within the first two or three days. Sometimes the puppies that die so young have just failed to develop fully or have a congenital problem that prohibits life outside of the womb. The rest of the time, whatever problems the puppies develop are usually under your control. We always feel that we have crossed one hurdle when the puppies survive to be one week old. You always feel bad about the puppies that don't survive. You can only take solace in having done your best to give them their greatest chance to live.

Before I get deeply into this subject, let me tell you a story that might relieve a concern that people new to breeding Saint Bernards may have. This happened a long time ago to a man who had just moved up to our area from California and had brought along a pregnant bitch. The lady who owned the sire asked me to look in on the newcomer and to let her know what I thought of the puppies. The puppies were born on a Thursday night, and the next Saturday I had to take some paperwork over to another man who lived just one block from the newborn puppies. I had called Bill the day before and said that I might drop by and was greeted rather coldly. Undaunted, I rang his doorbell and introduced myself. Bill told me that he really didn't want me to see his puppies, because he was afraid that his bitch had gotten with another breed of dog and the puppies were all mongrels. Knowing the kind of care the owner of the stud would have exercised, I thought that a mismating was most unlikely. So I asked Bill why he thought his puppies were mixed breed and he said, "They are all black and white and have pink noses!" Relieved, I laughed and told him that that is what newborn Saint Bernard puppies were supposed to look like. "Don't worry," I told him happily. "They will soon begin to look like real Saint Bernards." And they did.

There are concerns that the owners of brand-new litters need to worry about, but the color of the noses and markings is not one of them. So let's talk about the important stuff. It is critical that you watch the puppies' weights. Every day, after their first day and a half, should see a gain in weight. A puppy that fails to gain weight daily or one whose relative position in the litter (with respect to weight) drops down is a puppy with a very serious problem. Any puppy that fails to gain weight or loses weight is a puppy in the act of dying! You probably won't be able to save him, but you might see what a veterinarian can do.

Weighing Schedule. As soon as each puppy is clean and dry, record his birth weight. For the first two weeks, weigh each puppy daily and record the weight. From two to six weeks, record each puppy's weight twice a week. From six weeks to nine weeks, weigh the puppies about once a week.

A number of situations can cause a puppy to stop gaining weight. One of the most common is that one or two puppies will be weaker or smaller than their littermates. These puppies soon become exhausted from the competition for a spot at the dinner table and soon give up. When they stop eating, they stop gaining weight. These puppies just need solo time on their mother, or hand feeding, or both, until they get strong enough to hold their own.

Another common problem is that the puppy is sick and just doesn't feel up to doing battle with the rest of the gang. The usual causes of sickness are an infection of some kind or a severe trauma, such as getting crushed or chilled. These puppies also need special attention to see that they get enough groceries, and they will probably need veterinary assistance to identify the exact nature of the problem and the best remedy. Problems often can be solved easily when they are recognized early, and one of the surest signs of difficulty is not gaining weight. That is why you should closely monitor the weights of your puppies.

Of course, knowing that you have a problem is only step one. The next step is to identify the problem, and that requires some knowledge of what the puppies need for proper development and, indeed, for their very survival. Four conditions are of primary importance for brand-new puppies—staying warm, nursing, living in a sanitary environment, and avoiding flatness. Let's talk about them one at a time.

Staying Warm. Failing to keep your litter warm will result in dead puppies. Don't let new puppies get chilled; you must ensure that they maintain their body heat! Once the puppies lose body heat, they start to fail. Once they get to the critical point, only herculean efforts can revive them, and that often fails. We like to keep puppies in an environment

Two buddies sharing a serious discussion. It is a rule of nature that boys and dogs need each other, and this captured moment shows that their camaraderie can start when both are very young. There is, perhaps, no breed of dog that exceeds the Saint Bernard in forming this bond that makes them such wonderful companions.

that is kept a little above room temperature for the first thirty-six to forty-eight hours after whelping. By a little above room temperature, I mean in the range of 74°F. to 78°F.

The most important part of the puppies' environment, as far as temperature is concerned, is the surface upon which they lie. This is why you want to keep them on a heated surface for the first few days whenever they are not nursing. Be certain, however, that you don't cook the puppies! This is not a case of the hotter the better. If they struggle to get off the heating pad, it is probably too hot.

When the puppies are forty-eight hours old, we reduce their environmental temperature to normal room temperature—say 67°F. to 70°F. By the time the puppies are three weeks of age, they should be hardy enough to withstand normal outdoor temperatures, as long as they have littermates to help form a puppy pile.

A big part of staying warm is staying dry. Dry your puppies immediately after birth and then keep them that way. One of the biggest sources of becoming wet can be the puppies' mother. We have lost puppies whose mother licked them so much that they were continually wet. Sometimes you just have to intervene and stop the bitch from doing what she thinks she is supposed to do.

Nursing. You want strong, vigorous puppies that will start nursing immediately. If they were born by caesarean section, they will be groggy from the anesthetic for a while, but after that they should nurse with enthusiasm.

The first day's menu is a substance called colostrum rather than milk; this is nature's scheme for protecting the puppies. Colostrum is the source of antibodies for warding off the various diseases for the first six to eight weeks. Any puppy that is unable to nurse must be bottle or tube fed, but if he doesn't get a ration of colostrum, his chances for survival are diminished. You should expend a lot of effort trying to get the puppy to nurse on the bitch that first day.

Just a quick aside here to define tube feeding to those who are unfamiliar with the term. Tube feeding is the practice of putting milk into a puppy's stomach via a tube that has been inserted through his mouth, down his throat, and into the stomach. You can buy tube-feeding kits, but I recommend that you get instructions on the procedure before you try it yourself.

There are certain situations to which you should be alert. The newly born puppy should either be asleep or expending every effort to be nursing. If he just lies still when the rest of the litter is attacking the mother, he has a problem. Sometimes the puppy is small or tired or simply weak. If this is the case, you are going to have to bottle or tube feed him in an attempt to get him up to speed. A large percentage of the newly born that fail to nurse vigorously will die before they are a week old. Try to get them to nurse. Help them find the nipple. Hold them on the nipple and stimulate them by stroking. Protect them from their littermates, who will try to knock them off the nipple. If they fall asleep, wake them up. When all else fails, feed them by hand and pray that that will do the job.

Supplemental Feeding. The first caution here is to warn you not to feed human baby formula to your puppies. You need to see your veterinarian to obtain a supply of puppy formula. This is probably a good item to have on hand ahead of time just in case the need might arise. In an emergency, use goat's milk if it is available. We have, when all other options were not available and we needed to feed the puppy immediately, made our own formula of three ounces of condensed milk, three ounces of bottled water, and a tablespoon of corn syrup.

There are a number of situations in which you will be required to help supply sustenance to the puppies. The first is when the bitch's milk supply is not adequate. This may be because the litter is so large that the bitch cannot produce enough milk for each puppy. Sometimes the dam's milk supply simply fails to come in, or it comes in at an insufficient rate. It is not unusual for the milk supply to start slowly and then pick up speed in about a week; this is something that you need to watch. Whatever the reason, whenever we feel the need to help feed the puppies, we simply rotate the litter to give each a shot at nursing on the mother and either bottle feed or tube feed the ones whose turn it is to be off the dam. It is important for the puppies' development that the bitch try to clean and nurse the puppies and that they try to feed on their mother. You need to be an auxiliary helper to the process.

The second problem is one that you hope you never see. This is when the mother has no milk or you lose the bitch during whelping and you are dealing with orphaned puppies. I've already discussed the fact that the puppies will never receive their colostrum, so you will have to protect them from all exposure to infection and disease until they have had their first shots. Then there is the necessity of somebody devoting all of his or her time to taking care of the litter. Just like all babies, the puppies will start out by needing to be fed at three-hour intervals. Say goodbye to any thought of getting a good night's sleep for about three weeks. Remember to relieve each puppy by washing his genitals and anus with a warm washcloth just before feeding him. The puppy has a desperate need to nurse, so I strongly recommend that you bottle feed each puppy for a majority of his meals. Your mental well-being will be enhanced if you tube feed the puppies during the middle of the night. This can turn an hour-long session of nursing each puppy individually into a ten-minute procedure. You should be able to obtain a tube-feeding kit and instructions on its use from your veterinarian.

Sanitary Conditions. There are three things that will cause unsanitary conditions in the whelping box. Obviously, the puppies will do better if they don't have too much exposure to germs on their unhealed umbilical cords or at any of their bodily openings. These are all subject to infection, and you don't want that in your unprotected puppies.

The first source of contamination is the puppies' own excrement. This is usually not a problem, because the bitch will lick the puppies clean and clean up any droppings in the bottom of the whelping box. This may be enough to turn your stomach, but if you think about how wild dogs must keep their dens clean, you can understand how this instinctive behavior developed. I am discussing this here because it's important. You must understand this process or you risk losing puppies.

The only time a puppy will urinate or defecate is when his stomach, genitals, and anus are licked by the mother dog. If you have a bitch that won't do this (or if you have orphan puppies), you have to do it or the puppy may die! Now you don't actually lick the puppy, but you *do* use a warm, wet cloth to simulate the mother's licking of these areas. You must do this every time the puppy nurses, which will seem like all the time.

The second cause of unsanitary conditions in the whelping box is the mother dog. She will have a very dark discharge out of her vagina for the first week or so after the puppies are born. We simply shear away all of the hair on the underside of the bitch's tail and on the back of her thighs and hocks. If the hair is retained in this area, it will become stained a dark green and will eventually start to smell bad. The bitch will lose all of her hair anyway when the puppies are about seven or eight weeks of age, so there is no sense in trying to save her beautiful coat.

The real problem with this discharge is that the puppies will get into it. The most prolific nipple is always the hindmost one, so the puppies will compete for it. The cause of the problem is that they don't seem to be able to discern the difference between the bitch's vulva and the rearmost teat. Therefore, there will usually be one or two puppies in the green yuck whenever the litter is nursing. Of course, you must clean the puppy immediately if the mother doesn't. We try to redirect any puppy that goes looking for lunch too far far back, but it is impossible to always catch them before they get slimed. You just have to do what you can and clean up what you miss.

Another problem related to lack of sanitation is mastitis, an infection within a breast that involves the production of milk mixed with pus or simply no milk and all pus. Either way, it is poison to any puppy that sucks on that teat. What you need to watch for is any sign of an enlarged breast or one that feels harder than the next one. If you have a question about any teat, milk it to see what color fluid comes out. If it is milky white, breathe a sigh of relief. If it is cream colored or light yellow, start to panic.

Your first step is to ensure that no puppy uses that nipple. Clean the surface of the nipple, dry it, and tape it so that it can't be used. Then look over the litter to see if any puppy is in toxic shock. The bitch needs to see a veterinarian immediately, and the veterinarian needs to give her a treatment of antibiotics that won't affect the puppies. Any puppy in trouble needs treatment also, but his prospects are not great.

Avoiding Flatness. Try to avoid having any of your puppies go flat. "Flat?" you ask. "How do puppies go flat?" The answer is simple—puppies go flat when their mother lies on them. Every bitch is different, and many are good mothers that are very careful with their puppies. Then there are the other kind! Some bitches enter the whelping box, lie down, then start looking around the locate their puppies. If the puppy is only partly under the bitch and you are within earshot, you can usually respond to the puppy's screams in time to save him. If the puppy is dead center under the bitch or you don't hear the sounds of trouble in time, you will lose the puppy.

When you have a mother dog like this, you must have a plan. Always evaluate the bitch's maternal instinct before you trust her to be alone with her puppies. If she is a hazard to the puppies, somebody has to sit with her all the time she is with them. Some breeders have adopted the practice of leaving a "step-on" puppy with the bitch and removing the rest of the litter when they can't be right there. Of course, the "step-on" puppy is the one that you can most afford to lose. Somehow, this practice has never appealed to me. When we have a careless bitch, we never leave her alone with her puppies.

Dewclaws. Before we discuss how to remove dewclaws, I want to express a little personal philosophy on the subject of removing the dewclaws from puppies.

First of all, the only reason to remove dewclaws is for cosmetic reasons. Any reason expressed about how it is for the benefit of the dog is utter silliness that cannot stand up to rational scrutiny. Removing dewclaws is done only to make the dog similar to the rest of the dogs in the showring.

Second, AKC regulations prohibit any cosmetic surgery not specifically allowed in the Breed Standard. The Saint Bernard Standard only allows the removal of the rear dewclaws. If any judge had the courage to enforce AKC regulations, he or she would disqualify any Saint Bernard missing his front dewclaws. On the other hand, most Saint Bernard breeders customarily remove the dewclaws from all four legs. It is our practice to remove the rear dewclaws only, because a significant portion of the judging community will penalize a dog with dewclaws on the rear legs. I wish that the entire fancy could agree to abandon the fad of removing dewclaws.

If you are going to remove the dewclaws from your puppies, it needs to happen between two and six days of age. Before that, it is too much of a trauma for puppies struggling to just stay alive. After that, the operation becomes more serious; it is harder to stop the bleeding and some bone development or growth will be starting. Some people do this job themselves, but most people take the litter to their veterinarian. It is not a big procedure, but it does take some knowledge and skill, especially if there are complications.

Stage Two: The Nursing Stage

The nursing stage occurs between the end of the newborn stage, at six or seven days, until the puppies are weaned at approximately five weeks of age. The breeder's task during this time is to ensure that the puppies thrive, that the health of the puppies is optimized, and that the development conditions are the best possible.

Warning Signs. As discussed previously, the primary sign that one of the puppies has a serious problem is a failure to gain weight. However, there are other indicators for which you need to be alert.

Listlessness: Not as active or vigorous as the littermates. Usually this puppy is feeling ill and you need to identify the problem, especially if the puppy is either hot or cold.

Lone Ranger: The Lone Ranger is the puppy that is not with the rest of the litter. If all of the puppies are in a pile except for one, check that one closely. He most likely has a problem, and you need to solve it quickly before you lose him. Determine if he has been getting his turn on the mother. If he is smaller than the rest of the puppies, he may simply be exhausted from competing for a spot at the lunch counter, and you need to supplement his food intake. If he is cold, make him warm.

Swollen Limbs: Usually a sign of distress, such as an infection or trauma, such as a strain or a broken bone. This also applies to the tail. Swollen limbs are an indication to get that puppy under a veterinarian's care right away.

Swollen Belly: This is a hard problem to deal with, because you have to distinguish between a good swollen belly and a bad swollen belly. The belly of a puppy will normally be swollen and hard when he stops eating, and that is good. When you hand feed or tube feed a puppy, the belly becomes hard and swollen when you are done. On the other hand, if the puppy's belly is swollen and hard before he *starts* to eat, there is a problem—usually worms or an obstructed bowel. Again, the veterinarian needs to see the puppy quickly.

Loose Stools: You should see no signs of fecal material because the bitch will keep the puppy so clean that you won't see anything. This doesn't mean that you shouldn't try to determine the quality of the stools. If there is a problem with overly loose stools, the puppy may have a yellow- or light-brown-stained rear. If the puppy's rectal area, tail, and rear legs are stained, he needs to see a veterinarian.

Infections: Certain spots seem to be the most likely to become infected—the eyes (before they open), the umbilical cord, removed dewclaws, and between the toes. All of these areas need first aid immediately whenever they become swollen or weeping.

Sores: Get to the vet immediately.

Fleas: Puppies can become anemic enough to die if the flea population gets out of hand. Try to take care of this before the puppies arrive, because almost anything that will kill fleas will also kill puppies. After the puppies arrive, the only cleanser that I feel safe using is Ivory soap and water. The puppies also should be moved to new quarters.

Doesn't Walk: The entire litter should start walking within days of each other. If one of the puppies doesn't get up on his legs within a week of the rest, you need to get some expert analysis and advice. Unfortunately, you are probably dealing with a structural problem that isn't going to get any better. My advice is to see a competent vet who has extensive experience with Saint Bernard puppies to see if there is a remedy. If the problem can't be fixed, you will have to suffer through the trauma of putting that puppy down—never a pleasant experience after you have worked so hard to keep him going for so long.

Stages of Development. One of the most interesting aspects of the nursing stage is the number of developmental phases that occur during this time. At ten days, plus or minus a day, the puppies' eyes should start to open. At about eight or ten days of age, it will be necessary to clip the toenails on the puppies' front paws to reduce the damage to the teats of the dam, which is caused by the constant kneading of the breasts while the puppies nurse. The toenails should be clipped at regular intervals as long as the puppies are nursing.

At ten to twelve days, you can get your first indication about the eventual coat type. You need to look at the undercoat on the flank and upper thigh. You do this by running your finger against the grain. If the undercoat is beige in color, the dog will be a long hair; if it is gray, the dog will be a short hair. Personally, I have a hard time telling the difference, so I wait until the puppies are seven weeks old, when it is obvious which coat type they have inherited.

The puppies should make their first attempt to play at approximately three weeks of age. Between three and four weeks, their teeth should start to erupt, which will make mom a little less eager to have the pack chewing on her. At five weeks, the puppies should be weaned—more or less. If the puppies had their way, they would probably nurse until they were two years old.

We usually start the puppies on their first exposure to solid food at three weeks. We start with regular baby food—the pure rice type—mixed with powdered milk and water. Around our house, the first solid food that the puppies experience is almost a liquid, and we feel fortunate if we get as much inside the puppies as they get all over their outside. This is a very messy process! The fortunate part is that their mother is usually more than happy to clean them up. If she won't, you will have to literally wash the puppies after every feeding.

After three or four days on the rice and powdered milk, we gradually mix in puppy chow that has been put through the blender; we still keep the mixture almost a liquid. By the time the puppies are four and a half weeks old, we have them on pure puppy chow, but it is still put through the blender and mixed with powdered milk and water. At weaning time—five weeks—we switch to only puppy chow that has been soaked for approximately ten minutes in water.

The initiation to solid food often changes the puppies' stool so that it has a distinct odor. Many bitches will stop cleaning up puppy droppings at this stage. Guess who now gets to clean up after them!

Stage Three: The Postweaning Stage

Once the puppies are weaned, they seem to enter a period where they are at a reduced risk, but there is more work for the breeder. Keeping the puppies and their quarters clean gets to be an ever-increasing chore as the puppies get bigger and bigger. During this time, they will either be asleep, eating, or playing as hard as they can. Your concern as the litter's nanny is to control what they put into their mouths, keep them from injury, and optimize their socialization.

Pictured here is a three-month-old puppy that many puppy buyers would overlook. When evaluating puppies, search out the important qualities and don't be overly impressed by facial markings. This young lady, Ch. Stoan's Absolut of Cara, easily finished her championship before she was one and one-half years old.

Eating Dangerous Objects. Like little children, everything that catches the attention of a puppy goes into his mouth. If it seems the least bit edible, it is swallowed. Rocks, dried stools, sticks, rags, small chew toys, plastic utensils, dirt clods, sand, socks, underwear, carpet chunks, straw, and flowers are among the items we have seen pass through puppies in the last thirty years. The best you can do is to keep their pen free of such items and watch them closely when they are let out for a run. Even these precautions won't catch everything, so you must watch them continually for signs of an obstructed bowel. Almost always, they will pass anything that they can swallow. If they become listless and stop eating, you need to get them to a veterinarian as fast as you can.

The other category of dangerous items is toxic material. Pesticides, fertilizers, cleaning materials, and all such materials should be kept out of reach of the puppies. Even if eating some of these substances doesn't kill the puppies, it can cause severe and/or permanent damage to the liver and kidneys. Antifreeze is *always* fatal. The taste is sweet and the puppies will always clean the pan or bucket before they stop. They always consume a fatal quantity. This also applies to grown dogs. I can't emphasize this enough—antifreeze should always be treated as an extremely dangerous substance! The dogs think that it tastes good, they will almost never pass an opportunity to drink it, and there is no cure.

Too Big Too Soon. The puppies' food can be a problem for them if it is the kind that promotes excessive growth. With Saint Bernards, growing too fast is a bad thing—so bad that it can have repercussions for the rest of the dog's life. When the puppies are too heavy, their leg bones often develop in strange ways—crooked fronts, weak pasterns, cowhocks, and flat feet, to name a few. We also feel that there is a correlation between the puppies growing too fast and having problems with hearts, livers, and bloat when they become adults.

Our approach is two-pronged. First, we strongly believe in a self-feeding program for the dogs. This means that we keep food available to the dogs at all times and they just help themselves whenever they want to eat. By the time puppies are nine weeks of age, their food is dry kibble, so there is not a problem with spoilage when the food sits there for twenty-four hours. When we do this, the dogs don't think of their food as a rare commodity, and therefore it is not something worth fighting over. In our experience, every time a self-feeding dog becomes too fat, that dog has a metabolism problem that requires veterinary attention. Every time we have had an overweight dog, he has had a thyroid imbalance, and even this has been a very rare occurrence.

The next concern with feeding is the quality of the food. We do not like the very cheap brands of dog food, but we do not know anyone who has had a serious problem with these products. On the other hand, we have had to put puppies to sleep because of the structural damage that occurred when they were fed a brand of puppy food that was too rich. We avoid the premium brands of dog foods like we would some vile disease. We find that the middle of the road with respect to price and to the touted nutritional value of the dog food is the optimum for Saint Bernards. Many breeders have had problems with feeding a brand of dog food that was too hot. Saint Bernards thrive best on food that is mild, bland, and of just adequate nutrition. This is one instance where *better* is not as good as *just good enough*.

One other item of interest regarding Saint Bernard puppies: We start them off on a well-known, common brand of puppy food, and we let them continue on it until they begin to show a preference for the adult dog food. This usually happens by the time they are three months old. After that, they just have to get into the big dogs' food dishes when they want to eat.

Avoiding Injury. Puppies play hard, and hard play will result in some level of bumps, bruises, strains, and sprains. Because the puppies need this play for their proper development, it is better to suffer through these minor injuries than it is to protect them from every possible trauma. This live-and-let-live philosophy, however, doesn't extend to serious injury. Some things you simply don't want to risk.

You don't want the puppies hurting each other. Sometimes there will be a great difference between the sizes of the puppies, and you may need to offer some protection to the runt. I don't recommend separation, for they need their littermates, but I do suggest that you provide supervision while they are playing and a refuge for the little one where the bigger puppies can't get at him.

Another risk that puppies experience is drowning. Provide water in a wide, shallow pan rather than in a deep bucket. When the puppies are jostling with each other around their water, you don't want one of them to be pushed into the water and not be able to get back out. This can happen when a puppy gets his head down in a bucket.

The last hazard that I want to mention is falling. Puppies will climb up on everything they can. King of the mountain is a popular game among the young ones. Just be sure that whatever is available for them to climb upon doesn't have a side or feature that could lead to a traumatic fall. Dog-house roofs, porches, wood piles, and so forth are items that should *not* be available to a pack of puppies.

OTHER ASPECTS OF KEEPING THE PUPPIES HEALTHY

There are three other aspects of looking after the health of the puppies that you need to absorb—adequate exercise, worming, and immunization.

Adequate Exercise

Proper exercise is very important to the puppies' health and well-being. There is not much that you have to do to make the puppies exercise, but there are a number of inadvertent mistakes that you can make that will keep the puppies from getting the exercise required for proper development.

The first exercise that the puppies experience is a by-product of nursing. All the time they are nursing, their front feet are busy doing a tap dance on either side of the nipple they are working. I'm told that this is supposed to stimulate the flow of milk. All I know is that all of the healthy puppies do this all the time they are nursing, and it will cause scratches and sores on the mother's breasts if you don't keep the puppies' nails cut short. This pushing and prodding with the front feet tends to push the puppy off of the nipple, which means that all the time the front feet are working, the back feet are also working to push the puppy forward onto the nipple. This requires good footing. The other exercise that they get during this time is provided by the pushing and shoving that is part of the fighting with their littermates to hold onto whatever nipple they have claimed. This also requires good footing.

Now we get to your part in this scenario. Many people interfere with this nursing-related exercise by having the mother nurse her puppies on a surface that is so slick, the puppies can't get enough traction. Such a surface is usually chosen because it is easier to clean. This is a mistake that will cause your puppies to have retarded development of their leg muscles. They may eventually recover, but they never quite make it back to their full potential.

Indoor-outdoor carpeting is an excellent nursing surface. Other types of carpeting are too hard to clean and soon become unsanitary. Some people use towels or other types of cloth that can be put into a washing machine. The slickest acceptable surface is newsprint, which is also commonly used for lining whelping boxes. You can obtain end rolls from newspaper plants if you don't want to deal with ink on the puppies (it makes their legs and bellies gray).

Good footing is also necessary when the puppies start to walk and play. This is also the time to start thinking of their first exposure to the great world of outdoors. In nice weather, we start to put the puppies outside for a few hours at a time when they are about three weeks old. We gradually increase the out-of-door sessions as the puppies get acclimatized. If the nighttime temperatures are above 40°F., we try to convert all of the puppies to outdoor dogs about the time they are weaned.

Once the puppies are on their feet, their primary source of exercise is playing with each other and with their toys. We try to ensure that the bigger puppies don't traumatize the little ones too badly, but they need to mock fight with each other. Not only does this exercise their bodies, it also exercises their socialization—but that's another subject. Take my word for it, the pushing and shoving and growling are necessary for their development, both physically and mentally.

Toys are a secondary source of play for puppies. Little chew toys that lie around on the ground are of little use, for the puppies quickly tire of them or they become so fouled that you can't stand to let the puppies play with the nasty things. We usually hang a rag or stick from the roof of their pen so that one end is about four inches above the ground. That way they can have a gang tug-of-war with it, and when they tire of it, the toy will remain mostly off of the ground. It works for us! An old tire will also amuse the entire litter for extended periods.

Worming

I've been told that all puppies are born with roundworms. I can't verify this statement, but I can testify that it seems that way to us. The only variable seems to be whether the puppies have just a few roundworms or are so infested that their lives are at risk.

We start our worm control by worming the bitch about a month before she is to be bred. Our next step is to worm all of our puppies. Please understand what worming entails. Worming is the process of putting a toxic substance inside an animal. Hopefully, it is fatal to the worms and not fatal to the host animal. When puppies are less than three weeks old, the difference between fatal to the worms and fatal to the puppies is a very narrow gap. Sometimes the puppies are so badly infested that they must be wormed when they are just days old. The survivors of these premature wormings often will have permanent liver damage. I would never take on one of these early wormings without the services of a very experienced veterinarian.

Under normal circumstances, we worm our puppies at twenty-one days of age and then again ten days later. We almost always see dead worms in the puppies' stools at the first worming. If we see any evidence at the second worming, we repeat the procedure for the third time ten days later. That third worming has never failed to result in worm-free stools. I believe that we occasionally fail to get total success with the first worming because we try to use a little less than the recommended dosage. I just have this thing against putting poison in puppies. I know that this is irrational behavior, but I guess I'll just have to live with it.

A word of caution—if the mother dog is still cleaning up the puppy stools, she will have to be isolated from her puppies for thirty hours after they have been wormed. I don't know for sure that the dead worms or the worm medicine would do her any harm—it just seems to me that she shouldn't be eating them!

Immunizations

There are a lot of differing philosophies on this subject, so I'm just going to relate what works for us. We usually give the litter their first shots at seven weeks of age. We give a second shot at nine weeks of age, then we tell whoever gets the puppy to give a third shot when the puppy becomes four months old. We usually give the combination vaccine that is said to give immunization for distemper, hepatitis, leptospirosis, kennel cough, corona, and parvo. This is the so-called six-in-one shot that is so popular today.

We do not give rabies shots before the puppies go to their permanent homes at nine weeks. The veterinary advice that we have been given states that rabies vaccinations are not effective until the dog is six months old—so that's when we give the dogs their first rabies immunization.

MAKING CERTAIN THAT THE PUPPIES ARE SOCIALIZED

You want your puppies to become dogs that people like to be around—dogs that are people oriented and gregarious. Each puppy is born with an upper limit as to how social and intelligent he can become. The way you achieve the greatest potential is through proper socialization of the dog throughout his life. Like most aspects of any living being, the most important part of any development occurs at the beginning of life. This means that socializing puppies is very important. Now let's discuss how this is accomplished.

The Laying on of Hands

It is very important that your puppies become accustomed to being handled. They will fail to become quality pets if they do not come to think of the human hand as pleasant. Newborn puppies should be picked up and caressed at least twice a day. While the puppies are in the nursing stage, they should be picked up, petted, and held up to where they can smell your breath. After they are weaned, they should be picked up at every opportunity; that is, until they become too big to lift anymore. At that point, they still need to be touched and petted as much as possible.

Dogs in general, and Saint Bernards in particular, are touchy-feely beings. They feel something by putting it in their mouth. A puppy, and even an adult dog, will be comforted if you let him hold your finger or part of your hand in his mouth. I often sit and talk to a young puppy with my finger across his mouth just behind the canine teeth. For the rest of their lives, your dogs will seek contact with you whenever they are in a stressful situation. This usually means that they will press against your legs when the scenario frightens or disturbs them.

Talking to the Puppies

We communicate with our pets mostly by talking and by body language. Of the two, body language is of most use to your dog. Most body language seems to be instinctive with puppies, and the part that isn't is learned by associating your tone of voice with certain ways that you hold yourself, or gestures, or other signals of which we are not aware. Even the secondary communication mode—talking—is something that your dog learns after listening to you for a long time.

You should talk to your dog all the time. Start as soon as he can hear, and never stop. Baby talk is very good when you are dealing with young puppies. I think that this is just because baby talk is never ambiguous about how you are feeling and relating to the puppies. They seem to understand and respond to baby talk better than to normal conversation. I know that I feel completely foolish when someone catches me communicating with my dogs in this manner, but it seems to get the best results.

Puppy Play

Like children, puppies need play for proper development. They will instinctively play with their littermates and their mother before they can really sit upright. They will play with anything that comes within their focus of attention. This includes some items that are a little dangerous—objects that you need to keep out of their pen. We try to furnish toys that are too big to be swallowed and that are indestructible enough to prevent ingestion of anything harmful. Our most useful item is a branch suspended from the top of the puppies' pen so that one end is about four inches off the ground.

The puppies also need to play with their people. The litter owner should do this before the puppies go to their new homes. We encourage the puppies to play tug-o-war with us by pulling on a short piece of braided hemp rope or an old towel. Another activity that the puppies enjoy is going for a walk in the yard. They will try to catch you and bite your cuffs. Your part of the game is to dodge around so that they can't quite catch you.

ENSURING THAT THE PUPPIES GO TO GOOD HOMES

It would be a shame to raise a litter of puppies to be nine weeks of age and then see all of your efforts ruined by having the puppies end up in an environment that destroys their health, soundness, or temperament. That is the risk you take if you don't do everything in your power to ensure that the puppies go to good homes. Most homes will be just fine as long as you keep the new owners from doing stupid things out of ignorance. This means that you send puppies home with a good set of instructions, and they you try to keep in touch with the people to check on how the puppy is getting along. Your biggest concern is identifying the bad home. Note that a bad home for your puppy does not mean that it is occupied with bad people—it simply means that their life-style is not suitable for a puppy.

Signs of a Good Home

In general, you are looking for a home that will continue the socialization of the puppy so that his temperament will make you proud, that will provide a healthy place for the dog so that his quality of life is good or better, and that will be a safe place for the dog where he will not be subject to hazards.

Continued Socialization. The new family must have the time and space to make the animal a part of their family circle. A dog deprived of companionship will fail to be as gregarious and dependable as he should be. Make sure that the dog will spend most of his waking hours in the company of his family.

A puppy's development is greatly enhanced if he has a playmate. A positive sign is if there are children in the family who will bond with the dog, or if the family has other pets that will play with the dog when he is young.

One of the greatest contributions to the puppy becoming an integral part of his new family is to have the people make a commitment to take him to obedience class. Whenever new owners take their puppy to obedience class, the dog becomes much more socially acceptable. He becomes more pleasant to be around, so people tend to value him more and treat him better. The owners also learn how to relate to their dog and how to get him to behave the way they want. Everybody comes out ahead. What more could you want?

Healthy Environment. It is important that the new owners of one of your puppies have some common sense about keeping a dog in a healthy environment, and that they listen to your advice and heed it. The new owners need to understand some of the basic aspects of health maintenance and nutrition. You need to tell them about the schedule for shots and worming and about the kind of food that the dog will need for the rest of his life.

Beyond the basics, you need to be assured that they understand about sanitation and cleanliness. You will sometimes get dogs back because the people didn't realize that a Saint Bernard litters his yard with piles that can't be ignored or overlooked. Owning a Saint Bernard entails daily pick-up patrols and a disposal plan. (This may be a good time to explain about the life cycle of some of the intestinal worm varieties.) Keeping a Saint Bernard clean and groomed is another subject that most prospective puppy buyers fail to contemplate. Often you will hear back from your customers that they had no idea what a chore it is to bathe and dry a Saint Bernard.

It would also be to your benefit to help the new puppy owner identify the best veterinarian available to them. If you don't know the veterinarians in their area, give them some guidelines on identifying those who don't understand the special needs of the breed.

Safe Environment. You need assurance that the dog will live a life that is relatively free of some of the more serious and common hazards. Your first concern is whether or not the dog is going to be confined in a fenced yard. In this day and age, life is much too dangerous for a free-roaming pet. The probability of their living to a ripe old age when they are allowed to wander is exceedingly small. Even worse is the keeping of a dog on a chain or tether. Nothing will ruin a dog's temperament faster than this life-style. If the people don't have a fenced yard, they shouldn't get a puppy. When people without fenced yards want to get a puppy from us, it is our practice to hold onto the puppy until after the yard has been fenced.

You also should ask about their plans for protecting the puppy from inclement weather. Will the dog be a house dog? If he is going to be an outside dog (and there is no reason why Saint Bernards can't be outside in very cold weather), does he have a dry place to go when it rains, snows, or hails? Will he have shelter from the sun and heat? Will his exercise area be relatively clean and dry, or will the dog be up to his pasterns in mud (or worse) most of the winter?

You also need to identify what kind of hazard-free environment the new owners are going to provide for the dog. It may be worth your time to tell them about toxic materials such as pesticides, fertilizers, and antifreeze. You could warn them about leaving articles around that could be swallowed and subsequently cause the dog's digestive system to be cut or punctured or his intestine to become blocked.

Signs of a Bad Home

There are a number of danger signs that we have come to associate with homes that are a poor risk with respect to being suitable for a Saint Bernard.

Misbehaved Children. If the prospective puppy buyer has children, we always insist on meeting the children. If the children are adequately well adjusted and reasonably well behaved, then we have some expectation that any puppy will turn out the same way. On the other hand, if the children are snotty little brats, it is almost a certainty that the puppy will grow up in the same mold. An adult Saint Bernard that is out of control and does not mind is quite unpleasant to be around. It is almost a sure bet that this family won't be keeping the dog and that you will be getting him back! People who have no concept of what is required in the way of discipline for their charges should not be allowed to have one of your puppies.

Single Status. Single people are almost always in an unstable situation. While their present life-style may be suitable for a dog, you can count on a change happening that will make the owner unable to keep the dog. He will get married to somebody who is allergic to dogs, or he will decide to go back to school, or he will move to an apartment that doesn't allow dogs. The list goes on and on, but you see what I'm talking about here. Having to give up the dog is usually a trauma for both the owner and the dog. Of course, you end up with the dog coming back.

Inappropriate Desire to Breed. When an established breeder wants one of your puppies, be happy to give up one of your best. When someone else comes to your house and discusses future breeding plans, be on guard. There is no shortage of Saint Bernards—the world supply is more than adequate! To me, the only acceptable reason to add to the oversupply of dogs is an honest attempt to create a better Saint Bernard. People with one or two family pets will have difficulty convincing anyone that their breedings fit into the "honest" category.

So many people decide that they want to join the ranks of the breeders without having a clue about the purpose or processes involved. The only barrier between them and their avowed interest to create more puppies is *you*. I don't mean to imply that we don't want additional breeders—I'm just trying to say that the breed does not need more puppy producers. If you have any problem believing this, just visit your local animal shelter while they are killing the product of the puppy producers.

I have no problem with helping people get started in the breeder's role, as long as they are willing to take advice and promise to be responsible, *forevermore*, for everything they produce. I don't intend to save the world with respect to irresponsible puppy production, but I do think that it is my responsibility to ensure that it doesn't happen with any of my stock! At least I will make a 110-percent effort to see that none of my puppies or any of their progeny end up in the animal shelters.

Wrong Motives. There are a lot of reasons why people want a Saint Bernard. Many of those reasons sound kind of silly when they're spoken out loud, but you can usually relate to those motives and approve of them. Every once in a while, somebody will want to buy a puppy, and their reasons make the hair on the back of your neck stand up.

This usually is your signal to steer these people in another direction—maybe a different breed or a different hobby.

For example, if they just want the biggest, toughest guard dog they can find, they probably would be better off with some other breed. Saint Bernards are intimidating, but they do not make great guard dogs. Often you will be confronted with somebody whose dog has just died and they want to replace dear old Prince with a new puppy. You need to explain that Prince is gone and there will never be another one. You can sell them a puppy, but make them understand that he will never be Prince.

Then there are the bunch that are simply seeking to enhance their own image by owning the biggest dog on the block. People who just want to purchase a status symbol usually do not take very good care of their animals. They usually don't mistreat them—they just neglect them. You usually will get the dog back.

Put It in Writing

Two documents need to go home with every puppy—written instructions and a sales agreement.

Written Instructions. Tell the new owners that they need to immediately have their veterinarian give their puppy a health check. The veterinarian will need to know the puppy's health record—in other words, all of the health-related events that have occurred in the puppy's young life. Wormings, shots, illnesses, visits to a veterinarian, or anything else that is health related needs to be listed.

The next item that you should document is the puppy's eating schedule and diet at the time he goes to his new home. The new owners should be told that changing the diet or schedule abruptly will be upsetting to the puppy's digestive system. Explain the changes that should be made in the diet as the puppy matures and when the changeover should occur.

An item that many overlook when sending puppy instructions home with the new owner is an explanation of grooming. Recommendations as to frequency of bathing, types of shampoo, drying procedures, combing and brushing, and dealing with hot spots are subjects that are unknown to most new dog owners. Grooming is a subject that should be of interest to the new owners, and you need to give guidance.

Sales Agreement. This is sometimes referred to as the sales contract. I don't believe that the format, form, or phraseology is very important. What is important *is* that both parties fully understand what is expected of themselves and of the other party. Nothing will accomplish this better than writing down these items and both parties signing to acknowledge that they agree to them.

Over the years, we have evolved a sales contract covering most of the items that have been a problem in the past, and the format has been sufficient to keep us from having controversies with our honest customers. The other kind of customer is always a source of trouble no matter what sort of contract is executed. Your only hope with this type of customer is to avoid doing business with him. Anyway, a written agreement solves most of the problems most of the time, so let me tell you of some of the elements that we incorporate into our sales agreements.

The most important clause states that if for any reason the new owners are not able to retain the dog, he must be returned to you. I'll leave the details of refunds up to you, but we usually feel that puppies have a certain value at nine weeks of age which is either enhanced or diminished as the puppy grows, depending upon how the puppy develops. The whole point of this clause is that you must always be the primary contact for anybody who has one of your dogs. If you are going to be responsible for your stock, you have to be in a position to exercise some control. If you are a second party to someone's acquisition of one of your dogs, he will have little inclination to listen to you.

It is also necessary to control the restrictions on people breeding the animals that they acquire from you as puppies. Now that the AKC has begun to allow registration of pet-quality puppies on a limited registration, the situation is a little more under control. Prior to AKC's adoption of the limited-registration format, it was our practice to include in the contract a phrase to the effect that if the puppy was to ever be bred without our concurrence, then ownership of the dog and all ensuing offspring would revert to us. I doubt if such terms have much legal standing, but ever since we started including that condition in our contracts, we have had zero problems. Before that, we were continually having to deal with accidental breedings that were purported to be something that just couldn't be prevented!

Puppies need places to play and sleep. Shown here are three puppies from Janet Frick Mansfield's "I" litter, born at the La Casa Kennel in Stone Mountain, Georgia. Even as puppies, the Saint will seek out enclosed places to rest, showing their instincts as den animals. As adults, they will normally graduate to crates by choice.

Fairness is the next subject—these contracts should not be one-sided! Think about having your contracts be fair with respect to conditions that apply to you as well as to the buyer. Remember—the whole point of these contracts is to cover the areas of likely controversy. State the conditions of your guarantee as to AKC registrability, health, and congenital defects. Be very specific about what your guarantee covers and what you are going to do in case the puppy fails to meet expectations.

One area of misunderstanding is the definition of the term "show quality" used in the grading of puppies. It may be wise to include a statement that giving a puppy the grade of "show quality" is an indication of his potential development and is only an educated guess under the best of circumstances. Your customers need to clearly understand that the term "show quality" does not imply a guarantee that the dog will become a champion.

Co-ownership agreements are perhaps the biggest single source of controversy between the breeder and the people who purchase the puppy. This is because the conditions of the agreement are usually not clearly written and agreed upon before the sale. Co-ownership agreements that clearly define the purpose of the co-ownership, what is expected of each party (in great detail), and the consequences for not abiding by the agreement usually result in very little discussion.

One last item on sales contracts is the topic of rewards for achieving titles. It is in a breeder's best interest to have his stock gain AKC titles. We have lately adopted the practice of offering to refund a percentage of the selling price for every AKC title that the new owner puts on the puppy. I especially think it important for the owners to take their dogs through obedience training—it makes both the dog and the owner wiser and more pleasant to be around. And, obviously, the breeder's reputation is enhanced whenever one of the dogs becomes a champion. Think of this reward to your customers for putting titles on dogs bearing your kennel name as cheap advertising. In any case, it seems like a good idea to me.

Now you know how we approach the subject of puppy care. We want strong, healthy puppies that retain their health, vigor, and temperament throughout their lifetime and that go to homes that will enhance their development and quality of life.

Grading the Litter

The grading of litters is an art form—one in which almost everybody involved with dogs needs to become more skilled. Whether you are looking for breeding stock, a show animal, or just a family pet, you will increase your chances of getting what you want if you improve your skills at picking puppies. A very smart lady once told me, "To succeed as a breeder, you must develop some skill at grading your litters, for if you continually part with your best stock, your progress will be excruciatingly slow." I want to add my endorsement to this philosophy.

If you are simply looking for show stock to exhibit (and are foolish enough to insist on starting with a puppy), both your time and money will be wasted if you acquire mediocre or lesser specimens. If your goal in life is simply to get a family pet, it may seem like any choice is as good as another. However, if you get a puppy that grows up and eats one of your children, you may wish that you had made a better choice.

No matter what your perspective might be, you will be better off if you can avoid making large mistakes when choosing a puppy. Fortunately, for those whose expertise on the subject is less than mine, I am here to offer some wonderful (?) advice. Unfortunately, for those whose knowledge is equal to or greater than mine, I don't know where you or *I* will go for help—no matter how desperately we need it.

It has been almost thirty years since we picked our first puppy, and I still make mistakes. I take some solace in the fact that people with much more experience than me have also made mistakes. Nevertheless, these words are meant to share some of what has been learned over these years of involvement.

Let's begin by defining what age the puppy should be when you pick him. This, of course, depends on your perspective—on whether you are getting rid of the suckers or receiving one of the little darlings. If you are acquiring (or keeping) one of the puppies, the closer you get to having the litter be two years of age before making your decision, the better. The person simply interested in unloading the litter has a different point of view. At about five weeks of age, the mother is going to lose her enthusiasm for motherhood. Now the real expenses of having a litter on your hands begins. The outflow of time, effort, and money start to take on significant proportions!

Let's look at some middle ground. I don't feel that an honest job of grading a litter can be accomplished before the puppies are seven weeks of age. I also feel that a more complete job can be done when they are nine weeks old. Admittedly, most breeders have a pretty good idea of the litter's relative order from best to worst by weaning time, but at that time, the puppies have not been adequately evaluated in terms of head type, body proportions, soundness of limbs, or temperament to predict any one puppy's prospects in the showring. Because nine weeks is the very earliest that I am willing to choose the puppy I am going to keep, and because nine weeks is when I think that a good job of evaluation can be done, and because nine weeks is as long as I am willing to keep a herd of young puppies around, it should be no surprise that I recommend grading your litter at nine weeks of age.

Now let's tackle the subject of how to grade a litter. In doing so, I am assuming that you are looking for the best prospect for a successful show career. First, check for conditions that are unacceptable. Do the males have two testicles each? Are any of the puppies either deaf or blind? Do any have a hernia or a cleft palate? Do any have either a blue eye or a brown nose? Are the puppies apparently in good health, free from mange, worms, fleas, and any other observable problems? Does the litter owner claim to have had the puppies wormed and inoculated?

Next, just observe the litter as a whole. Note if each puppy is outgoing or shy, aggressive or timid, sober or playful, dominant or submissive, noisy or quiet, a boy or a girl. It is my practice then to divide the litter into a boy pile and a girl pile. I evaluate each pile separately in order to put them in order of best to worst. Next, I decide if the best available boy is better than the best available girl. Finally, I decide whether I want the best available boy or the best available girl.

To commence the actual grading process, start with a look at the head. If the head is not exciting at this age, it probably will be wanting as an adult. Are the ears set high? Are the eyes dark and set more to the front than to the sides? Does the skull look wide? Is the muzzle substantial? Are the flews the correct shape? How are the proportions, both with respect to parts of the head to each other and to the head size fitting the body size? You must answer these questions correctly in order to begin a proper evaluation of the head.

Next, use your hands to check for actual head structure rather than the appearance given by the fluffy exterior seen by the eye. When I start putting my hands on a puppy, I first feel for the top skull by cupping my hand over the puppy's head. I am looking for the largest skull with respect to width and length. Simultaneously, you can feel the depth of stop and check the furrow between the eyes and the development of the cheekbones.

Then, using two fingers, feel the width, length, and depth of the muzzle. Look for a square block of a muzzle, a deep muzzle, and a muzzle that does not taper. Open the puppy's mouth and observe the distance between the canines. The canines must be far apart with the incisors lying in a nearly straight line between them. If the canines are close together and the incisors lie in an arc equivalent to the edge of a fifty-cent piece, the puppy probably will have a tapered muzzle when he is mature.

Reject any undershot mouths! If they are undershot at this age, they will be disasters as an adult. Also avoid an even bite or a significantly overshot bite where the jaw seems malformed. Just remember that the lower jaw will probably grow as much as or more than the upper jaw, but never the other way.

Having evaluated the head, continue the feeling process to check the length and diameter of the neck. Avoid thin necks, for they will grow to be thin

La Casa's Isaiah (on the left) and La Casa's It Had To Be You bred by Janet Frick Mansfield of Stone Mountain, Georgia. These are two fine examples of shorthaired puppies at an age suitable for grading.

dogs. Pay particular attention to the relative length of the necks, for it gives an indication of shoulder layback—that is, the greater the relative length of the neck, usually the greater the front angulation.

Check the shoulder blade and upper arm to make sure that neither is undersized. A short upper arm is a common problem that you want to avoid.

Feel the substance and straightness of the front legs. They will never have heavier bone than they do now, so it better be adequate at this point. If the fronts are malformed to some extent, there is some hope that they will straighten out, but sometimes they get worse. I always feel more comfortable when the puppy has fewer problems initially.

Next, check the overall width of the puppy. You are looking for a puppy that will be a massive adult. The puppy should feel wide at the shoulders, ribs, and hips. Do not, however, confuse a barrel chest with the kind of width for which you are looking. Any puppy that has a wide chest because he has a barrel chest should be rejected with no further consideration. The loin and belly area should be short in length and large in diameter.

Because you are holding the puppy, get a sense of his density. Is he lightweight, or does he seem dense and somewhat heavy? Remember that you are looking for a massive adult and not fluff.

Check the quality of the skin. It should be neither as loose as a Bloodhound's nor as tight as a Doberman Pinscher's.

Then comes the important part—the puppy's hiney! The amount of muscle on the ham is only slightly behind the quality of the head in importance when determining the quality of the puppy. Just remember that a big butt is a good butt, and the bigger the better! Consider the mass of muscle on the upper thigh, and the firmness. Look for as much firm, hard muscle as possible here. Avoid any puppy that lacks significant and impressive muscle mass on the upper thigh! Without this massive rear end, your dog will never be strong and powerful.

This completes the evaluation by feeling the puppy. Now it is time to return to simply observing the subject. First, get down to eye level with the puppy as he stands naturally, and get a real sense of his proportions. Is he tall or long? If he is not as tall as he is long (that is, withers to ground equal to sternum to pinbone), the puppy will never have correct Saint Bernard proportions.

Observe the rear angulation now, for it will never get better than what you see on this day. Rest assured that it will only become straighter if it changes at all.

Look at the pasterns and feet. Sometimes weak pasterns and flat feet can be corrected, but usually not. This is a problem that you want to avoid given some sort of option.

Finally we come to the really hard part. How does the puppy move? The trick is to put the puppy on the ground and then, somehow, get him to walk or run so that you can evaluate his movement. Because puppies are never leash trained at this age, it can take some real innovation and persistence to get little short glimpses of each puppy's true movement.

Even after you have been successful in observing the puppy's gait, you still have problems. Some aspects of puppy movement are accurate predictors of his expected adult performance. Other aspects, however, are practically useless. For example, adult length of stride usually correlates pretty well with what it was when the dog was a young puppy. To some extent, you can say the same thing about the limbs operating in a plane when viewed from the front. On the other hand, the rear action is different in that a cowhocked puppy (with good muscle mass on the rear legs) will often run straight and true as an adult. A word of caution—if the puppy lacks that muscle mass, he probably will be cowhocked for the rest of his life.

Usually a hackneyed or high-stepping action on a puppy will be the same when he becomes an adult. Likewise, a sickle hock now is a sickle hock forevermore. (Note that a sickle hock is one that seems locked so that it neither opens nor closes when the dog is moving.)

One feature that doesn't correlate very well with expected adult action is the puppy's grace and style

Ch. Forever Moxie at eight weeks of age. This lovely puppy, owned and bred by Sara and Terry Temple, went on to finish her championship at the Saint Bernard Club of America's National Specialty Show, where she was awarded Best of Winners and Best of Opposite Sex over many champions entered at that show.

while moving. In the adult dog, an easy, fluid movement depends greatly on conditioning and attitude, both of which are affected by the way in which the dog is raised and kept. Still, you look at a puppy and decide if he moves like a clod or a gazelle. I just don't recommend letting this aspect override some more important one.

On the other hand, I can't remember seeing a puppy that moved like a gazelle and subsequently grew into a plodding, shuffling adult. In the same vein, I fear for the future of any puppy that slides his feet along the ground or moves with a roached back. Even more frightening is the hopping puppy! I strenuously recommend that you reject any puppy that moves with both rear feet in unison—the so-called bunny-hop mode of locomotion.

I suppose that I let myself be too much influenced by the puppies' movement when I'm grading a litter, but I think it is important in the adult. If you are going to follow my lead, just remember that we tread on very unreliable ground here.

Now that you have looked at all the pieces, you must sit back and consider each puppy as a whole animal. No matter how lovely the pieces, you can't

(Above):
In this over-the-shoulder shot we see a future champion, La Casa's Fiesta v. Stoan, owned and bred by Janet Frick Mansfield, who has her La Casa Kennel in Stone Mountain, Georgia. Fiesta is one of the many champions of the two matings of Ch. Stoan's Fortuno of Copper Mountain, HOF, POE, to Ch. Stoan's Isabelle v. Encore, HOF.

(Left):
Waiting for a ride in her wheelbarrow is nine-month-old future Australian champion Elkeef Cutencuddly. Her owner is Judy Teniswood of Tasmania, Australia.

highly rate any puppy that is going to grow into a fear biter. A beautiful head and great movement are not sufficient to make a show dog out of a dog lacking substance. While I am not personally concerned about markings and color, I must recognize that pale-colored animals and seriously mismarked Saint Bernards have to be extra good to compete. Fortunately, they very often are!

Now that the litter has been evaluated, the litter owner must go out on a limb and decide if and where the term "show quality" applies. I have seen litters where no member was of show quality, and other litters where most of the puppies were destined to become champions. Most well-planned litters fall in between these two extremes. Most poorly planned litters have no show-quality puppies, and most litters fall into this category.

It is up to the litter owner to use good judgment and a sense of integrity in making this decision. If the litter owner has some measure of integrity, he must recognize that the litter is probably not 100 percent show quality, and that there is a range of values (and hence prices) within the litter.

If you are getting a puppy, keep in mind that the litter owner has an economic motivation for claiming show-quality status for as many in the litter as possible. Remember that pick of the litter is not the same thing as show quality! Be aware that well over 99 percent of the puppies designated as pick of the litter never become show dogs, let alone champions. Be especially wary of any offering in which there is more than one pick of the litter.

Always bear in mind that grading puppies has no resemblance to a scientific procedure. The entire process of puppy evaluation is only an educated guess at best, and an exercise in the breeder's self-delusions at worst. No matter how it is done, picking out the future show stopper is a gamble and, as gambles go, this is not a very good one. That is why you must pay three to eight times as much for a show-quality adult as you do for a show-quality puppy. I estimate that any given show-quality puppy from a reputable breeder has but one chance in twenty of maturing into a worthy show dog, and one chance in a thousand of becoming a great show dog. If you want to calculate the numbers, you will soon discover that buying show-quality adults is a lot better of a deal than buying show-quality puppies.

I wonder, then, why it is that everybody (including me) still lusts after beautiful puppies. I suppose it is because we are not rational beings or we wouldn't be involved with the dog game in the first place.

Cache Retreat Mia, shown here in March 1994 as an eight-week-old longhaired bitch puppy, was bred by Ivan Palmblad at his Cache Retreat Kennel in Providence, Utah.

Guidelines for Buying a Puppy

Obviously, you have decided that you want a Saint Bernard puppy or you wouldn't be reading this book. So far you have made good choices, but you are facing the opportunity to make some poor choices. I have some advice to offer that may help you realize your goals.

You are acquiring a puppy that is to be your companion for many years, and you want that to be a happy episode. Even with the best of intentions, many prospective owners fail in the acquisition process, as witnessed by the number of Saint Bernards that are dumped in the animal shelters, euthanized, returned to the sellers (when they will take them back), sold dirt cheap, given away, or simply abandoned. The problem is that most people believe in the generic dog myth—that any Saint Bernard puppy will grow up to be the well-mannered, obedient, loving member of the family seen in the movies or on television. Even people who have had Saint Bernards before think that they can simply buy another that will grow up to be a duplicate of their previous dog. This belief in the generic Saint Bernard does not allow for the many factors that cause a puppy to develop into a very distinct, highly individual adult animal.

It is truly fallacious to believe that all Saint Bernards are alike regardless of factors such as pedigree, bloodlines, how they are raised, how they are trained, or the environment in which they must live. This is no more true for Saint Bernards than it is for people. There are innate differences between the individual animals, and those differences are made greater by the great range of skill and understanding (or lack thereof) among the breeders and owners.

Every puppy is born with a specific potential with respect to temperament, intelligence, character, health, beauty, and physical soundness. Some puppies were well planned so that their potential for success is pretty high, and some puppies just sort of happen without much thought being expended by the breeder. Obviously, not all puppies are born equal, nor do all puppies get an equal shot at optimum development. Not every puppy will grow up to be the healthy, happy, loyal family companion envisioned at the time of purchase, because not every puppy will benefit from skilled care and training from the very start. Your dog can only perform at the level allowed and encouraged by the people in charge of his life. Just as neglected or undereducated children seldom reach their full potential, so it is with puppies and dogs.

It is when you end up with a puppy that has very low potential or one that doesn't get the chance to reach his potential that you experience acquisition failure. Whether your puppy was born a bum or was made into a bum by his environment matters little—a bum dog represents a failure in being the optimum family pet. You need to make intelligent choices if you are to get the dog that best fits you and your family. Most pet "failures" are the result of inappropriate choices, impulse purchases, and lack of early training and socialization for the puppy. If you can avoid these obstacles, there is a greater likelihood that you and your new Saint puppy will have a long and satisfactory life together. Let me offer you a few suggestions to help you make good decisions and to locate the right place to buy your puppy.

THE RIGHT DOG FOR YOU

Even after you have decided to buy a Saint Bernard puppy, you still have some choices to make—baby puppy, older puppy, or a young adult? Male or female? Longhaired or shorthaired? Pet quality or show quality? These questions may need answers before you pick a puppy. Then again, answering these questions may not be all that important. Many people simply take a shine to a certain puppy in a litter. It's love at first sight and the details just don't matter to them. Assuming that you want to make these choices, let's look at the factors involved.

The Right Age

The first decision that you can make is how old the dog should be when he joins your family. No responsible breeder will let a puppy go younger than seven to nine weeks of age, so that is the youngest age you can consider.

Most people prefer to start with a young puppy, because they want to experience that cute puppy stage. They enjoy the appealing aspects of puppy behavior and believe that only a very young pup will bond permanently with them. Of course, with a very young puppy, you also get a creature that is not trained, housebroken, or completely socialized. He needs constant attention, frequent feedings, and trips outside. He is dependent on your providing extensive care for his very life. You have to schedule two to five inoculations beyond what the puppy receives while with his breeder, and you may have to deal with neutering the dog. You must survive the chewing stage that all puppies go through. You will have to handle the transitions from puppy to adult teeth and puppy to adult coat. It will be your job to train the dog to calmly tolerate grooming, tooth cleaning, and nail clipping. If you have the time and inclination to perform all of these tasks, then a young puppy is probably the best choice for you.

If, however, the scope of the extensive care required by a baby puppy is more than you want to take on, or if a very young puppy would require more of your time than you have available, you might consider an older puppy or even an adult. Many people seem to worry about taking a dog past the age of a few months, fearing that the dog will not bond to the new owner. This is particularly *untrue* for a Saint Bernard, especially if he has been properly socialized by the breeder. A well-bred, well-socialized Saint Bernard is very people oriented, and such a dog only asks for a family of his own to love and protect. Once this dog has learned to trust and love human beings, it is quite easy for him to move to a new home. A Saint Bernard taken from one home to another goes through an adjustment period, but generally no more than a few days to a couple of weeks.

The one thing that breeders can count on is that Saint puppies are cute! These little angels are Lynchcreek's Nancy (on the left) and Lynchcreek's Nordstrom, bred by Candace Blancher, owner of Lynchcreek Kennels in Eatonville, Washington.

The Right Sex

A male will grow into a larger and more substantial animal. A female will grow into a more graceful and less blundering adult. Which aspect is more important, or which sex is better are questions for which I have no answer. A male will tend to be a little more macho, but that behavior is usually a façade that disappears as soon as he needs to behave in a manner befitting Saint Bernards. If there is any slight distinction, it might be that a female takes a little more readily to training. This is really much more dependent upon the individual dog's temperament than upon his sex. A male will devote himself to watching out for children as eagerly and surely as a female. A female will rise to the occasion when danger threatens her family just as quickly and effectively as the biggest male. When it comes to factors such as aggressiveness, bravery, strength, health, concern for children, and affection for the family, I do not see a significant difference between a male and a female.

If your dog is to serve only as a pet, he should be neutered. Once neutered, the distinctions between females and males becomes even more blurred. It seems to me that deciding between a male or a female is a choice that you must make based upon something other than logic.

The Right Coat Type

The longhaired variety, often called the rough coat, and the shorthaired variety, commonly referred to as the smooth coat, are both recognized in the Saint Bernard breed. Each individual dog will be either one coat type or the other, and it is common to have both coat types in any given litter. In this situation, you will have a choice to make. I'm afraid that this, too, is based upon personal preference rather than logic.

The longhaired Saint will appear to be bigger and bulkier than the shorthair, even though putting the dogs on a scale will most often show that just the opposite is true. Many people consider the rough-coated Saint to be flashier and prettier than the smooth-coated variety. The movies and television have glamorized the longhaired dogs to the point that many people have trouble accepting the shorthaired animal as a real Saint Bernard. This prejudice continues in spite of the fact that the original dogs used in the Alps were all shorthaired. The long-hair gene was introduced into the breed later by crossing with Newfoundlands, and it was soon discovered that the longhaired Saints were not suitable for that harsh working environment. Until recently, a number of breeders considered the longhaired Saint Bernard to be a mongrel rather than a purebred dog.

Grooming is the key to making the choice between coat types. If you have the time and temperament for grooming your dog on a regular basis, then you might opt for a longhaired Saint. If removing mats, dealing with extensive washing with prolonged drying at regular intervals, and combing out your dog once or twice a week is not your idea of fun, then you might be better off with a shorthaired Saint Bernard.

In this 1970 photograph we see John Cox's new puppy "Nicklus" in the entrance to his penthouse ready to come to the rescue of anyone needing a keg of brandy. Who could have predicted the many titles this youngster had in his future?

I can usually wash and dry three shorthaired dogs in the time it takes to groom one longhaired dog. In the winter, all of our dogs get wet and muddy. As soon as the weather clears and the dogs dry out, the shorthairs simply shake the dust out of their coats and they are relatively clean. The longhairs are another story! When they dry out, they are nothing but dry mud balls full of mats and in bad need of a bath. If Saint Bernards were articles of clothing, the smooths would be identified as "wash and wear," while the roughs would be labeled "dry clean only."

One last thought on the subject of grooming. Grooming is often ignored by pet owners because they fail to recognize that it serves more than a cosmetic purpose. Unkempt dogs are apt to have skin problems, infections, parasites, excessive shedding, and an unpleasant odor. If your dog is going to live in your house, you need to bathe him about once a month to keep the doggy odor within reasonable bounds. Further, if you have a longhaired Saint, you need to completely comb the dog about once every week or ten days if you hope to stay ahead of the mats.

The Right Quality

I hesitate to use the term "quality" here, for it means something quite different to the general public than it does in the vernacular of the dog fancy. Almost all breeders are convinced that the puppies in any given litter can be graded into two categories—pet quality and show quality. The implied theory here is that a show-quality puppy has a very high potential for becoming an adult animal that will be competitive in a dog show. The other side of this theory is that pet-quality puppies probably will not stand much of a chance in the showing when they grow up. Hence, it is customary for dog breeders to grade their litters assigning the term "show quality" to some of the puppies and "pet quality" to the others. I discussed this topic in some depth in the previous chapter, "Grading the Litter," but want to address here how you choose the right quality for you and your family. Keep in mind that the term "quality" in this context has nothing to do with features such as temperament, intelligence, health, strength, or any other aspect associated with being a family pet and protector.

The question that you need to answer is simply: Do you intend to have the dog compete in dog shows and/or produce puppies? Unless you intend to breed or show him, your puppy should be neutered as soon as possible. Once he has been neutered, he is automatically pet quality, so there is no advantage to buying a show prospect. For many people, there is absolutely no advantage to procuring a show-quality puppy. On the other hand, if you are looking for a dog that will eventually win prizes at dog shows, then you need to buy one with very good prospects. Unfortunately, you will most likely be disappointed. The odds that any particular show-quality puppy will develop into a seriously competitive adult range from 2 to 1 against to about 1000 to 1 against, depending upon the breeder with whom you do business.

My advice to anybody looking for a true show-quality animal is to avoid buying a young puppy, because it is nothing but a gamble with very bad odds. The older the puppy, the less likely he is to go through some development that will ruin his show career. The risk (and price) levels out when the dog is about two years old. At this time, he is almost a dead cinch not to degrade, and he has an excellent prospect of becoming a little better as he matures. The cost of a show-quality adult will be three to eight times as much as the price of a young show-quality puppy, but that cost will be trivial compared to the cost of buying and raising a puppy that doesn't turn out to be show quality.

THE RIGHT PLACE TO BUY YOUR PUPPY: CHOOSING A BREEDER

There are good sources for puppies, and there are those "other places." If you choose one of the other places, your chance of being unhappy with your purchase is rather great. Pet shops, puppy brokers, and other commercial outlets for puppies are traditionally poor risks. Your first choice should be an owner/breeder, but even then you must make a distinction. You are looking for an owner/breeder who has real integrity and in-depth knowledge of his art and who feels a deep responsibility for each individual dog produced by his kennel, no matter how long the dog has been gone from the kennel or who has owned him since he left. This sort of person will seldom be found in a newspaper advertisement, and he will probably have a waiting list for his puppies.

Clean and Sanitary

Look for a kennel that is clean and free of offensive odors. Do business with a breeder who has healthy stock being raised under healthy conditions. A well-maintained kennel shows a level of concern for the dogs' well-being and happiness. Another factor is that puppies raised in a clean, sanitary environment are much easier to house train when they move into your home.

Alert and Friendly Dogs

Look for a kennel where the breeder is glad to have you interact with his stock. All of the dogs should appear happy, friendly, and healthy. If the dogs seem aloof, unfriendly, or lethargic, take your business elsewhere. A Saint Bernard should be a gregarious animal anxious to make new friends. Anything else is either a failure to breed for the correct temperament or a failure to properly socialize the dogs. Another possibility is that the dogs are all sick. No matter what the cause, look for someone who cares a little more about the dogs and what is being produced there.

Behavior of the Dam

It is very important to interact with the dam and, if possible, the sire of the puppies. You can judge how your puppy will look and act as an adult from the appearance and behavior of his close relatives. The dam may not be very happy about strangers around her new puppies, but she should not growl or threaten visitors. Once the puppies are weaned at about five weeks, the bitch should display the typical Saint Bernard gregarious and friendly demeanor. Never accept the excuse that her aggressive behavior is simply concern for her puppies.

Good Reputation

Look for a kennel with a good reputation. You want to do business with an owner/breeder who has integrity. The question is, how do you discover information about breeders? Check with your veterinarian to see if he knows the reputation of various Saint Bernard kennels in the area. In most localities, there are local all-breed clubs that usually have a referral service or, if not, they will have knowledgeable members who will know local Saint Bernard people whom they can recommend. The best source may be either a local Saint Bernard club or the national club, the Saint Bernard Club of America. Attending any of the local dog shows is another excellent source of contacts. Attending dog shows will let you observe dogs in and out of the ring, and it will give you the opportunity to meet the breeders and exhibitors. I recommend that you ask other Saint Bernard breeders who they consider to be fair and ethical. I've never met a serious breeder who would concede that a competing breeder had better dogs than himself, but he will allow that there are other breeders who they respect for both the quality of their produce and their ethics. Such faint praise should be sufficient recommendation for you to check out that breeder.

Concern about the Dogs

Look for a kennel that really cares about the animals produced there! You want to do business with an owner/breeder who has a sense of responsibility for his animals and for their quality of life for as long as they live. Look for someone who has cared for each animal and provided him a loving home until he goes to his new home. Seek someone who uses great care in selecting homes for each animal that leaves the kennel. This means that he even refuses to let a dog leave unless he is convinced that the potential owner can provide an excellent home.

A concerned breeder will screen potential buyers in order to ascertain the mutual suitability of dog and buyer. Caring breeders ask many questions, some of which may seem intrusive. They will inquire about issues such as your history with dogs and other pets, and if the entire family is comfortable with the new acquisition. Are your children of an age that they will not injure the puppy accidentally, or accidentally be hurt by the puppy's needle-sharp baby teeth? Be prepared to explain why have you selected a Saint Bernard to join your family. You will be asked how you intend to socialize, exercise, and train your new pet. The breeder will ask about your home, its location, and security provisions for the dog, such as a fenced yard and an enclosure for when the dog is to be left home alone.

This degree of concern may strike you as inconvenient or even offensive. Your lack of initial appreciation will change after the sale to a realization

John Cox's Utility Express! Here we see Nicklus as an adult dog of eight years, pulling a cart full of his offspring. By now he has become Am. Can. Ch., Can. OTCh. Cherryacre's Nicklus von Hyden, Am. Can. UD. His children in the cart are Can. OTCh. Lovecraft's Nita Nicklus, Am. Can. UDT, and her brother, Can. OTCh. Frederick von Hyden, Am. Can. UDT.

that this screening process is the greatest protection a dog purchaser can have. When you find a breeder who puts you through this careful screening, you have found someone truly worth visiting.

Return Policy

Equally important to the screening process is the breeder's willingness, nay, insistence, to have the dog returned to him if the dog is no longer wanted. This willingness to accept the dog back, whether in two weeks or eight years after the sale, is the single most important distinction between puppy mills and reputable breeders. It shows a clear indication that the breeder is more concerned about the dog's welfare than he is about the money.

Full refunds are not usually offered after you have had the puppy more than ten days. It is unreasonable to expect a refund simply because you have decided that you don't want the dog. Most reputable breeders will take a dog back and offer to resell the animal, returning to the original owner the money received from the sale less some nominal commission. Understand that the value of puppies either goes down or up with the passage of time. There is a glut of older, mediocre dogs, and their value is about fifty dollars. On the other hand, if the dog develops into a show-quality animal as he approaches maturity, his value will be three to eight times the price of a show-quality puppy. Don't, however, get your hopes up or expect to get more than you paid for the puppy, because almost all puppies fall into the first category.

Knowledge of the Breed

Look for a breeder who is both knowledgeable and truly concerned about the breed. This is someone who not only knows in great detail which aspects of temperament, intelligence, health, soundness, and physical features of breed type are ideal for the breed, but he must also seek to incorporate those virtues in his stock. It is only when the breeder understands the ideal dog and seeks to incorporate that vision in his breeding program that you can depend upon the dogs to mature into truly saintly Saint Bernards.

SELLER RESPONSIBILITIES AND BUYER RIGHTS

Most people have some idea of their legal rights and responsibilities whenever they enter into leasing a car or buying a house. Yet, there are many horror stories associated with the ordinary business of buying and selling dogs. Most people apparently do not use the same amount of common business sense when the transaction involves a living animal.

Let me suggest some of the items that you, the buyer, should expect from the seller. You should receive a pedigree, a registration application form, a written sales agreement, a written guarantee, the puppy's medical record, and written instructions on the care and feeding of the puppy. In some instances, there may also be a separate co-ownership agreement or a separate breeding contract that both the buyer and seller sign.

The Pedigree and Registration Form

Basic to the sale of any purebred dog is certification that the parents are registered with the American Kennel Club and that the ensuing puppies are registrable with that body. A word of caution is called for here. There are other organizations within the United States that register dogs. It has been my experience that only shady operations use these other stud books. In my limited experience, I have never seen a Saint Bernard of even minimal quality that was registered outside of the AKC umbrella. Of course, this does not apply to the AKC-recognized dog registries of foreign countries.

The certification of registrability is usually a pedigree that has been certified as being accurate by the breeder. Expect the pedigree to show at least four generations and to indicate which of the puppy's progenitors were AKC champions. Along with the pedigree, the seller owes the buyer the so-called blue slip. This blue slip is supplied to the breeder upon his registering the litter with the AKC, and it is the form that you must use to apply to register your dog. AKC rules prohibit the breeder from selling the blue slips. They may be withheld from the buyer only on the condition that a signed sales agreement so stipulates, but the seller cannot charge an extra amount for the application form. It is not uncommon for a breeder to procrastinate so long that he does not have the blue slips back yet from the AKC when it is time for the puppies to go to their new homes. In this case, you need a written statement that the blue slip will be delivered to you when it is received by the breeder.

The Sales Agreement and Guarantee

It is my opinion that any breeder who fails to provide a written sales agreement is behaving in a very foolish manner. The breed clubs are always being asked to referee emotional disagreements between the seller and buyer of dogs and puppies. Almost every one of these arguments could have been avoided with a simple written sales agreement.

The agreement doesn't have to be a legal work of art—it simply needs to state the details of the sale, the description of the dog, and the terms of any guarantee. With these facts adequately described, all parties know what is promised or implied, and what is not. The details of the sale should include the date of the transaction, a statement about who is the seller and who is the buyer (plus addresses and telephone numbers), the selling price of the dog, and any fees or taxes collected.

The description of the dog should include the breed, the date of birth, the sex, the coat variety (longhaired or shorthaired), and a simple description of markings and coat pattern. The description should also include other pertinent details if they are known, including the dog's registration number, his name, and the breeder's evaluation of the puppy's quality (pet quality or show quality).

The guarantee should state specifically what is guaranteed and the recourse if the terms of the guarantee are not met. As a minimum, a sales agreement should guarantee that the dog is registrable with the AKC, that he will successfully pass any veterinarian's health check made within ten days of delivery, and that he will not within two years develop any congenital defect that will prohibit his ability to function as a family pet. These defects should include hip or elbow dysplasia, epilepsy, the failure of any major organ (heart, liver, or kidney) or certified autoimmune deficiency.

Because many disagreements arise over the buyer's expectations rather than specific claims made by the breeder at the time of the sale, we find it necessary to include some words about what we do *not* guarantee. This is why our sales agreements state that we do not guarantee that any dog will be able to win awards at dog shows or successfully produce puppies. These items depend more on how the dog is raised after he leaves the breeder's kennel than they do on situations that can be controlled by the breeder. A puppy sold as show quality only means that the breeder believes that the puppy has good prospects of such potential if he is raised correctly.

When the conditions of the guarantee are not met, most kennels will give a replacement puppy of equal value as opposed to a refund. It is necessary to have this stated clearly in the sales agreement, because this does not usually meet the expectations of most puppy buyers.

Any special conditions of the sale should also be included in the sales agreement. If the dog is supposed to be neutered by a specific age and before the registration papers are to be delivered, that should be stated. Every sales agreement should contain a clause stating that the dog must be returned to the breeder if for any reason the buyer cannot keep him.

Often, breeders will retain some interest in the better-quality puppies in a litter. In this case, a separate co-ownership or breeding agreement should be rendered. Again, this document needs to be specific about what is expected from each party in order to prevent misunderstandings. Details such as who has possession of the dog at various times, who pays for what expenses, and how breeding decisions are to be made should be spelled out. This agreement should also define penalties for failure to abide by the agreement—for example, what the monetary compensation will be and who will own the puppies if the dog is bred to another dog not approved by the breeder.

Health Record and Instructions

Some states have laws that govern the sale of puppies, but most do not. Either way, you have a right to expect a health record and written instructions from the seller.

Health Record. Within one or two days after receiving your puppy, have him examined by your veterinarian. The seller should give you a document that you can show to your veterinarian about the puppy's medical history, including:

1. When and if the rear dewclaws were removed.
2. When the puppy's inoculations were given and how many were given (one or two). These puppy shots should vaccinate your puppy against distemper, hepatitis, leptospirosis, parvovirus, coronavirus, and kennel cough (parainfluenza).
3. When and if two treatments for worms were administered (should be ten days apart).
4. A list of any other treatment by a veterinarian.

Here we see Am. Can. Ch., Can. OTCh. Cherryacre's Nicklus von Hyden, Am. Can. UD, at the age of seven years, clearing a jump set at his shoulder height of thirty-two inches. Nicklus was owned and trained by John Cox of Seattle, Washington.

Instructions for Care and Feeding. The seller should assume that you are not an expert on the subject of raising puppies. Therefore, he should provide a written statement that:

1. Tells what specific brand of food the puppy has been eating and defines the accustomed feeding schedule.
2. Recommends when the puppy should transition to adult food and an adult feeding schedule.
3. Recommends a process for dealing with the trauma of the puppy leaving his littermates to live with his new family.
4. Recommends a schedule of inoculations and worm treatment.
5. Recommends how to deal with early training such as housebreaking and puppy socialization.
6. Encourages the buyer to freely return to the seller with any questions or concerns about the puppy.

Now you have sufficient information to do an intelligent job of buying a puppy. I hope you understand that when you get a puppy from a responsible breeder who has seen to the puppy's neonatal care, socialization, veterinary needs, cleanliness, and affection, you acquire a treasure. When you take a puppy that has not had the benefit of this care, you risk ending up with a problem for which you might be ill prepared. Finding an honest breeder sometimes takes a little effort, but it is well worth it. Acquiring the knowledge to make informed decisions also takes effort, but the payoff is that you will be much happier with your new puppy.

Vicki Graves and her Saint "Uba" (Mountain Shadows Cinnamon N Spice, CD, WP), enjoying a hike through the woods of the Pacific Northwest.

The Rewards and Risks of Inbreeding

When I was only a few years into breeding Saint Bernards, I found myself at the National Specialty and in a late-night conversation with one of the more famous of the East Coast breeders. After I told him that I aspired to be a successful breeder of Saint Bernards, he asked me if I had read the book titled *Ten Easy Steps to Becoming a Successful Breeder*. I told him that I had never heard of it, which surprised me, because I thought that I had read just about everything ever printed on the subject. He laughed and said, "Small wonder! Such a book has never been written and it never will!"

He then poured himself the last of the beer from the pitcher and remarked, "Breeding is not something that has a set of rules to follow. Nor is it something someone can tell you how to do. If you are a real breeder, it's something you feel in your gut, and if you don't have that gut feel for the job, you'll never be a breeder!" He drained his glass, and as he got up to leave, he concluded quietly, "And don't ever forget—breeding dogs is not for the lily-livered set. If you are going to make your mark, then you have to make tough decisions—and many of them will break your heart."

I have learned to appreciate the wisdom of those words. On more than a few occasions since that time, it has occurred to me that it would certainly be nice if there was a universally accepted "how to" manual on breeding dogs. Wouldn't it be grand if the best methods had been identified and documented? Many books and articles have been written on this subject, but they seem to have been of little use to most of the more successful breeders. Successful breeders who have discussed this subject with me have told me that they learned primarily by making their own mistakes and, secondarily, by being able to recognize good advice when they came across it—and then being able to follow that advice.

There lies the problem. There is a lot of advice available, both from those who have experienced success and those whose success has been not particularly notable. The really unfortunate part is that some of the most profound advice comes from the weakest sources.

Even if you are able to limit your intake of advice from those whose success is well proven, you will find that there are as many divergent opinions on how an animal should be bred as there are breeders. I have heard many successful people say that they never inbreed. Others say that they never outcross. These opinions are literally poles apart, yet they represent the firmly held opinions of these declared experts. Everyone has an opinion on breeding, and they all seem to be different.

My solution to this dilemma is to ask myself, "Just what is a successful breeder?" The answer that best satisfies me is that a successful breeder is a person who has a vision of perfection with respect to Saint Bernards and a plan for producing generation after generation in order to make steady progress toward that goal. This answer has led me to the opinion that anybody who can show progress in the quality of their stock is somebody to whom I want to listen. I may not accept all of their opinions, but I must respect them.

Almost everyone who fits my definition of a successful breeder will tell you that the job entails taking good-quality animals and improving upon them. It is in the details of this plan where we run into conflicting advice.

I belong to the set of breeders who believe that the most effective plan for producing high-quality Saint Bernards involves the use of controlled inbreeding combined with a coldly rational and hard-hearted selection process. I also believe that the ability to do this is limited to people who not only care a lot for their dogs but are also willing to suffer, without flinching, through the heartaches that come with the job. My purpose here is to convince you that there is a lot of merit in this line of thought.

Let's discuss the process of taking two high-quality animals and mating them. How do you make the decisions that go with this process? The easy plan would be to take two animals that have the features you want and breed them together. Does like beget like? That is the question that concerns most breeders. I'm afraid that the answer is, "Not usually."

Life would be so much simpler if we could depend upon our dogs to produce puppies that looked like their parents! In the vernacular of the dog people, there is a word for dogs like that—prepotent. Prepotent sires or dams are worth their weight in gold, mostly because such animals are extremely rare. They are so rare, because no matter how good any given animal is, his genetic makeup is usually so scrambled that it can never truly reproduce itself.

Ch. Sanctuary Woods Kleona, whose outstanding breed type, massiveness, soundness, and power made most people forgive the fact that she had inherited her daddy's very short legs. Kleona, who to this day has a very large fan club, was awarded Best of Opposite Sex at three consecutive SBCA National Specialties. Kleona was owned by Bob and Mary Tarlton of Shelton, Washington. This picture was taken at the 1972 National Specialty and depicts the SBCA president, Fred Anderson; the judge, Georgean Raulston; and an unidentified young and inexperienced handler.

Most breeders realize that when they are breeding dogs, they are dealing with genes and not with the dogs themselves. Yet, we all tend to forget this extremely important aspect of breeding. We all have looked at several dogs, or perhaps litters of puppies, and wished that we could take a head here, a front there, a rear from another, and a neck or top line from yet another, and build a perfect dog. It's all right to build dogs this way in your mind, but when you return to real life, you must face the fact that this is not how it works. In any breeding, you must work with two individual dogs, and you must accept the fruit of their union as pure chance dictates.

There is some good news, however. You *can* have some effect on these chance happenings if you understand a few genetic principles. By paying as much attention to genetics as you do to appearance, you stand a reasonable chance of realizing your goals.

Every trait possessed by any biological entity is inherited in duplicate. A dog gets a gene for every trait from each of his parents. He will show one trait that is more like one parent, and another trait that is more like the other parent. The combination of genes inherited from the two parents in any individual puppy will often result in the expression of one trait similar to that of one parent and a second trait similar to that of the other parent. This explains why a puppy can have the eyes of one parent and the ears of the other.

The trait that is exhibited, or that you can see, is referred to as dominant. The trait that is not exhibited is referred to as recessive. The dog can pass on the recessive traits as easily as he can the dominant ones. This is the source of surprises. Whenever a dog gets a recessive gene from both parents, the trait will be displayed in its recessive form. For example, Saint Bernards are either longhaired or shorthaired. The gene that controls this feature comes in two varieties—longhaired, which is recessive, and shorthaired, which is dominant. A Saint Bernard cannot be of the longhaired variety unless he receives the recessive longhaired gene from both parents. If he receives one longhaired gene from one parent and a shorthaired gene from the other, he will spend his entire life as a shorthaired dog. This is the simplest of cases. Many traits are a combination of more than one gene—that is, one gene will affect the expression of another gene. If you need this concept clarified, I recommend almost any textbook on the subject of genetic inheritance.

Then there is the extremely complex cases that monopolize the attention of the breeders. Most traits that people seek are not singular entities but are a combination of traits that are controlled by a combination of genes. For example, a head is a combination of many independent features that are each independently controlled by their own gene. This will come a shock to some, but there is *not* a gene for good heads. Each bone of the skull and muzzle is controlled by its own gene. There is a separate gene for nose color, one for whisker length, one for eye size, one for ear shape, and one for every other aspect of the head. A good head is the melding of many good features. I estimate that there are at least thirty genes that control those aspects that we call a good head. Just contemplate trying to control thirty genes at the same time—the magnitude of the task is mind boggling.

Contemplate a single gene pair that controls the appearance of some particular feature—say eye color. Half of that gene pair comes from the mother and the other half from the father. The two halves of any gene pair are not necessarily identical, so it matters a lot which half of the gene pair is inherited. One gene half may say, "Have brown eyes." The other gene half may say, "Have blue eyes." Because brown eyes are dominant, the dog will have brown eyes. The offspring, however, may have blue eyes if they get a blue-eyed gene from this dog and another blue-eyed gene from the other parent.

There is no way to control which gene half is going to be inherited by any individual offspring. Like flipping a coin, the laws of probability are the only control that governs which half of any gene pair will be passed on to any particular individual in the next generation. And every puppy in the litter is defined by a separate and independent flip of the coin for every gene pair. One puppy will have blue eyes and the next one in the same litter will have brown eyes. One puppy will be undershot and the rest may have a scissors bite. Everything about each puppy depends on which gene he inherits from each parent.

Now broaden your perspective to consider the thousands upon thousands of aspects of each dog and the identical number of gene pairs that control the form that each feature takes. Perhaps this will give you some inkling of the breeder's folly in thinking that he or she has a lot to do with the results. The most that a breeder can hope to accomplish is to influence the outcome of relatively few features.

The question is, "How do you accomplish this influencing of the features in which you are interested?" A tool is available to those who aspire to be breeders. It is called inbreeding. Inbreeding is the mating of closely related animals to one another. Closely related means: (1) parent to offspring, (2) grandparent to granddaughter or grandson, (3) full siblings to each other, (4) half-siblings to each other, (5) aunt to nephew, or (6) uncle to niece. For this discussion, if the two parents are related to a lesser degree than these, such matings will be defined as linebreeding rather than inbreeding. I realize that many will see an article on inbreeding and think of taboos that are applicable to the human race. If there is a principle misunderstood by even those who advocate its use, it is inbreeding.

Do not confuse inbreeding with linebreeding! I have heard some jokers claim that if it works, it is inbreeding, and if it doesn't, it is linebreeding. It is my feeling that linebreeding is a half-hearted attempt to obtain the benefits of inbreeding without taking as great a risk. It has been characterized as a scheme to achieve vast goals using half-vast methods!

It has been well established that both desirable and undesirable features will be accentuated by inbreeding. Because there is a large risk of producing bad results, breeders tend to outcross or, at best, linebreed. The one true danger of inbreeding is that it will so set some undesirable trait that it will be almost impossible to eliminate. Inbreeding is not a game to be entered into lightly, and you must be ready to find another approach toward your goals at the first sign of a real problem.

Detractors to inbreeding can easily point to examples that have resulted in out-and-out disasters, and they use this as an argument against the practice. They fail to note, however, that it is extremely easy to find examples of both linebreedings and outcross breedings whose results are just as bad or worse. These detractors point out that there are two alternatives to inbreeding. The first is the mating of outcrossed dogs based upon their phenotype alone. The second, and the one in almost universal use, is the try-it-and-see-what-happens scheme. There are advocates of both of these plans who have experienced a degree of success. If you produce enough puppies, these methods can produce dogs that win in the showring, but seldom are they able to produce quality offspring.

Inbreeding is done for one particularly compelling reason, and that is to reduce the variability involved in the genetic makeup of the dogs in your breeding program. If you don't have some sort of handle on the genes, every mating becomes a total crapshoot, and any progress is either exceedingly small or of a negative nature. A side benefit of inbreeding is the identification and, hopefully, the elimination of any recessive faults that may be lurking in your gene pool.

The practice of inbreeding is not restricted to dogs, or even to animals. Nor is it a new tool. Neither is it an unproven, wild-eyed theory. Superchickens, miracle rice, and patented roses are all products of this tool. Yet, for some unknown reason, it is a tool that is misunderstood and avoided by most of the dog fancy.

To inbreed or not to inbreed, that is the question. Inbreeding, like any tool, is subject to misuse, especially by the inexperienced and by those poor souls who just never seem to learn. The inexperienced may persist until they do indeed become experts, but the nonlearners (and the easily discouraged) will muddle around for awhile and then drop out of the dog game. Just remember that all who survive in any trade must first take their lumps and then become the master of their tools.

If you inbreed, always be alert for the first signs of negative results. When serious problems within a strain are revealed, your selection process must be ruthless! You must cull with a heavy hand. You must stand ready to go backward two or three generations to clear the problem. While you are in the game, you risk both glory and grief. If you seek the glory of having your stock admired and your kennel renowned, then you better be willing to stand up to the grief that will be your lot on regular intervals.

If you don't, the results can corrupt your line and, indeed, become widespread within the breed. This is not just idle speculation. There are some specific breeds in which inbreeding has been used unwisely, and present-day breeders in those breeds

Almshaus Hollywood Raz'l Daz'l (aka Hollywood) is shown here at the age of sixteen months being awarded Best in Sweepstakes by Judge Carol Varner Beck. Hollywood is co-owned by his breeder, Elizabeth Surface, and his handler, Melissa Diaz-Getty. This impressive young dog has some big boots to fill, for he is the son of Ch. Almshaus Double The Pleasure, HOF, and the grandson of Ch. Sweetholm's Heartbreak Kid, CGC, HOF, POE.

have an impossible job facing them. The virtues that were sought were indeed set in the dominant bloodlines, but some health problems are also apparent throughout the breed that are simply heart-breaking. A ruthless selection process is mandatory whenever you indulge in playing God with your dogs. No matter what other good qualities you achieve, if you generate a line with bad hearts, nonfunctioning kidneys, autoimmune problems, or blindness, you will have done a grave disservice to your breed.

Rest assured that there are indeed lumps associated with any breeder's use of inbreeding. Some of the lumps are very hard to take by those who are emotionally involved with their end product. And if you are not emotionally involved, why are you breeding dogs? If you are doing it to make money, I expect that you will end up being disappointed. If you are doing it out of your love for your animals, you must be prepared to suffer the heartaches that go with the rewards.

Now let's discuss some examples of success that involve the use of inbreeding. When the Santa Gertrudis breed of cattle was being developed in South Texas, the ideal bull was produced. He was bred to his daughter, and to her daughter, and to her daughter, for six successive generations. Finally, the last generation produced a cow that had 127/128ths of her genetic material donated by the original bull. This is very close to creating a clone of an animal.

The Santa Gertrudis is one of the hardiest and largest of all breeds of cattle. Descendant cattle were just as big and had the same temperament as the original stock. There was no loss of size or of good temperament resulting from this type of concentrated inbreeding. Because you are not introducing any new combinations, this method cannot cause faults. It does, however, allow you to identify any hidden faults and then remove them from the existing breeding stock.

A specific application of this plan was used by a gentleman of my acquaintance whose interests involved another breed. Peter had in hand a stud dog of very good quality and a plan for a breeding program that was to produce a gene pool with that dog's virtues, but without many of his faults. Peter began by conducting a study of the dog's pedigree. He wanted some understanding of which ancestors were most responsible for the qualities that he admired—for the features that he wanted to be universal in his line. He first acquired a bitch of the best quality, which meant: (1) having the virtues that defined the breed, (2) not having faults in common with the target dog, and (3) one that shared ancestry with some of the dogs behind the target animal. The second step was to breed the bitch to the target dog and obtain a litter of puppies. The third step was to identify the best bitch puppy of the resulting litter. "Best" meant not having the faults of the sire but having the most virtues. His fourth step was to take that best bitch puppy and breed her to her father. The fifth and final step was to take the best bitch puppy resulting from the father-to-daughter mating and breed her to her father/grandfather. The result was a very uniform litter of five puppies that had 87.5 percent of their genetic material from the original dog and that had very few faults in common with their sire. While Peter was very lucky, he used a plan that let him take advantage of his good fortune.

Peter's plan was a good one, even though it was vulnerable to bad luck and to the breeder making poor choices. People who use this plan, who make good decisions, and who do a proper job of selection should end up with better animals than the original dog. But the most important result is that these animals should also prove to have a great deal less genetic variability. That is to say, a much higher percentage of their gene pairs will have two identical gene halves.

One of the problems with this and similar plans is that our dogs often do not live long enough to breed puppies to their grandfathers or to older generations. When this happens, you must find the best-quality son of the dog upon which you are building and breed to him. If no son is available, you must find the best-quality grandson. This is not as efficient as breeding to the original dog, but it is effective in that you still increase the percentage of the original dog's genetic contribution in each succeeding generation. Remember that your goal is to create puppies that have as much of the original dog's genetic makeup as possible, but without his faults.

You will find that, as time goes on, certain characteristics are not available in the gene pool with which you are working. This is when you consider using an outcross. You must approach outcrossing very carefully, because you risk losing all that you have gained from a very careful inbreeding program. While you may, with a little luck, get some outstanding puppies in that first outcross generation, you may also pick up some undesirable recessive characteristics that will crop up again and again in future generations.

Nevertheless, when you need a greater lay back of shoulder and it is not in the dogs related to your stock, there is no choice but to go outside your comfort zone and look for it. You should first identify a class of all of the candidate dogs that have the feature you seek. Then you must evaluate the class and put each possibility in order of quality. Remember that quality means not having faults in common with the bitch, having the virtues of the breed, and having as many ancestors in common with your bitch as possible. In this case, quality has another aspect—you want the dog to which you outcross to be as linebred as possible. That is, avoid any dog that is simply a flyer from some wild outcrossing program.

Let me relate another example of a successful Saint Bernard breeding program that I observed in another country. This breeder took a half-brother-to-half-sister cross to produce a litter of two dogs and one bitch. The resulting bitch puppy was bred to one of her littermates, and that produced another puppy bitch that was bred back to her double uncle—the littermate of her two parents.

Many examples of this type of breeding or variations of it are found in the preeminent lines of many breeds. It has been demonstrated frequently that these practices yield much success when done with insight, good planning, fortuitous selection, and the guts to keep going when your efforts turn out puppies that need neutering.

Patience is the key. No breeding program is going to turn out the ultimate dog after only one or two generations. What you should see, though, is a consistent improvement generation after generation. More and more, as the years go by, you should see uniformity and consistency within your litters. You expect to see more uniformity from an inbred litter than from any other kind of breeding. This is simply because there are fewer genetic variables involved.

Choosing a Mate for Your Dog

Before you choose a mate for your dog, you need to define all of the characteristics associated with a Saint Bernard of quality. This, of course, assumes that you have garnered sufficient knowledge of our breed to make informed decisions regarding various qualities required for your breeding goals. If this is not the case, please wait until you are better educated before you start putting puppies on the ground.

It is not easy to explain how we decide on breedings. One breeder I know states very clearly that she breeds her bitches only to dogs that are successful in the showring. Pedigrees are relatively unimportant to her. Personally, I would not purchase a dog from her, given these selection criteria. Nonetheless, she has produced several big winners in her own right. If your aim is to produce winners, this simply illustrates that there are other ways to achieve such goals.

It is my belief that any serious breeder needs to have more selection criteria other than just winning in the showring. We have always placed considerable importance on the dog having a sound mind in a sound body, on having a beautiful animal that lives a long and useful life, and on having our dogs able to reproduce their finer qualities. These are goals not easily achieved, but I suggest that they should be the target sought by anyone interested in the breed.

I recommend that you seek in your animals overall quality and let success as an exhibitor be a by-product of your efforts rather than a goal. It is relatively easy to breed for show wins only, for the aspects required for success in the ring are comparatively few. Overall quality is more difficult to obtain, but it's a much more worthy achievement.

It is interesting to note that breeders have generally been successful at achieving the features that they think are important. The other side of the coin is that they inevitably lose characteristics that they think to be *not* important. That is why so many people who operate with a limited perspective inevitably lose some specific qualities in their stock. They lose important criteria such as good temperament, breed type, the ability to perform the breed's original purpose, the ability to function as a family pet, general health and soundness, the propensity to live a long, full life, and the ability to pass on the accumulated virtues to following generations.

If you aspire to be a breeder of quality, it is necessary that you establish your selection criteria with the *entire dog* in mind. If you don't, you could end up with a strain that has serious shortcomings. This is where so many people go wrong. They ask themselves, "What are the important qualities for which I am searching? Do I want a lot of shoulder angulation, or do I want a more moderately angulated shoulder? Do I want a beautiful head no matter what else I have to give up in order to get it? Do I want a friendly disposition, or does it matter to me?" This approach means that you are looking at pieces and not the entire dog. Please don't fall into the trap that this sort of thinking represents.

In order to develop a method that allows you to look at the entire dog, you must have some insight into the genetic aspects of the characteristics that you can see. That is, you need to know a bit about the parents of the dog under consideration. A number of tools will give you this sort of visibility. Two that I have found to be of the most utility are the Feature Pedigree Diagram and the Stoplight Chart. The Stoplight Chart is the easiest to fill out. Both of these charts are included in this chapter.

The Stoplight Chart is simply a table of the features being evaluated with a column for the dog under evaluation, a column for the sire, and another for the dam. The list of features being evaluated should cover the entire dog but not every possible individual feature. For example, the front assembly is a collection of many features plus their interaction with each other—in short, a collection of features.

Ch. Sanctuary Woods How-Cum-Zit, a dog of great dignity and nobility, at the age of nine years under his tree at Bea Knight's Sanctuary Woods Kennel near Drain, Oregon. Bea felt that this dog epitomized the term "masculine"; she always stated, "You'd never mistake How-Cum-Zit for anything but a stud dog!"

Ch. Stoan's Firenze of Miyou being awarded Best of Winners at the SBCA's 1991 National Specialty by Judge Marcia Carter. Also pictured are Minnie Horlings and Ray Horlings, show chairman. Firenze's primary assets are good balance and proportions.

To fill out this form, simply make a small colored circle in the appropriate box opposite the feature being evaluated. The circle is green if it is correct, red if it is incorrect, and yellow if you don't know, if you can't make a determination, or if it is a mixture of both good and bad.

It is my practice to modify this scheme a little. I use dark green if the feature is correct and light green if it is almost correct or just barely acceptable. Similarly, I use dark red if the feature is incorrect and light red (pink) if it is better than incorrect or close to being acceptable. I leave the feature uncolored (white) if I simply do not know, and yellow for characteristics that are a mixed bag—for example, a rear assembly that seems to function correctly but lacks muscle mass.

The Feature Pedigree Diagram is a pictogram of different aspects of the dog under consideration, his sire, and his dam. As in the Stoplight Chart, you simply color in the pictogram for each feature as it is evaluated. The appeal of the Feature Pedigree Diagram is that it is a little more graphic than the Stoplight Chart, and perhaps this allows you to achieve a better mental picture of the entire dog.

The purpose in filling out these forms is to allow you to gain visibility on the whole situation when you are trying to make a breeding selection. When you undertake a breeding, your goal should be to take a step toward creating an animal whose chart is dark green all over, not just for himself but for the sire and dam as well.

Remember the old saw that states that the dog will more often resemble his grandparents than his parents? I wholeheartedly endorse this philosophy! I believe that it is almost more important to consider the four grandparents than it is to consider the two immediate parents of any potential breeding under contemplation. You are trying to build an animal that has a complete set of virtues and very few faults, but the virtues must be from the grandparents or they will not be passed on to the next generation (and following generations) with any assurance. You seek a perfect animal, but it will be of little value if he can not reproduce himself.

Your quest should motivate you to ensure that every step you make is *toward* your goal. Always move forward and never backward by choice! The whole point in breeding selection is to hang on to the virtues in hand while trying to eliminate the faults. It's sort of like building a house of cards—you're trying to add to what you have without losing all of the previous work.

Ch. Stoan's Dudley Do Right of Jay-U, Am. Can. CDX, WDCh.,WPS, Agility Dog, DD, owned by his trainer, Lia Greendale of Bend, Oregon. Dudley is the first dog in the history of Saint Bernards to combine an AKC championship with the SBCA's Working Dog championship.

Now let's get into the mechanics of how to use these charts. Let's assume that you have a bitch that you want to breed. The first step is to fill out the Stoplight Chart for her. The next step is to fill out a form for each of the stud dogs that are under consideration. Then, look at each stud dog and evaluate how many virtues each one has in common (how many green lights) with your bitch, and how many of the bitch's faults (red lights) each male might correct. It has been my experience that once you fill out these forms and hold the stud dog's form next to the bitch's form, the decisions almost make themselves. It is usually very obvious which dog you should be using.

The exception is when you are using a bitch of such poor quality that any worthy male looks like a good breeding choice. If you find yourself in this situation, and if time and money are important to you, I recommend that you consider not breeding that bitch. You will be many years and a ton of money ahead if you go out and buy a quality bitch with a good pedigree. The only true measure of your success as a breeder is how you compare with your competitors. Why would you want to start in the second sub-basement when you could be starting out on the first or second floor with the rest of your competition?

Then there is the opposite problem. That occurs when your bitch is of such high quality that it seems like every available male would represent a step backward in your breeding program. This is not a trivial kind of incident, nor is it all that rare. The better your bitch, the fewer sound choices you will have when it comes time to breed her. When you find yourself in this predicament, all you can do is make a choice that will put greater depth behind the virtues and hope for a lucky roll of the dice with respect to the faults. My advice is to always be more concerned with retaining virtues than in eliminating faults.

One last problem that breeders face when trying to make a selection for a breeding is not knowing the parents of the dog they want to use. This is the handicap that people with less experience must face when they decide to become breeders. Anyone in this situation obviously needs to seek assistance. You can talk to the owner and breeder of the dog that you are thinking of using. You can talk to people who have seen the sire and dam of the dog, particularly if they have had dogs that competed against the dog in which you have an interest. The dilemma is deciding who to believe—who is not kennel blind or who has a tendency to hide negative aspects of their animals. I can't help you with this problem. You will have to use your own skills in evaluating people. Some people are knowledgeable, truthful, objective, and willing to help. Some are not! I recommend that you make a great effort to find people who are.

Sometimes looking at old pictures will help, but that is a poor substitute for actually seeing the dogs or being able to go over them in person. You must do the best you can with what information you have and resolve to have greater depth of information for the following generations. And there must be following generations or you have not made the commitment to be a breeder of quality. Remember that a breeder of quality is someone who first has a mental picture of perfection that involves the entire dog, then evaluates his stock objectively and completely, and then makes his selections so that generation after generation are ever closer to that ideal. Being a breeder of quality is a lifelong commitment or it isn't a worthy effort.

STOPLIGHT CHART FOR: ______________________________

(Name of Dog)

SIRE: ______________________ DAM: ______________________

Date of evaluation: ______________ Evaluator: ____________________

FEATURE BEING EVALUATED	FOR THIS DOG	FOR THE SIRE	FOR THE DAM	REMARKS
Temperament				
Quality of Offspring				
Intelligence				
Proportionately Tall				
Overall Size				
Substance				
Balance				
Muscle Tone				
Movement				
Free Stance				
Excessive Skin				
Markings				
Color				
Bite				
Muzzle				
Flews				
Eyes				
Skull				
Ears				
Neck				
Chest				
Top Line				
Loin				
Croup				
Belly				
Tail				
Scapula Length				
Upper Arm Length				
Front Assembly				
Thigh Mass				
Rear Assembly				
Feet				
Hips and Elbows				

FEATURE PEDIGREE DIAGRAM

Sire: ______________________

Name

date of birth

Dam: ______________________

EXPLANATION OF FEATURE PEDIGREE DIAGRAM SYMBOLS

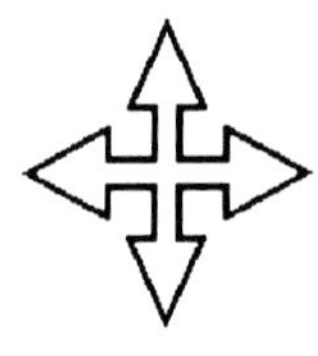

Proportions: Height at withers equal to length of body

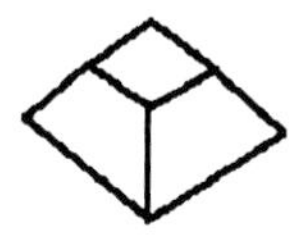

Massiveness of entire dog

Bone: diameter of legs

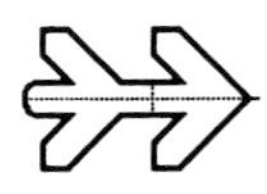

Feet pointing correctly

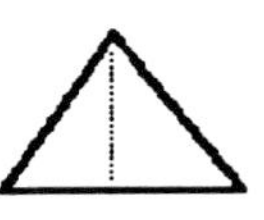

Angulation: Front-Rear

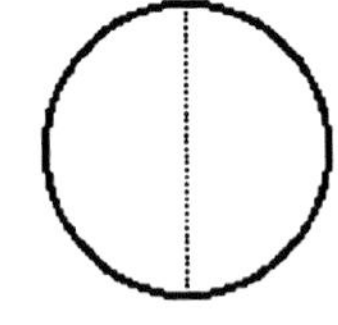

Coat Type: L/L(Long/Long);
S/S(Short/Short) or L/S(Long/Short)

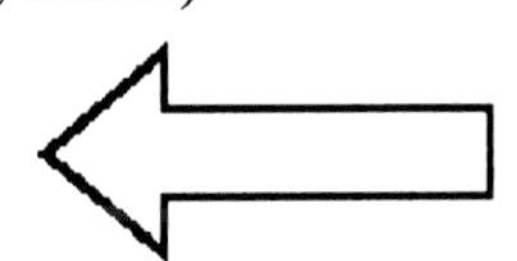

Correct Movement

Coat (Quality)

Mask and/or Markings

Temperament

Intelligence

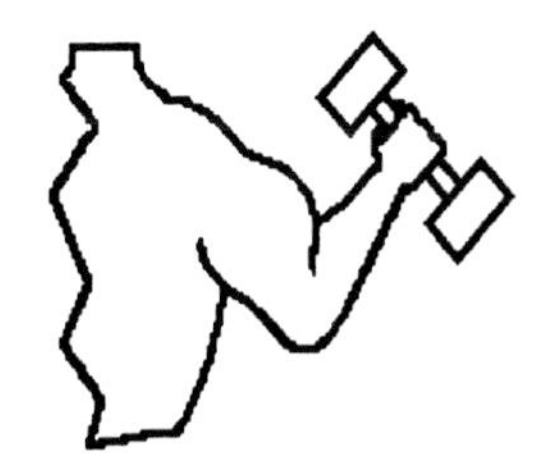

Strength or quality of muscles

Teeth - Bite

Quality of Offspring

Advice for the Less Experienced Breeder

One day a few summers ago, while sitting out on our deck, drinking iced tea, and watching the dogs play in the yard below, one of our visitors asked if we were happy with the quality of our dogs in general. Without the slightest hesitation, I brashly replied, "You bet!" I then had second thoughts and added lamely, "Well, for the most part, I suppose, for there are some features we would like to enhance and some problems we would like to eradicate." "Oh, I see," responded my guest inscrutably. "What troubles me most," I continued conjecturally, "is that had we started out knowing a few of the many pitfalls of being breeders, we would undoubtedly be much closer to our goals at this point in time." "Would it not be wise," queried my guest sagely, "for you to write down a list of these pitfalls so that others might avoid them?" "What a good idea!" I exclaimed excitedly. "I'll do just that!"

And this is it—my advice to newcomers to the Saint Bernard fancy who want or need a little help in becoming an accomplished breeder. There are really two roads to that place called "Success." One is "Quantity" and the other is "Quality." The "Quantity" method requires producing something like a thousand puppies in order for blind luck to create ten or twelve really good dogs. The other path is much harder and may not produce many more truly great animals, but it will result in a great deal less "dog-pound fodder."

Assuming that you are interested in the welfare of the breed and in the welfare of every individual puppy that you produce, I will discuss the "Quality" road. This path is a test of your ability to care, your ethics, your perseverance, and your industry. It is also a never-ending learning process. There are no real shortcuts, but there are a few guidelines to mark the trail for you.

The following is a list of principles that will blaze this trail toward becoming a successful breeder. These principles originated with articles I have read, some good advice I have been given, and some bad experiences through which I have had to suffer.

1. If you forget all else, remember this one guiding principle: Breed only out of love for your dogs, or for your happiness and pleasure, but never for profit, because if you do, your accounts will never balance.
2. It is absolutely essential to have a mental picture of the dog that you want to produce. Begin with the silhouette of the entire dog, then fill in the details as they become clear to you. If you don't have this kind of clearly defined goal, you will find it very hard to make any significant progress.
3. You must develop an appreciation of true type and learn to recognize it at a glance. This is a breeder's greatest asset and one that you cannot do without. Ask successful breeders to discuss this subject with you, because there is no better way to learn.
4. Do not fall into the trap of thinking that type is confined to the head, for type must be embodied in the entire dog. While it is extremely important to have a Saint Bernard head, you must also have a Saint Bernard neck, Saint Bernard feet, a Saint Bernard loin, a Saint Bernard rear—all parts of the dog must be typical for the breed.
5. Don't take advice from people who are unsuccessful breeders; opinions worth having are proved by successes, not words. The dog fancy's lore is replete with information that just isn't true, and this misinformation is preached as if it were gospel by these pseudo-experts. For example, if someone tells you that it is in the best interest of the breed to allow only six puppies in any litter to survive the first day, recognize that you are dealing with someone who advocates utter nonsense.

6. Don't join the ranks of those who worship pedigrees. You will often come upon some proud owner who tries to impress you by reciting all of the famous dogs behind his animal. It is foolish to be taken in by such nonsense. Having famous dogs behind an animal does not in any way indicate the worth of that particular specimen.
7. The tools of a breeder are called inbreeding (which the timid refer to as linebreeding) and outcrossing. You must learn the dangers and benefits of each before you can master these tools.
8. A breeder understands the basic rules of genetic inheritance but does not worship them. Both blind ignorance and blind faith in these rather imperfect tools will lead to fallible conclusions.
9. The use of indiscriminate outcrosses is a shortcut to grief. A well-chosen outcross can be of great value, but a poorly chosen one can produce a collection of every imaginable fault. Faults established in this manner are much harder to eradicate than they were to collect.
10. Don't inbreed just because that is what successful breeders do. Inbreeding with complimentary types can lead to great success, but if you try it with unsuitable animals, you are not going to be very happy with the results.
11. Don't try to recreate some dog by inbreeding on it. That dog is gone forever and you should limit yourself to trying to recapture virtues that the dog possessed. Nor should you try to inbreed on two dogs at the same time, for you will end up by inbreeding to neither.
12. When planning a breeding, study the potential parents and grandparents in great detail, but do not waste your time with contemplating the great-grandparents and older generations. The influence of animals more than two generations removed is so diluted that it has become trivial. The littermates and offspring of your proposed parents will give you a much better clue about the genetic recipe you are cooking up.
13. There are two edges to the breeder's sword! The front edge is called "mating," and the back edge is called "selection." It is not sufficient to be skillful at choosing the right stud to be bred to some particular bitch, because the true mark of a breeder is the ability to select. You must remember that you had a particular purpose for the mating, and you need to select from the resulting puppies so that your purpose is realized. This is one real area that can significantly handicap your progress if you aren't careful.
14. Don't lose track of the puppies that you produce. You must continually hone your skills at choosing matings and at evaluating young puppies. You can only verify the correctness of your decisions two years after they have been made—and you need to see all of the results, not just a biased selection.
15. Always remember that your future as a breeder is invested in the puppies on the ground, and you must do your best to ensure that they achieve the optimum development of mind and body. You must understand what is involved in the socializing of puppies and see to it that the puppies receive the handling and personal attention that they need. Don't send puppies to their new homes too soon, and try your best to see that they only go to families that will provide properly for them. If possible, raise two puppies together in order to provide the correct amount of exercise and stimulation required for them to grow into the best possible adult animals.
16. Don't try to find a substitute for the animal that has the qualities you desire. When some particular dog or bitch has the virtues that you seek, do not fall into the trap of thinking that breeding to a littermate will bring about the same results. It very seldom works out that way.
17. Don't mate animals that have the same serious faults, because if you do, you will have a difficult time trying to undo that bit of mischief.
18. Don't use mediocre animals for breeding. Bear in mind that the absence of a fault does not in any way signify the presence of its corresponding virtue, and a lack of virtue is by far the *greatest* fault of all.
19. Don't mate noncomplimentary types. This means, do not mate dogs that not only have the same faults but also lack the same virtues.
20. Make your breedings only between animals of complimentary types, and don't be frightened of breeding from an animal that has obvious faults as long as his mate has the compensating virtues. You must seek these virtues actively rather than simply attempt to breed away from faults.

21. The mating of extremes with the expectation that things will average out is fallacious thinking. Breeding an overshot bite to an undershot bite is not the way to achieve a perfect mouth.
22. Always remember that you are dealing with the entire dog and not just the part that concerns you at the moment. If you forget one virtue while searching for another, you will lose everything. I have lost count of how many Saint breeders there were when we first started who concentrated on trying to eradicate hip dysplasia from their stock. Inevitably, they soon had such untypical animals that they could no longer compete in the showring. Further, these people also lost any claim to soundness that they might have started with! Everything was lost simply because of that focus on only one part of the dog.
23. Don't allow yourself to be kennel blind. When someone is accused of being kennel blind, it means that they credit their own dogs with virtues that the dogs don't possess and/or they are blind to the faults of their animals. Kennel blindness is an indulgence that you cannot afford.
24. Make sure that your animals carry the characteristics of their sex, not those of the opposite sex. A stud dog can have no greater fault than a failure to be masculine; it is extremely rare for such an animal to have quality offspring. Doggy bitches often have trouble becoming pregnant. Bitchy dogs and doggy bitches will bring you grief in the long run.
25. Don't evaluate a stud dog by the worst of his progeny. To properly assess his worth, you must look at the overall results when he is bred to a good bitch, but not when he has been bred to a poor or uncomplimentary female. Any stud will sire poor progeny when he is misbred, but when he is well mated, there should be some outstanding puppies in every litter, and a majority of the rest of the puppies should be of good quality.
26. Don't allow your feelings to influence your choice of a stud dog. If the dog is right for your bitch, he is right no matter who owns him or how much you dislike his owner. On the other hand, if the dog is wrong for your bitch, he is wrong no matter how much your dear friend wants you to use his stud dog.
27. Don't ever become so enamored with any stud dog that you are blind to his faults. Everyone finds dogs that they greatly admire, but if you take a noncomplimentary bitch to such a dog, you will soon regret your blindness. Every dog has faults. Just make sure that you are aware of them whenever you plan a breeding.
28. Guard the reputation of your stud dogs! It is very tempting to adopt the philosophy of, "If I don't breed her, they will just go down the street and breed her to a lesser male, and the resulting puppies will be poorer, and I owe it to the breed to not let that happen!" This sort of thinking is a trap that will bring you to the depths of regret. I will long remember the first time that I resorted to this kind of rationalization. A man who owned a bitch arrived upon my doorstep one day and informed me that my dog had the good fortune to have been chosen to sire her first litter. I was able to resist the temptation to tell him that his bitch should never be bred only by telling myself that I would be doing the breed a great disservice if I caused the alternative male to be used. While the bitch was greatly lacking in type, she did have the redeeming quality of being very prolific—she had thirteen live puppies of very poor quality—and each of those thirteen puppies grew to inherit their mother's talent of producing large quantities of puppies so *un*true to type that they made your face hurt! To this day, whenever someone walks onto the premises with some dog that totally lacks type, I know I am going to be told that the dog is related to my stock and that I should help them to decide upon a fitting mate. That breeding happened a very long time ago, and I am still haunted by that one encounter.
29. A breeder's job is to seek for each specific mating the best stud available, which means the dog that has the virtues you need and/or that you want to keep. Don't search for the perfect dog as a mate for your bitch, because such a dog doesn't exist—he never has and he never will.
30. It is usually a great mistake to chase after the famous champion or the winner of some prestigious show. Just because a dog has won a particular award means only that he was best in the ring, not that he is best for the breed or, especially, that he is just right for your bitch.

A portrait of the proprietors of the Saint Bernards of Stoan Kennel with one of their dogs. Pictured are the author and his wife, Joan Zielinski, along with Ch. Stoan's Firenze of Miyou, who was awarded Best of Winners at the SBCA's 1991 National Specialty.

31. Avoid using a flyer (an outstanding dog from an otherwise poor litter or out of a very poor family) on your bitch unless his worth as a stud dog has already been established. Such animals are usually very poor producers. A good male from a good family is a far better bet than a similar male from a poor family.
32. To a breeder, the only true treasure is a great bitch. A great stud dog is silver, but a great bitch is gold. To succeed as a breeder, you must be a treasure hunter who always seeks to acquire such gold. No price is too high to pay, and you never have enough. You must be a gold seeker whose greed knows no bounds!
33. If your kennel space is limited, every spot is much too valuable to be occupied by a male. If being the best breeder possible is your aim, you need to let those who are more interested in servicing their own egos keep and feed the stud dogs.
34. If your kennel space is limited, every spot is too valuable to be occupied by a poor or mediocre bitch. If the puppy that you kept or bought turns out to be less than you expected, it is time to let her become somebody's family pet. You can't make up for lost time, effort, or expense by breeding her.
35. It is not enough to limit your concerns to aspects that contribute to winning in the showring. You must consider the health and vigor of your stock. You must seek animals that are easy keepers. You must worry about all of the elements that enhance or detract from the desirability of owning dogs with your kennel name on them. If there is no market for your dogs, you will not be long at the breeder's table.
36. Be concerned about the whelping problems and the after-whelping recovery rates exhibited by your bitches. Excessive inbreeding can cause these problems to ever so slowly creep up on a breeder and make life very difficult. You want healthy puppies being raised by a healthy mother, because your sanity depends on not deviating too often from this scenario. Of course, you can cause whelping problems by mismanaging your females. But if you refrain from breeding females that are not in optimum health and/or condition and do not overbreed them, you should more easily be able to identify the source of any problem.
37. Select for dogs that display quality during their older years, for you must seek dogs that look good and feel good beyond that first bloom of youth. If you breed dogs that you would rather

not put on display when they get older, then you probably have your priorities misplaced. You must strive for Saint Bernards that live both a long and fulfilling life if you want the kind of reputation for your stock that enhances your chances for success.

38. You must breed for sound dogs that live to a ripe old age and die from any cause other than being put to death because they are too crippled to walk anymore. You do this by breeding for large muscle mass on loin and thigh and by selecting for hard, firm muscle tone. Avoid "wetness" like the plague.
39. Do not worship at the altar of that false god known as "OFA!" No good has ever come from subscribing to the teachings and philosophies preached by those who promote this religion. This does not mean that breeding unsound dogs is acceptable—it only means that you do not define soundness as the shape that some shadow takes on an X-ray plate.
40. Don't ever forget that a Saint Bernard without a saintly temperament is no Saint at all. There is no other single feature of a Saint Bernard as important as this. Your poorest specimen should make somebody a marvelous pet. If you ever have to make any excuse for any dog's behavior, you need to take another look at your stock.
41. Remember that each and every mating should bring you closer to your breeding goals. If you find yourself selling off entire litters or the best stuff you produce, perhaps you should reassess your direction.
42. Remember that the first, and maybe the second, breedings of any dog or bitch must be considered a test breeding, for only after the puppies have been on the ground for a couple of years can the true value of a mating be determined.
43. Capturing and maintaining a beautiful head must be one of your primary concerns. If you don't make every effort to preserve head quality, it will vanish like a dream, and like a dream, it will be very difficult to recapture.
44. A great head plus soundness should be one of your aims. Any novice can breed one without the other.
45. Massiveness plus quality should be another goal. Massiveness means having a reasonable size and adequate substance; quality means excelling in both type and soundness. If your dogs lack either massiveness or quality, you should not take a great deal of pride in your stock, because you have a long way to go.
46. Don't wait to recognize a mistake until you make it the second or third time—profit from the first experience. If a dog or bitch is obviously a poor producer, get rid of that animal and don't try another combination to see what happens.
47. If you aspire to be a successful breeder, you must compete in dog shows. Win or lose, you must exhibit. Your dogs will all look great in their own backyard. It is only in the showring that you can compare your stock with what the other breeders are producing. The realities of competition clear your vision and give you the "breeder's" eye.
48. It is not possible to succeed as a breeder and avoid the National Specialty Show—you *must* go every year! Nor is it enough to simply attend—you must make a statement to the rest of the Saint Bernard fancy by putting your stock on display. I can't explain why this is so—it is just something that I have observed.
49. If you truly love Saint Bernards, you will malign neither the good nor the great specimens of the breed. These dogs should be a source of aesthetic pride and pleasure to all true Saint Bernard fanciers, and if you are going to accomplish anything as a breeder, you must be honest and objective about your competition. Besides, if you pay homage to that which is good and refrain from volunteering comments on the flaws that you see, you will have much less trouble explaining your words when they get repeated to ears that were never intended to hear.
50. You must never be satisfied with anything but the very best, for second best is never good enough. If you ever become complacent about the quality of your animals, you might as well admit that you have given up and are just coasting.
51. Learn! Learn! Learn! Never miss any opportunity to become more educated. You will never know enough, and you will continually be inundated with new information. Be always alert for these opportunities to get smarter. Also, remember that you will never meet anybody in the fancy so stupid or uninformed that

Ch. Lynchcreek's Bravo Nicholas at the age of six years (he lived to be ten years of age) being awarded Best of Opposite Sex by Judge Ken Nelson at the Great Salt Lake Saint Bernard Club's 1990 Specialty. Nicholas, who was handled here by Gareth Chabot, was co-owned by Elizabeth Surface and his breeder, Candy Blancher. Those who knew Nicholas were impressed with his wonderful disposition, his excellent breed type, and his marvelous balance and proportions.

they do not know something that you would be better off knowing. It is your job to find out that information; it is not their job to spoon-feed it to you.

52. Don't try to live in just your own cozy little world so that you don't have to cope with all of the unpleasantness that comes from dealing with people who do not share your likes and dislikes. It is very important for you to observe your competitors' efforts. When they choose a mating, try to understand their reasons and closely watch the results. Continually monitor the efforts of all of the other breeders. Note what is good and bad about what they have done, then use that information in your program. Life is too short for you to make all of the mistakes yourself.
53. You must personally look after the care and welfare of your dogs—this is not something that you can hire to be done. You must be the one who picks up the dog droppings and knows that it is time to break out the worm

medicine. You must be the one who discovers the sick and the lame, and the one who knows when the last vestige of dignity has gone and it is time to call for the green needle. If you do not know your dogs better than anyone else, you do not know enough to be a breeder.

54. You must have the respect of all of the players in the dog game, and producing good dogs is only the starting point. Rather than bemoaning the many frustrations that you will encounter, you must learn how to earn that respect. You must master the politics of becoming a known quantity to be reckoned with. This means that you will have to learn to speak and write effectively, and you must contribute articles to as many publications as you can. You must attend and contribute to educational meetings and seminars. You must join clubs and contribute to them. You must give of yourself without expectations of compensation. The rewards for following this plan are success in the showring and the ensuing respect of the rest of the dog fancy. But remember the part about starting by producing good dogs!

55. Resolve to persevere. If you don't, you will probably never become a breeder. When your best plans result in disaster, learn from your mistakes and move on. When the actions and words of others overwhelm and discourage you, resolve to still be breeding Saint Bernards after they have dropped out of the game. Through all of the disappointments and mishaps, press on! If you cannot do this, you will not realize your goals.

There it is! A collection of the easy steps to becoming a breeder. There probably are other important steps that should be listed here, but this list is already longer than anyone could possibly absorb. Now that you know so many of the secrets of those who have been successful over the years, there is no reason why you cannot now become one of the really big guns in the breed. That is, there is no reason as long as you are willing to expend the time, effort, and money required to wear the breeder's hat.

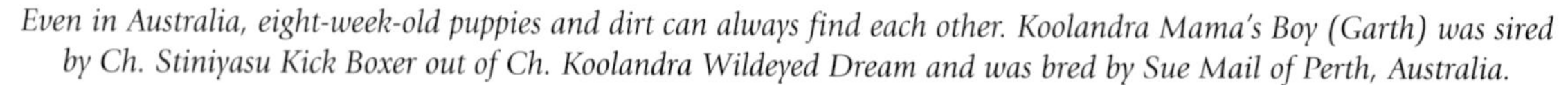

Even in Australia, eight-week-old puppies and dirt can always find each other. Koolandra Mama's Boy (Garth) was sired by Ch. Stiniyasu Kick Boxer out of Ch. Koolandra Wildeyed Dream and was bred by Sue Mail of Perth, Australia.

A Short Course on Judging Saint Bernards

Are you a judge of Saint Bernards? If you come to your judging of this breed with a background in another breed, this chapter is intended to help you in your quest to judge Saint Bernards with some confidence. Because most people judging the Saint Bernard do not have an extensive background to truly evaluate the entire dog, the question must be asked, "What few features, when properly evaluated, will go the farthest toward identifying the best Saint Bernard in the class?" It is my suggestion that you won't go far astray if you can properly evaluate the following features (not necessarily in order of importance): (1) powerful build, (2) sound body and mind, (3) correct proportions, and (4) proper head.

Of course, a list of important features does little good without an explanation of the intricacies of each. These subjects need to be considered in some detail to explain the finer points.

POWERFUL BUILD

Things To Look For

If there is one word that clearly expresses the essence of a Saint Bernard, it is "powerful." As a judge, you should look for the dog that is the most powerful. One of the best of the tests for this feature is the touch test. Much of the quality of the dog is determined via the laying on of hands, for the body must not only have great substance, it must also feel firm and muscular during the examination.

The loin should be commanding in its presence, enough so that you should get the impression that you could lift the dog by grasping him by the loin with both hands. If you are not impressed with the mass of muscle on the rear legs then you probably aren't dealing with one of the better specimens of the breed. The same could be said for the nape of the neck, the shoulders, and the forearms.

Not that you should ignore the information gathered visually. Your eyes should tell you, when gazing upon a good Saint Bernard, that this is a strong, powerful, massive animal. The width, when viewed from the top, should be the same for the shoulders, the ribs, and the rear quarters. Bone must be substantial without being cloddy in appearance. There should be so much muscle development in the neck that you get the impression that the dog has a short neck. A word of caution here: The neck should not really be short—it should only *appear* to be short. The neck should form a smooth transition into the broad shoulders, and from there into the wide, flat back, loin, and croup. Even the tail should be so powerful in appearance that it looks as if it could be used as a weapon.

What You Should Penalize

General Lack of Substance. While it is not required that a Saint Bernard be overly tall, he must be strong, massive, and powerful. Lacking these properties, the dog lacks breed type.

Pseudo-Substance. Of course, you must not be caught mistaking pseudo-substance for the real thing—for example:

Wetness: Epitomized by sloppy, loose-hanging skin and soft, spongy muscle and body tissues. This excess of skin to the point of dripping wrinkles is a severe problem in our breed. The Saint is not a breed with tight-fitting skin, but neither should it ever be Bloodhoundlike in appearance. Loose, flabby skin is an indicator of loose muscle and ligamentation. Normally, when viewing such an animal, you get a sense of a weak, sloppy, clumsy animal that no amount of conditioning can make right.

Excessive Weight: Found in dogs that are packing too much lard. Don't ever mistake fat for substance. A Saint should be athletically built in order to perform his historical functions.

Barrel Chest: In seeking a massive dog, you must not confuse a wide dog with a misshaped one. The dog must still be able to function without having to reach around some huge barrel to reach the ground.

Faulty Temperament. Aggression in any form, be it directed toward people or other dogs in the ring, is not appropriate. Temperament on a Saint Bernard becomes faulty long before the AKC definition of attempting to bite comes into focus. The dogs should not resent the judge or fear him. Because shyness and aggression are the two opposite sides of the same coin, neither is acceptable for the breed.

SOUND BODY AND MIND

Things To Look For

You should need little guidance in recognizing soundness of body with respect to a Saint Bernard. Keep in mind, however, that a proportionately tall dog absolutely must have moderate angulation in both front and rear; therefore, the correct movement must be compatible with that construction. In other words, the great reach and drive sought in the German Shepherd ring is not appropriate in the Saint Bernard ring. However, this does not mean that a short stride is acceptable. The length of stride must be as great as possible without overreaching. The other point that needs to be made is that a Saint Bernard needs to single track without rolling his body to reach the ground.

Now the subject of soundness of mind needs more detailed treatment. Remember that this breed was intended to be sent out unescorted in packs of two or three adult males to find foot travelers who, while trying to cross a high and dangerous mountain pass, became lost and in danger of freezing to death. The dogs could not indulge in fighting with each other, nor could they attack strangers. They were supposed to *save* strangers, not eat them! Therefore, the hallmark of the breed is a gregarious, friendly attitude toward both people and other dogs whenever they are in a businesslike environment. Proper breed type includes a wagging tail.

What You Should Penalize

Faulty Movement. Again, I assume that you know movement faults and need little guidance on the subject. Any aspect of movement or static balance that would be faulty on the generic dog is also faulty on a Saint Bernard.

TALL PROPORTIONS

Things To Look For

The first paragraph of the Standard calls for a proportionately tall dog. This means that it is not a proportionately long dog. This is not a requirement for a lot of altitude, but rather a statement of the proper proportion of height to length. Much that is erroneous in the breed is a direct result of the fancy ignoring this one important feature.

- This is the feature that requires moderate angulation and all that it implies.
- Proper balance is a direct consequence of the dog being tall rather than rectangular.
- The inherent nobility of the breed follows from the logical step-by-step requirements dictated by this one property.

What You Should Penalize

Penalize any deviations from the dog being proportionately tall. Being a rectangular dog is wrong, whether he is short on leg or long in body.

Having said that, I must note that I find real fault with extremes rather than with small deviations from the ideal. While you must guard against a degree of angulation unsuitable for a proportionately tall dog, you should also not accept a dog that is so short coupled that he would require straight stifles and vertical shoulder blades for compatible movement. As to my personal philosophy, I find that a just barely perceptible degree of extra body length is found in what I consider to be very good specimens. However, I never accept short legs as being anything other than a serious fault. Neither do I accept as correct any obviously rectangular animal. Correct breed type demands that the dog must have the correct proportions for a Saint Bernard.

Ch. Mia Faithful Friend, HOF, POE, owned and bred by Dick and Dinah Tull of Mia Kennels in Rockville, Maryland, is shown here as a very young dog by owner Richard Tull under Judge Lee Pierce. Friend's soundness, beautiful balance, and tall proportions were passed on to his many champion offspring.

This photograph shows some of the offspring of Ch. Mia Faithful Friend, HOF, POE, and the SBCA Stud Dog of the Year for 1984. From left to right are Joan Zielinski with Ch. Stoan's Nadia of Klafa, HOF; Stan Zielinski with Ch. Stoan's Nicholas of Klafa, HOF, POE (himself SBCA's Stud Dog of the Year for two consecutive years); Mike Strasser with Ch. Mistihil Friendly Nature; Bill Oliver with Ch. Revilo's Bogart v. Holly, HOF, POE; Pat Kinser with Ch. Revilo's Bonus; and Marlene Oliver with Ch. Revilo's Better Yet v. Snowland.

PROPER HEAD

Things To Look For

This is a subject that could be the sole focus of an entire book. Because a lengthy treatment is not appropriate here, I will focus on a few features that, if correct, will usually indicate that the entire head is acceptable. Let it be noted that the Saint Bernard is a head breed every bit as much as are Collies, Shetland Sheepdogs, and Boxers.

Furrows. Without furrows, all else is a waste of effort in evaluating a Saint Bernard head. The very shallow furrow along the top of the muzzle is prerequisite to a correct muzzle. The extremely deep furrow between the eyes serves the same function with respect to the skull—that is, no deep furrow means that you have an improper head. It is not that the furrows in their own right are all that important, but rather that without them the construction of the rest of the head is seriously faulty. You may occasionally find a faulty head with furrows, but you will never find a good head without them.

Bumps. You absolutely must have bumps over the eyes and below them. The bones both above and below the eyes must be very pronounced to give the head the chiseled appearance required for this breed.

Boxlike Muzzle. The muzzle must be substantial, square-sided, deep, wide, and short in length.

Massiveness. The head must be big and wide, even for a big dog. The mass of the head should be imposing. The ears, when at attention, should be set so that they form a continuation of the top line of the skull, thus enhancing the sense of width there.

What You Should Penalize

Not only should you penalize the negative of those features described above (lack of furrows, flat cheeks and weak eyebrow ridges, small or tapered muzzle, small skull, etc.), but you should watch out for features that appear to be correct but are really faults.

Ch. Stoan's Awesome Sofie v. Hahn being awarded Best of Winners by Judge Donald Gill. The trophy presenter is the late Mary Begshaw, whose Encore Kennels made a significant contribution to the breed. Sofie had magnificent proportions; she was the epitome of the term "proportionately tall" demanded by the Standard.

Excessive Flews. The Standard calls for a muzzle that is deeper than it is long. The depth being discussed is the distance from the top of the muzzle to the bottom of the lower mandible—that is, a measurement made bone to bone. The depth of the flews is often confused with the depth of the muzzle. Don't make that mistake! Excessive flews can also be found on a dog with a good muzzle. Any flew that extends more than two inches below the bottom line of the lower mandible is faulty.

Man-Made Heads. It is a common handler practice to gather up all of the excess skin that he can pull from the head, face, and neck, then pile it all up just ahead of the collar to simulate a massive, wide head. Just ask the handler to drop his death grip on the collar of such a dog and you will be amazed at the transformation.

Markings. Markings are not a requirement in our Standard, so the subject should be of little concern to a judge.

These guidelines should in no way substitute for a thorough understanding of the breed and the breed's type. Also be aware that there are a myriad of features not discussed here that are also very important. It is hoped that correctness in those features will tend to be found in dogs that score high in the qualities discussed here.

Ch. Titan von Mallen, a two-time winner of the SBCA National Specialty, is the prototype for many Saint Bernard kennels across the nation. He is shown in this picture being handled by his breeder and owner, Lou Mallen, as he was awarded Best of Breed at the SBCA 1972 National Specialty.

The Perspective of a Judge Who Also Exhibits

Once upon a time, which was about two months before a particular judging assignment, I received a letter from a potential exhibitor asking what kind of dog I would be putting up at that show, and requesting my response before the closing date so that she could decide if she would enter her dog. I did not answer that letter, but it started me thinking about how I could respond if I was so inclined.

I wondered if I could explain what kind of dog would achieve awards when exhibited under me. How would I arrive at my determinations, and what reasoning would explain those decisions? For my own information, I decided to write down what, how, and why I do what I do in the ring as a judge. It is presented here to see if it sounds like a rational process.

First, let me relate the official AKC position. This quote was taken from *The Complete Dog Book*, the official publication of the American Kennel Club.

> The standard portrays what, in the minds of its compilers, would be the ideal dog of the breed. Ideal in type, in structure, in gait, in temperament —ideal in every respect. Thus, the standard is not the representation of any actual dog, but a concept. It is against this concept that a dog show judge must measure every competitor of that breed.

It should be sufficient to say that I try very hard to do exactly what the American Kennel Club, with the preceding statement, says that I must do. This is, of course, a generality that any judge will tell you. Let me try to be more specific.

Whenever I start to judge a class, I first move the entire class around the ring together to see if any of the exhibits need to be excused for lameness or to see if any individual dog is going to really make an impression with his spectacular movement.

Then I begin to evaluate the individual dogs as they stand posed in a group. My very first step is to stand away from the dogs and observe each overall silhouette with respect to balance and proportions. The next step is an almost unconscious evaluation of just how pleasing to my eye are the curves of the neck, withers, back, croup, belly, chest, and legs. The truth is that any dog that gets low marks during this first glance will have a hard time doing well under me.

I then usually move closer to the dog and look at some of the details (such as head type, expression, substance, size, coat condition, detail proportions, and static balance) and try to compare this overview of the dog to the Standard with particular emphasis on the very first part of the Standard labeled "General Appearance."

At this point, I try to have established which dogs in the class rate an "Acceptable or Better" with respect to the Breed Standard. It is among those dogs that I attempt to make my award based upon a hands-on examination of structure (skeletal features) and muscle (mass and quality), plus a visual examination of the dog's movement.

Movement? Yes, indeed—movement! It is not the static dog that is so beautiful, because if this was so, we would be better served by photographs or statues. The dynamics of motion—the way in which the dog uses his body and face to communicate, and the sense that this is a dog with strength, ability, intelligence, and purpose—are what make me truly appreciate the quality of the dog. While the way in which a dog moves is not any more important than fitting the description found in the Standard, it is not any less important either.

Having looked at each dog from afar, made an up-close examination by eye and by hand, and watched the dogs moving, I then try to sort the dogs in order of quality and beauty. I try to look for the overall dog and not overemphasize some particular feature. I try not to dwell overly long on faults, for the most terrible fault of all is a lack of virtues. Proper judgment must be made by looking passionately for virtues that define the breed.

Of course, the greatest virtue of all is harmony of the whole. This describes a dog notable for neither excess nor deficiency, but rather one whose beauty rests on the foundation of the features necessary for his historic work. Philosophers through the ages have ascribed beauty to that which is simple, does not have superfluous parts, exactly answers its ends. Show me a dog with all parts correct and ideal so that they fit and flow together—nothing exaggerated or out of synchronization, no factor protruding through excess and by absence—and I will show you a dog that I think to be beautiful!

Now I would like to turn to the subject of what it takes to be a good judge. Most would agree that the judge's purpose is to find the best animals in the ring. We have all seen judges who seem not to understand their purpose. All shortcomings in manners, courtesy, procedure, gentleness, ring presence, keeping to the schedule, etc. can be forgiven for the judge who always finds the best animals. On the other hand, any judge who fails to find the best animal is a poor judge no matter how many other sterling qualities he may possess.

I have always felt that some of the worst jobs of judging are performed by some truly nice people. Given the choice of showing under a pleasant, fun, and enjoyable but incompetent judge, or a grumpy, obnoxious person who gives the awards to the best dogs, I have never had a problem making the decision. I want to compete under the competent judge. Judges should assume that most exhibitors feel that nothing is more important than having the best dogs win.

There is, however, another aspect to this equation. The total experience of having the lesser dogs being put up over better animals is not entirely the fault of the judges. Bear in mind that the exhibitors and breeders also have a big influence on these events. It is as frustrating for the judge to have to make his evaluations based upon inconsistent and misleading information as it is for the exhibitor to lose with the better dog. All judges receive regular and confusing communications telling them what they should be placing in their awards. Advertisements, letters, and just ordinary conversations all

Ch. La Casa's Victor, HOF, was owned and bred by Janet Frick Mansfield of Stone Mountain, Georgia. Victor is shown here being posed by his admirer, Don Dvorak. Victor is noteworthy for his handsome proportions and his superb front assembly. Notice his proper forechest and correct depth of body not coming below his elbows.

inundate the judges with what appears to be contradictory advice.

This holds especially true when the people in control of the parent club and the exhibitors being guided by the Standard are breeding an entirely different kind of dog. It is this sort of situation that makes many judges put proper breed type at the far end of their priorities. Having breed type ignored or minimized is what most often generates feelings among the exhibitors and spectators that the wrong dogs have won.

Does all of the abuse and the conflicting pressures heaped upon our poor judges excuse their looking only at generic dog qualities when making awards? Is it all right for a judge to make awards based primarily upon movement, condition, grooming, showmanship, and/or presentation skills of the handler and to minimize aspects of breed type? I believe that judges who resort to this sort of philosophy do a disservice to the dog fancy. Let me give you an example. Suppose you were judging a class of mediocre or poor Saint Bernards and somebody had entered the ring with the world's most perfect Akita. The Akita would have to be placed at the end of the line. No matter how much style, elegance, breed quality, and soundness he might have, the Akita has no Saint Bernard type. Those qualities that make him a wonderful Akita also make him a failure as a Saint Bernard. A correct job of judging must always place breed type as the first priority in making awards. Knowledgeable breeders and exhibitors generally look for judges who not only are competent, but who also understand this point. They know that the great judges are made in this mold.

I fully understand the thinking that makes people wonder about the competence of judges, for I have been there often myself. My self-image has me primarily as a breeder and exhibitor who occasionally judges, and my empathy is with those who suffer under judges who do not do a proper job. As a breeder, there is nothing more distressing than having a good dog passed over by a seemingly incompetent judge. This holds true whether the best dog is the one you are showing or not. It offends a good breeder to see a top-class dog beaten unjustly, no matter who owns the dog.

Sometimes I think of ways to improve the dog game, and it has occurred to me that one of our problems is that the dog world is divided into camps, neither of which empathizes with the other side's point of view. We seem to have one side doing the judging and the other side being the target of

Ch. Stoan's Yvonne von Yondo finishing her championship under Danish Judge Karl Otto Mastrup. Yvonne had many admirers and had an easy time completing her championship. However, her breeder and owner considered her to be a little too rectangular in proportions and too angulated to be considered correct.

that judging. It would be better if each group had constant reminders of just what is important.

If I had my way, every judge would be required to finish at least one dog every year. It would keep them ever-mindful of how hard it is to breed, or even to acquire a good dog, and how devastating it is to have a good one missed through inattention or incompetence by the judge, or put down for political reasons. Further, I would give the novice exhibitor five years in which to exhibit under the "parasite" status; thenceforth, he would be required to judge at least once a year in order to be eligible to enter dogs into exhibition. Anyone not willing to do their share of the judging would have to stay out of the showring. That would make the exhibitors aware of the necessity of courtesy—courtesy that does not interfere with the judging process or with the other exhibitors and that does not display poor sportsmanship when the better dog goes over the poorer dog.

I'm sure that my plan will never be adopted, but it doesn't really matter as long as we all are seeking the best interests of the sport of purebred dogs. It doesn't matter whether you serve in the capacity of exhibitor, breeder, and/or judge as long as you seek this goal. I firmly believe that if we want to realize a betterment of our game, we should all try to have a greater understanding of each other's perspective. There are no shortcuts—you have to get there step by step. Just remember that all of us are trying to get up the stairs together.

A part of that getting up the stairs involves people becoming fanciers of the breed in the truest sense of the term. This means having a clear and unbiased appreciation of quality in our sport and in our breed. Let me give you an example of what I mean. Sometimes I go to a show, and when somebody's dog wins over mine, I get my nose out of joint. I tell myself that my dog was the finest in the ring, and therefore his losing must be attributable to either a lack of ethics or a shortfall in competence on the part of the judge. I usually don't have to search far for a sympathetic ear. And therein lies the shoal that has scuttled many a breeder's dream of sailing upon the ocean called "success in the dog game."

We must guard against depending upon excuses to make losing in the showring palatable, for it can get to be a way of life that leads you downhill and away from your objectives. Once or twice a year, you may be the subject of judging gone awry, but the rest of the time, the person in the ring has tried to do an honest job. Rather than blaming the loss on the judge, always take time to sit back and really evaluate your competitors' dogs whenever your dog gets beaten.

Ask yourself if it could be that the other dog really had some particular virtue not as keenly expressed in your dog. Did you present your dog in his best light? Does your dog sport some problem that is small in your eyes but horrendous to most of the dog fancy? Is there some new direction your breeding plans should take in order to make your dogs more competitive in the future? If these questions don't yield the reason for your dog's lack of success, make a truly honest attempt to answer the really important question: "Have you eliminated kennel blindness from your personal list of problems?"

If you cannot appreciate a good specimen of the breed that is not related to your dog, then you should not classify yourself as a fancier of the breed. You are only a fancier of some particular kennel. While we are all aware that of the existence of different bloodlines, I'm not absolutely sure that we all understand how all of the various strains have their strengths and their shortcomings. We have variety in our breed and in the showring, and that is good! It is more than good—it is wonderful!

To a honest fancier of the breed, the most enjoyable times are those spent drinking in the beauty of a truly great animal. However, you can have too much of a good thing, for uniformity and sameness tend to dull your appreciation of such beauty. I actually would not enjoy seeing only my favorite style of Saint Bernard every time I put on my judge's hat and stepped into the ring. Variety is essential to hone your appreciation.

I grew to my maturity as a Saint Bernard fancier in the shadow of Sanctuary Woods, and my heart remains there. But I value virtue in every dog—I appreciate the good Saint Bernards of the entire world. If you are a true fancier of the breed, you, too, must admire every worthy Saint Bernard—no matter who owns him or what dogs are found on his pedigree chart.

Judges Who Fail to Put the Emphasis Where It Belongs

Who would like to tell me just what is the judge's job? I'll bet that your first inclination is to tell me that the task is to judge dogs. That doesn't tell me very much, because you haven't explained your terms. Let me offer a description.

We can all probably agree that we want the judge to carefully evaluate each dog and then give the top award to the best dog or dogs in the ring. We also want the judge to be pleasant, attractive, and of great renown. However, we are usually willing to forgive shortcomings in these areas as long as the best dogs win.

Standing outside the ring, many are not convinced that this happens much of the time. Many exhibitors are convinced that there is trouble with the judging of Saint Bernards. They observe that one day one dog will win, and the next day he will be out of the ribbons. Why is this? Those with a shallow perspective would have you believe that one of the judges has done a competent job of judging and the other has failed in his duty.

I want to present a different point of view. I am not going to discuss the unethical judge or the incompetent judge, but rather that 90 percent of the judging society who are reasonably competent and honestly trying to do a good job when they are making their awards.

Why is it, then, that when certain dogs are judged on two or three consecutive days, a different dog wins each day? I contend that the judges simply fail to place their emphasis on the same points. One judge will think that soundness is of utmost importance, the next will not place a dog with an inadequate head, and a third judge will prefer great size and substance. In my opinion, they are all in error. Judges who operate in this fashion just don't understand what makes one dog more deserving than the next. They fail to understand that the most important aspect of each individual dog is the overall package. They fail to understand that their favorite parts, aspects, or features must be a secondary consideration to the *total* dog.

In order to add to our understanding, I want to examine some of the thought processes that are used by various types of judges. One type of judge can be called the "fault judge." He will recognize a bad head and eliminate the dog from consideration immediately. Next, he will eliminate the badly proportioned and unbalanced dogs. Then he will move the dogs and eliminate the poor-moving animals. He will then make his placements among the remaining dogs. Because this method of judging is reasonable, rational, and readily understood, it is a dirty, rotten shame that it almost never identifies the best dog in the ring. Instead, this process of eliminating all of the dogs in the ring that have an obvious fault usually finds a fault-free, mediocre dog and gives him the top award.

So what is wrong with a fault-free dog? If the dog show is supposed to reflect the breeder's viewpoint, then finding a fault-free dog is not what dog shows are all about. The mediocre, fault-free, generic dog is an animal that no competent breeder would ever consider using. What breeders and, hence, judges, should be looking for is the dog with the greatest collection of *virtues*. The fault judge fails to understand that a lack of outstanding virtues is the greatest fault of all. The argument that this kind of judge usually fails to give the awards to the best dog is a strong one.

The next kind of judge is the "small-bucket judge." This judge is generally admired as being consistent. What makes this person consistent is that he has a limited number of features that are going to be evaluated. For example, this judge may want a very good head plus a great deal of substance, and nothing else matters. Serious problems in other aspects of the dog, such as bad temperament, poor proportions, or lack of soundness, will not affect this judge's placements.

I have more problem accepting the small-bucket judge than I do the fault judge. This type of judge becomes popular because he makes the exhibitors' and breeders' jobs easier. If only two or three aspects have to be correct, then the exhibitor's act of choosing a dog to show is simple. But it is the breeders who really benefit, because breeding for only a few aspects changes the breeder's task from a most excruciatingly difficult endeavor into a simple game of chance and numbers. This kind of judging makes the breed a collection of shallow, two- or three-dimensional animals. When the breed is afflicted with three or four of these kinds of judges, those few features become exaggerated. Once exaggerations become a requirement for winning and become well established in the breed, the breed loses its ability to accomplish its historic job and, hence, breed type is lost.

Can either the fault judge or the small-bucket judge find the best dog in the ring? Of course he can! It would not be that unusual for the fault judge to officiate in a ring where the best dog also has the fewest faults. In a similar vein, the small-bucket judge may occasionally face a collection of dogs wherein the best dog has among his outstanding virtues those few items that the judge of the day demands. Does this make having one of these judges an acceptable situation? I think not! These judges more often than not give the top award to a lesser animal. I just wish that they wouldn't do that!

Now, let's return to the seldom-used concept of the total dog and the rare judge who looks for this package. I refer to this type of person as a "total dog judge." This judge considers a dog to be more than a collection of pieces; he understands that any animal is greater than the sum of his parts. This judge tries to evaluate every significant aspect of every entry in the ring and then places the dogs in order of overall quality.

This style of judging is difficult and complex, especially when there is pressure to keep to a schedule. Should we accept any other style of judging? That depends. I personally accept any style of judging that results in my dog winning; I never refuse the points no matter what my opinion of the judging. However, I don't want you to adopt my rather self-centered philosophy. Most exhibitors, including me, feel that all is right in the dog world when the best dog wins, regardless of who owns that dog. My purpose here is to urge each of you to demand only that kind of judging.

Ch. Almshaus Just Joe Kool, CD, DD, WP, WPX, WPS, at the age of two years demonstrating his skills in an agility match. Joe was owned by Ray and Barbara Slish of Kent, Washington, and was bred by Libby Surface.

Ask yourself, what is the purpose of a dog show? Is it a contest for determining who can groom the best? Is it to find the best showman in the ring? The best trainer or handler? Although you have to wonder if these are not legitimate objectives after watching some judging performances, the consensus is that this is *not* why we have dog shows. Dog shows are a showcase for the breeder's art, and the point of dog shows is to demonstrate progress in breeding dogs and to identify worthy candidates for perpetuating the breed. We must then conclude that we are looking for the dog whose total being has the most virtue. Therefore, we must ask that the dog receiving the top award in every ring be the best overall specimen of the breed.

If this is what most of us want, why doesn't it happen more often? Why is it that judges almost never place the emphasis where it belongs—on the entire animal? Two things motivate judges *not* to adopt this philosophy. The first is that it is harder to evaluate twenty or twenty-five aspects than it is to just weigh the merits of three or four features. So sheer laziness explains why some judge this way. The other thing that pushes judges away from using the whole-dog concept is that they soon get the reputation for being inconsistent. Judges who want to be popular avoid the inconsistent tag like it was poison ivy. If a judge adopts the point of view that no single feature is more important than the collective merit of the entire animal, then he will be labeled inconsistent, incompetent, and/or unethical.

One of the reasons why judges who evaluate the entire dog get these labels is because it is very difficult for outside observers to follow the judging. The usual rap on a judge who can't be followed by the ringside experts is that there is something wrong with the judge. Have you ever noticed that no judge ever goes outside the ring to do his judging? Is it obvious that there is a reason why the judge does his job entirely while inside the ring? Could it be that it is not possible to evaluate the entire animal from any other location? Yet many a ringside expert will soundly denigrate a judge's awards based upon only that evidence available to him from outside the ring. This attitude fails to recognize that, while some features are readily determined by standing well away from the dog and simply looking at him, most judging also requires a close-up observation and putting your hands on the dog.

Let me give you a few examples. The person outside the ring probably can't tell that the dog with the great-looking head has a wry mouth, or that

Ch. Lynchcreek's Executive, CGC, DD (Boss) is owned by Clyde and Kathy Dunphy of Carlinville, Illinois, and was bred by Candy Blancher of Eatonville, Washington. Boss has had an outstanding show career: he was the number-one Saint Bernard for 1995 in almost all rating systems. He was awarded "Select" at two SBCA National Specialty Shows and was Best of Breed at the 1996 National Specialty. Boss also earned his Draft Dog title and was awarded the SBCA's Stud Dog of the Year at the 1996 National Specialty. This dog's greatest assets in the showring are his great proportions and his extremely good movement.

Ch. Sanctuary Woods Litany being awarded Best of Breed by Judge John Carey at the Greater Washington Saint Bernard Club's 1975 Specialty Show. Her breeder, Beatrice M. Knight, is standing between the judge and the handler. This event happened on the day after Litany was awarded Best of Breed at the Saint Bernard Club of America's 1975 National Specialty. Because the judging of the National Specialty the day before was completed in the dark with the ring lighted by the headlights of exhibitors' cars, there are no good photographs of that event. Litany, co-owned by Elizabeth Surface and Stan Zielinski, was also awarded Best of Opposite Sex the year before at the 1974 National Specialty. Of interest is the fact that Litany whelped a litter ten days after this picture was taken.

the dog with great substance has only hairspray and a blow dryer to thank for his appearance, or that the great massive dog is only overly fat and has the muscle tone of a newborn baby. Those outside the ring should keep in mind that what you see isn't necessarily what you get! Those inside the ring should learn to live with the slurs on their reputation and just judge dogs the right way.

Now, let's discuss the process of finding the total dog. There are three aspects of the total dog that need to be understood: beauty, soundness, and temperament. All must be correct or the dog fails to be an adequate representative of the breed. A dog must be scored "adequate or better" in each of these categories or he should be dismissed from consideration. After having found the dogs that score "adequate or better" in each category, then, and only then, should the judge start looking for the dog with the most merit.

This search for the best dog can be accomplished in many ways. You could have a score card and a point scale for various virtues, and use these to arrive at a tally of points. This is much too cumbersome of a method to be used by a judge in the ring. It is, however, a great learning tool for novices who have not yet developed their judge's eye. I highly recommend that you try to do this at least once.

The judges whom I most admire go through a process that is almost like this tally procedure. When I ask for a description of their process, they all tell me of a method of unconscious and automatic score keeping that happens as they examine their classes. Their eye observes the total dog and rates him with respect to his competition without their having to put any conscious effort into thinking about it. Oh, how I wish I could do that!

Let me tell you about the mental gymnastics that I have to go through while evaluating a class of dogs. I start by creating a mental dog in my mind. This dog is to serve as an imaginary mate for the dogs in the ring. Therefore, when I'm judging males, the mental dog is a bitch; when I'm judging females, my mental dog is a male. My mental dog is a plain, brown-paper-wrapper sort of animal that is not spectacular in any aspect, but he is free of any significant faults. Every feature of this dog in my mind's eye would be graded as "good" or "correct."

Then I start my game. I tell myself that I am to get the pick puppy from my mental dog, and my job is to choose the mate for my mental dog from the dogs in front of me. In short, my judging process consists of answering the question, "Which dog would I choose to be bred to my mental dog, assuming that I want to produce the best litter possible?" This makes me concentrate on the virtues on display in that ring without being overly concerned with faults. This thought process also compels me to look at the entire dog rather than just my favorite pieces

I don't know if my judging method would be of any use to anybody else, but it works for me. I have included it here simply as food for thought and, perhaps, a topic of conversation among those with nothing better to discuss. The important message is that the judge's job is to find the best overall dog, and this requires that the *whole* dog be judged, not just the judge's favorite features.

Still, some will claim that dog shows are naught but beauty contests. "Not so!" I must decry loudly. Let those who feel thus involve themselves with porcelain statuettes! Leave the real dogs to those who believe that you maintain breed type by producing dogs able to perform their historic tasks, to those who understand the importance of the total-dog concept.

Taking a ride in an antique auto are Lontanpark Colbran and Australian Champion Elkeef Cutencuddly, both owned by Judy and Susan Teniswood of Tasmania, Australia. The car is a 1906 Alldays & Onions automobile.

The Essence of Breed Type

A few years ago, while attending an educational seminar for dog-show judges, I heard a Poodle breeder claim that anyone who wanted to do a good job of judging in any breed had only to understand the first paragraph of that Standard and find the dog described there. It was his contention that the opening paragraph of each Standard gave the general description of the breed and that the description invariably contained the essence of the breed. He further claimed that a judge's sole responsibility was to rank the class before him on how close each individual animal came to being a Poodle, a Collie, or whatever breed was supposed to be in the ring.

His words made me think—an unpleasant activity that I do only under duress—about the Saint Bernard Standard. I had to conclude that his statements held true for my breed also.

Although others have made a point of the importance of our Standard's first paragraph, I felt obliged to add my thoughts. First, let me quote that paragraph.

> Powerful, proportionately tall figure, strong and muscular in every part, with powerful head and most intelligent expression. In dogs with a dark mask the expression appears more stern, but never ill-natured.

These words place four unique demands upon breed type:

1. *Physical Character of the Overall Dog:* Is described by the phrase, "Powerful . . . , strong and muscular in every part."
2. *Body Configuration:* Is defined by the term, "proportionately tall figure."

Ch. Chad's Raleigh with one of his kids. Raleigh is showing his son how to stand on a grooming table to get ready for a show. They live at Chad's Kennels in Chandler, Arizona, with Jack and Carol Terrio.

(Above): Ch. Revilo's Curly Sue, owned and bred by Diana and William Oliver, being shown to the Best of Breed award. Curly Sue is an example of correct type in a longhaired bitch. (Below): Ch. Dein Hard's Kleona, bred by Karin Byrevik of Oesterbybruck, Sweden. This bitch has a lovely expression, broad muzzle, and wide skull.

3. *Uniqueness of the Head:* Is required by the phrase, "with powerful head."
4. *Personality and Temperament:* Is implied by the phrase, "and most intelligent expression. In dogs with a dark mask the expression appears more stern, but never ill-natured."

PHYSICAL CHARACTER OF THE OVERALL DOG

In dealing with the phrase, "Powerful . . . , strong and muscular in every part," let's examine the word "powerful." I interpret "powerful" to mean having great power or force—being physically strong and imposing in size. "Powerful" here is used in the same capacity that you would use it when referring to a bulldozer. Synonyms that might have been used are "forceful," "strong," "mighty," "potent," and "massive." The word "powerful" suggests great force or strength. It also suggests capability of exerting great force or overcoming strong resistance

Now let's add the phrase "strong and muscular in every part" to the word "powerful." To some, this may seem to be simple repetition for emphasis. To me, the combined phrase, in this context, conjures up a picture of a large, strong athlete. Because Standards, by their very nature, are a description of the ideal, I maintain that this phrase calls for an animal with the strength, agility, grace, coordination, and soundness of a world-class athlete. Obviously, it is describing an athlete that can easily jump over obstacles, scramble up steep, rocky slopes, or plow through chest-high snowdrifts.

Because it is essential for a Saint Bernard to be powerful, we must recognize that quality and not become confused. The argument has been made that simply being big or massive fulfills this requirement. Let us denounce such foolishness. A dog with adequate size can fail to be powerful. An unsound dog is not powerful. A dog that slides his feet along the ground rather than picking them up and putting them where they belong is not powerful. A soft, lumbering, sloppy, clumsy clod of an animal is not powerful. Obviously, Saint Bernards can be too small to be powerful. In the context of their historic task of traversing deep snow and mountainous terrain, dogs that are too small would be at an extreme disadvantage. There is no purpose in belaboring this point.

There is a less obvious condition that needs our attention. Saint Bernards can also be too big! Extra size can come in two configurations—massiveness and altitude—and either can be incorrect. If the massiveness is created by the accumulation of large amounts of fat or other soft tissue, the dog is not powerful. The consequences of that condition should be so patently obvious that the subject of fat or soft dogs needs no further discussion.

Then there is the dog that is too tall. Just like people, dogs can have an extremely large frame (skeleton) and inadequate muscles and tendons to make it work. It is hard for these dogs to be athletic; they simply lack the vigor. If the dog's entire supply of energy is just barely sufficient to get him from one spot to another, he fails to fit the picture of "powerful."

BODY CONFIGURATION

Now let's look at the term "proportionately tall figure." You may wonder at the reason for including this phrase as an essential ingredient of correct breed type. Wolves, coyotes, feral dogs (Dingoes, etc.), and Doberman Pinschers are examples of proportionately tall figures. German Shepherds, Rottweilers, Golden Retrievers, and Cocker Spaniels are examples of proportionately long figures.

The correct locomotion of any breed is dictated by its ideal configuration. The way in which a dog moves is determined by the way in which parts of the body fit together and work together. Body proportions, the relative lengths of various bones, and the attachment points of muscles and tendons all play a big role in determining details of gait. One obvious example is the American version of the German Shepherd. This breed's long bones, long body, and extreme angulation impart a mode of locomotion that is unique for the breed. Indeed, the German Shepherd gait is considered an essential part of breed type. Examples of extreme conformation dictating correct locomotion for the breed include the waddle of the English Bulldog and the light, quick step of the Fox Terrier. Once correct conformation for a breed is defined, then a unique form of locomotion is dictated.

In asking for a proportionately tall figure, the authors of the Standard have demanded a unique conformation characteristic that says much about

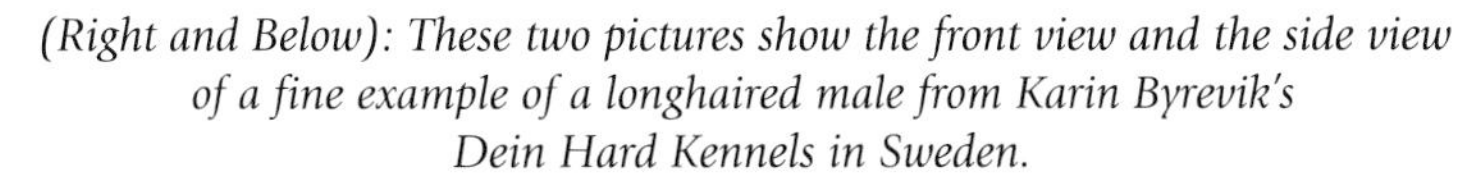

(Right and Below): These two pictures show the front view and the side view of a fine example of a longhaired male from Karin Byrevik's Dein Hard Kennels in Sweden.

Saint Bernards love to ride in cars. Here, a handsome shorthaired male, bred by Karin Byrevik of Sweden, has decided that he's staying in his Volvo station wagon.

how the breed is to move. Many fanciers of Saint Bernards admire the exaggerated gait of the German Shepherd Dog and hence strive to incorporate the long body and extreme angulation of that breed into ours. My response is that a German Shepherd body is not correct for a Saint Bernard, and a proportionately tall figure is an essential part of correct Saint Bernard breed type.

UNIQUENESS OF THE HEAD

A lot is implied by the phrase, "with powerful head." It is again the use of the word "powerful" that needs discussion. Synonyms that might have been used are "imposing," "impressive," and "massive."

To be imposing requires the Saint Bernard head to be large, massive, and big. To be called "powerful," the head of a large dog must not only be large, it must also be large in proportion to the dog. A Great Dane is a large dog, and, in general, the Great Dane is larger than a Saint Bernard. A correct Great Dane has a very large head that matches his very large body. You would not, however, use the term "powerful" to describe the head of a Great Dane. A correct Saint Bernard head is more massive, both proportionately and actually, than the head of a correct Great Dane and, hence, is correctly described as "powerful."

"Powerful" also implies the concept of imposing or impressive. To the true connoisseur of Saint Bernards, an imposing or impressive head is both massive and correct. I, of course, equate beauty and correctness whenever I discuss Saint Bernard head type. It follows, therefore, that a head that is big and ugly fails to be impressive and thus is not powerful. This opening paragraph does not spell out the details of correct head type; those details are fleshed out in the body of the Breed Standard. You just need to remember that the phrase "with powerful head" implies a head that is both big and beautiful is essential for correct breed type.

PERSONALITY AND TEMPERAMENT

My contention that the phrase, "and most intelligent expression. In dogs with a dark mask the expression appears more stern, but never ill-natured," is talking about personality and temperament has caused some disagreement. Some people say that this part of the Standard discusses only the expression and nothing else. I simply don't agree.

Why is it that we put any importance on expression? The reason is because we look at expression as a mirror of character and temperament. We are offended when anybody or anything looks friendly but acts vicious. Surely, nobody would advance the argument that it is all right for a dog to be highly reprehensible in character, nature, or conduct as long as he has a friendly, intelligent expression. It seems obvious that this part of the Standard demands that Saint Bernards actually be intelligent and never be ill-natured; it is not sufficient to have just the external signs of being so.

Now look at that part that says, "In dogs with a dark mask the expression appears more stern." Have you ever considered the implication here—that in dogs without a dark mask, the expression does not appear more stern? I have always interpreted this phrase to mean that not having a dark mask is an acceptable feature of the breed. In this context, I believe that "stern" was used to mean serious, not bad tempered. Otherwise, this sentence from the Standard would make little sense.

Any dog that fails any one of these four criteria has nothing but his registration papers to uphold his claim to being a Saint Bernard. If you want the term "quality" to apply to your Saint Bernard, he must incorporate correct breed type as defined by the four essential ingredients of the first paragraph of the Standard.

Ch. Stoan's Nadia of Klafa, HOF, who represents the kind of pedigree excellence that is essential in producing a line with merit. Nadia was the SBCA's Brood Bitch of the Year; her littermate, Ch. Stoan's Nicholas of Klafa, HOF, was the SBCA's Stud Dog of the Year for two years; her sire, Ch. Mia Faithful Friend, HOF, was awarded SBCA's Stud Dog of the Year; and her dam, Stoan's Klara of Duf, HOF, was the SBCA's Brood Bitch of the Year.

The Three Varieties of Saint Bernards

I have a friend who judges dog shows but comes from another working breed. Sometimes I have to wonder about my friend, because he takes great delight in harassing me. The last time we were on a panel together, he accosted me at the judges' dinner with his new philosophy about the Saint Bernard breed.

"Hey, Stan," he exclaimed loudly, "I bet you think that Saint Bernards come in two varieties, don't you?" Since he now had the attention of most of the other judges, I retorted heatedly, "You're damn tootin! The official Standard says that there are two varieties and I, as an expert on the breed, concur!" "Well, you and your Standard are both wrong!" he said laughingly to the now-gathered crowd of judges. "I think not!" I retorted doggedly.

Then, with a nasty grin and a twinkle in his eye, he challenged, "I'll bet you a bottle of Jack Daniels that I can get both you and everybody here licensed to judge Saint Bernards to agree that there are three varieties of Saint Bernards." I was so indignant at this that I agreed to the bet and told him that he had set himself up for a losing argument.

This, then, is the gist of what he said to us.

> I've noticed on a couple of occasions when Stan and I judged Saint Bernards on successive days that not only did we put up different dogs, but also that we had different dogs shown to us. Since I'm a much better judge than Stan, I could attribute the different dogs winning to the fact that Stan's judging was not quite up to the quality of mine! However, I did not understand why dogs entered one day were not entered the day before or the day after. When I asked him why he thought this happened, Stan told me that he, as a breeder judge, attracted the good specimens, while the bad dogs awaited some jerk to judge that would not know the difference.
>
> Not being one to accept such an insult quietly, I asked Stan why, since he was such an attractive judge to the good dogs, were not the big winners from the local specialty show being exhibited under him? Stan's answer was that I should take in a couple of specialty shows and arrive at my own conclusion. So I did just that.
>
> What I found was another kind of Saint Bernard. In talking to some of the exhibitors, I was informed that here was the real quality in the breed! And, of course, I had never seen dogs such as these entered under me, as they were only shown to those experts with the special insight that recognizes the essence of the breed; to those few knowledgeable judges with an appreciation of a truly superior quality.

Ch. Slaton's Piece Of The Action, CD, CGC, HOF, POE, with owner Jerri Hobbs giving cart rides at a company picnic in 1992. Here is a great example of a wonderful disposition combined with working ability. As if that were not sufficient, he later became the nation's top Saint Bernard in the showring, setting the breed's record of twenty-two all-breed Best In Show awards.

Excalibur's Dream Weaver, UD, four-year-old bitch, owned and bred by Barry and Judy Roland of Ellenwood, Georgia, participating in an agility clinic in spring 1990.

Upon contemplation of this revelation, the reality of the situation became clear to me. There are really three varieties of what I had previously considered to be one breed. There were the dogs to which I gave awards, there were the dogs that Stan Zielinski puts up, and there were the dogs upon which only the anointed passed judgment.

My friend's discourse thus completed, I looked around the group of listening judges and retorted, "Does anybody know where I can pick up a bottle of Jack Daniels at a good price?" I was tempted to tell my friend that there were also at least two more varieties in Europe but decided that he should not be given any more ammunition with which to harangue upon the subject of Saint Bernards.

Nevertheless, I thought that I would take this opportunity to document this concept that we, here in the United States, are dealing with three different philosophies about the ideal Saint Bernard. My names for the camps that champion these three philosophies are "The American Show Dog," "The American Specialty Exhibit," and "The Functional Saint Bernard." We have zealots in each of the camps who believe strongly that perfection lies in the direction advocated by themselves.

THE AMERICAN SHOW DOG

This is the generic fault-free dog that goes to the group with major expectations of winning. Much of what constitutes breed type is very often forgiven in these dogs; that is, they can have adequate breed type or not—it's not important. This dog's essential requirements for success for are: (1) he has great presence or showmanship combined with a talented handler, (2) he has an impressive side gait, which means that he has great reach and drive while moving with a strong back; in short, he moves in a manner appropriate only to the American style of German Shepherds, and (3) he has a good bite and a set of four reasonably sound legs.

THE AMERICAN SPECIALTY EXHIBIT

This is the dog of gross exaggeration that is entered with high hopes under certain select breeder judges. Considered as being unimportant in this animal is any tendency toward athleticism or soundness; also of little value is correct temperament. Necessary and sufficient factors for success are: (1) an exaggerated, large head and muzzle, (2) the illusion of substance given by aspects such as elephantlike legs, spongy muscles and other tissue, and folds of loose-hanging skin (which is the description of a wet dog), and (3) a long, luxuriant coat that has been fluffed and sculptured into the latest style or fad; short-haired dogs are almost universally barred from this category.

THE FUNCTIONAL SAINT BERNARD

This is a dog that looks like a Saint Bernard yet retains the ability to perform his historical tasks. This dog features a sound mind in a sound body. You want and expect this dog to have the intelligence and temperament to be both a family companion and a

Here is a demonstration that some dogs can do it all—obedience, drafting, and conformation championships. Ch. Keepsakes Bonneville, CD, DD, TDD, and his dam, Ch. Cache Retreat Up Tempo, CD, DD, pull a wagon with their owner, Larry Jech, in a local parade. The Saint Bernard Club of Greater Phoenix participates in this event every year.

Ch. Stoan's XL Duncan de la Casa at three years of age is owned by Jim and Debra McCracken (shown in picture) and Joan Zielinski, who all live in Kent, Washington. Duncan is a very masculine, shorthaired male weighing 185 pounds and measuring 32 inches at the withers. Duncan was sired by Ch. Stoan's Fortuno of Copper Mtn out of Ch. Stoan's Isabelle v. Encore. He was bred by Janet Mansfield and Joan Zielinski.

protector of the children. The important features of this dog are: (1) he conforms to the Standard without either exaggerations or shortcomings, (2) he is a sound and athletic animal, and (3) he has a truly saintly disposition.

It should go without saying that I belong to one of these camps, and my choice of words in describing the categories should make it so obvious that I need not mention it. The only significant question before us is, "Which of these camps (or should we say religions?) represents the true path to enlightenment?"

Answering this question is the equivalent of arguing which religion is the true one. The members of each camp have their reasons or rationalizations for their positions, and they are not subject to being persuaded that their logic is in error. I can make this statement because I have tried, on many occasions, to convert some of my heathen brethren

These two pictures were taken at the Saint Bernard Club of Puget Sound's 1997 Weight Pull and Harness Match event. The top picture shows the course used for the event called the "Travois Maze." This is a timed event with severe penalties for each pin knocked over. The lower picture shows Vicki Graves and her four-month-old puppy, Vicdory's Amber, completing a very good turn with only a few pins dislodged. Some dogs knock down most of the pins.

and sistern without the slightest bit of success. I have found that there is no hope that those who do not believe as I do can be transformed into reasonable, rational human beings. And I want to wish a lot of luck to anybody who thinks that they can convert me!

Is there some middle ground upon which a compromise is possible? I'm afraid that the answer is, "Probably not." The American Show Dog usually is of a rectangular construction so that it can move like a German Shepherd. The American Specialty Exhibit is almost always too wet to be functional or athletic. The Functional Saint Bernard is normally too short-coupled and too moderate to fit into the other two categories. Occasionally, some dog will be a reasonable compromise between two of the categories, but a dog fitting into all three categories is almost never seen. I would like to think that we are all looking for that rare animal that would be successful in all three categories, but that's not what I believe. I am afraid that the individuals involved in the fancy are all working very hard to make the three varieties more and more diverse.

The best we can probably do is agree that we disagree and applaud, with some sort of enthusiasm, the successes of those in the other camps. We only have a problem when all three varieties are competing in the same ring. Everybody wants to win, but that is impossible. Everyone argues that the reasons why their dog fits into their chosen variety or category is the reason why they should win. This is, of course, utter nonsense. Winning is only the expression of the judge's privately held opinion and has nothing to do with how well your dog fulfills the requirements of your favorite variety.

While your opinion will often differ from some particular judge, it is your very own personal opinion, and you have the right to both retain and defend it. So, go ahead and proselytize among the unbelievers, for there is nothing wrong with you advocating your position as long and as loud and as hard as you can.

On the other hand, there is nothing to be gained by any of us getting excessively emotional about our personal version of correct breed type. Let's all lighten up a bit! Let us resolve to smile and congratulate the winner, and to save our recriminations until after we have cleared ringside. There are good Saint Bernards in all three varieties, and maybe we should all learn to appreciate the real quality Saint Bernards whenever and wherever they occur—especially when such dogs appear outside of our comfort zone.

Ch. Skycroft's Lady Kristal, owned by Mr. VonArmin, is being awarded Winners Bitch by Judge Alfred Moulton at the Northern New Jersey Saint Bernard Club's 1968 Specialty Show. This is an example of a champion quality shorthaired bitch of that era and demonstrates the change in philosophy of the mainstream Saint Bernard fancy that has occurred over a thirty-year time span.

List of Abbreviations Used in This Book

Abbreviation	Translation of Abbreviation	Remarks
"A" match	A match held under the "A" set of rules	A mock dog show held under AKC rules at which no points or titles are awarded. Usually such matches are considered to be a qualifying event prior to a club being allowed to put on a real dog show.
AKC	The American Kennel Club	The internationally recognized governing body of dog-show activities and stud-book registration in the United States.
AM. CAN.	American Kennel Club and Canadian Kennel Club	The award (a conformation championship title or an obedience trial title) has been granted by both organizations.
AX	Agility Excellent	A title awarded by the AKC for successfully competing in an Agility Trial.
"B" match	A match held under the "B" set of rules	A mock dog show held under AKC rules at which no points or titles are awarded. Usually such matches are considered to be practice for the exhibitors, the dogs, the judges, and the show-giving clubs.
BOB	Best of Breed	An award given at each show (and in each breed at all-breed shows) to the dog adjudged to be the best specimen of the breed.
BOS	Best of Opposite Sex to Best of Breed	An award given at each show (and in each breed at all-breed shows) to the dog of opposite sex to the Best of Breed dog that is adjudged to be the best specimen of that sex.
BOW	Best of Winners	An award given at each show (and in each breed at all-breed shows) to the dog adjudged to be the superior between the Winners Dog and Winners Bitch.

Abbreviation	Translation of Abbreviation	Remarks
CD	Companion Dog	A title awarded by the American Kennel Club for performance in the obedience ring. This is the first and simplest in a series of obedience titles.
CDX	Companion Dog Excellent	A title awarded by the American Kennel Club for performance in the obedience ring. This is the second and more advanced title in a series of obedience titles.
CGC	Canine Good Citizen	A title awarded by the American Kennel Club. This title is primarily given after testing the dog's temperament and behavior in controlled situations.
Ch.	Champion	This dog has been awarded its Championship title. Unless otherwise noted, this award is given by the American Kennel Club.
DD	Drafting Dog	A title awarded by the Saint Bernard Club of America for successfully completing the requirements at a cart-pulling event.
DKCh.	Danish Champion	A title awarded by the Kennel Club of Denmark.
FCI	The Federation Canine International	The governing body of most dog shows held outside of the United States, but does not control any of the stud-book registrations.
HOF	Hall of Fame	A title awarded by the Saint Bernard Club of America for Excellence. The awards are given for both producing offspring of quality and/or outstanding accomplishments in the showrings and other areas of performance.
INTUCh.	International Champion	A title awarded by the FCI.
NA	Novice Agility	A title awarded by the AKC.
NUCh.	Norwegian Champion	A title awarded by the Norway Kennel Club.
OTCh.	Obedience Trial Champion	A title given by the American Kennel Club for earning a set number of points in obedience trials.

Abbreviation	Translation of Abbreviation	Remarks
POE	Plateau of Excellence	A title given by the Saint Bernard Club of America for performance significantly beyond the requirements for entry into the Hall of Fame.
RWB	Reserve Winners Bitch	An award given at each show (and in each breed at all-breed shows) to the female dog adjudged to be the superior of the dogs entered in the regular classes after the dog awarded Winners Bitch has been eliminated.
RWD	Reserve Winners Dog	An award given at each show (and in each breed at all-breed shows) to the male dog adjudged to be the superior of the dogs entered in the regular classes after the dog awarded Winners Dog has been eliminated.
SBCA	The Saint Bernard Club of America	The official AKC parent club for the Saint Bernard breed and a member club of the AKC.
SBCPS	The Saint Bernard Club of Puget Sound	The regional Saint Bernard club licensed by the AKC to put on dog shows and to promote the interests of the breed in the Seattle area. (There are over thirty such regional Saint Bernard clubs throughout the United States.)
SUCh.	Swedish Champion	A title awarded by the Kennel Club of Sweden.
TD	Tracking Dog	A title given by the AKC for successfully competing in a Tracking Trial.
UD	Utility Dog	An advanced obedience trial title awarded by the AKC.
UDT	Utility Dog/Tracking Dog	A title given by the AKC for dogs who have both their UD and TD titles.
UDX	Utility Dog Excellent	An advanced obedience trial title awarded by the AKC.
UK	United Kingdom	Another term for England.

Abbreviation	Translation of Abbreviation	Remarks
VST	Variable Surface Tracking Dog	An advanced Tracking Trial title awarded by the AKC.
WB	Winners Bitch	An award given at each show (and in each breed at all-breed shows) to the female dog adjudged to be the superior of the dogs entered in the regular classes. (Note: Does not include the dogs entered in the BOB class or in the Veterans Bitch Class.)
WD	Winners Dog	An award given at each show (and in each breed at all-breed shows) to the male dog adjudged to be the superior of the dogs entered in the regular classes.
WDCh.	Working Dog Champion	An award given by the Saint Bernard Club of America for combining specific awards in the fields of weight pulling, draft tests, obedience trials, and tracking trials.
WP	Weight Puller	A title awarded by the Saint Bernard Club of America. This is the simplest of the awards given for performance at weight-pulling events.
WPS	Weight Puller Superior	A title awarded by the Saint Bernard Club of America. This is the third and most stringent of the awards given for performance at weight-pulling events.
WPX	Weight Puller Excellent	A title awarded by the Saint Bernard Club of America. This is the second and more advanced of the awards given for performance at weight-pulling events.

Index

(Page numbers in brackets denote picture captions.)

abbreviations, 169
abilities and instincts, 3
ability to perform, 2
acceptable or better, 150
accomplished breeder, 138
accumulated virtues, 131
Actongold, [66]
adequate or better, 157
adult coat, 117
afterbirth, 96
aggression, 146
aggressive, 34
aggressiveness, 42
agility, 155, 160
agility trial(s), [38], [78]
AKC registrability, 110
AKC registration, 109
AKC titles, 110
Almshaus, [49], [74], [129], [155]
alterations, 32
altitude, 161
American Kennel Club, 150
American show dog, 165, 168
American specialty exhibit, 165, 168
angulation, 1, 13, 31, 36, 112
antifreeze, 103
appreciation of quality, 153
appreciation of true type, 138
Arthur Hessar, [67], [69]
athlete, 160
athletic, 25
athletic animal, 167
athletic endeavor, 4
Australia/Australian, [80], [144], [158]
avalanche/avalanches, 3, 4, 5
avoiding injury, 104
awards, 151, 154

baby talk, 106
baby teeth, 63
back, 9, 30, 33, 37
bad temperament, 154
bad tempered, 163
badly proportioned, 154
balance, 5, 25, 33
barrel chest, 112, 146
Beatrice Knight, [iv], vii, [53], [81]
beautiful curve, 66
beauty, 116, 157
being handled, 106
belly, 9, 30, 36, 112
Belyn's, [2], [28], [39], [57], [61], [68], [84]
Benbaron's, [78], [83]
Bergundtal, [92]
Bernesgarden's, [70]
best litter possible, 158
best overall dog, 158
biased selection, 139
bicycling, 34
big, 5, 49, 160, 162,
big winners, 164
bitch, 100, 101, 102, 105, 133
bitchy dogs, 140
bite, 29, 65
black-faced, 84, 85
blaze, 9, 11, 33
blind, 111
Bliss Farms, [84]
blow dryer, 157
blue eye, 111, 127
blue slip, 122
body, 30
body configuration, 159, 161
body language, 79, 106
body length, 26
body proportions, 161
body type, 4
bond, 117
bone, 1, 5, 47
born strong, 95
Boroniahil, [x]
boxlike muzzle, 148
bred back to, 130
breech births, 96
breed, 126
breed quality, 152
breed standard, 150
breed type, 69, 121, 145, 151, 155, 158, 159, 161, 162, 165
breeder/breeders, 108, 111, 120, 123, 139, 152, 153, 155
breeder of quality, 131, 134
breeder's art, 155
breeder's eye, 142
breeder's job, 140
breeder's viewpoint, 154
breeding agreement, 123
breeding contract, 122
breeding dogs, 125
breeding goals, 131, 142
breeding program, 130, 134
breeding stock, 111
breeding to a littermate, 139
bridge, 14
bridge of the muzzle, 61
brindle, 11
brisket, 30
broken, 11
broken muzzle, 14
brown eyes, 127
brown nose, 111
bumps, 148
bunny-hop, 114
Burestubli, [67]
burr, 8, 11, 81, 82
bushy, 10, 32
buyer rights, 121
buying a puppy, 116

Cache Retreat, [47], [54], [58], [64], [115]
caesarean section, 96, 97, 99
canine teeth, 63
care and feeding, 124
care and welfare, 143
care of puppies, 95
carting events, 90
Chad's, [40], [72], [92], [159]
champions, 115
character, 34, 162
cheek bones/ cheeks, 7, 11, 16, 28, 54, 57, 69, 70, 72, 76, 112
Cherryacre's, [121], [123]
chest, 9, 30
chewing, 117
chiseled appearance, 148
choosing a breeder, 119

choppy steps, 34
cleft palate, 111
clip the toenails, 102
clod, 160
cloddy, 145
clumsiness, 25, 33
coat/coat type, 9, 32, 102, 118
collagen, 45, 46
collar, 9
color, 9, 32
colostrum, 99, 100
combination vaccine, 106
comfort zone, 130
commercial outlets, 119
compensating virtues, 139
competence, 153
competence of judges, 152
competitors' efforts, 143
complimentary types, 139
concerned breeder, 120
conditioning, 4, 114
conformation, 4
congenital defects, 110
conjunctiva, 77
consistent improvement, 130
convergent, 62
coordination, 160
co-ownership, 110
co-ownership agreement, 122–123
coronavirus, 123
correct breed type, 163, 168
correct conformation, 161
correct height, 52
correct movement, 146
correct proportions, 145, 146
cowhocked/cowhocks, 10, 11, 37, 103, 113
crabbing, 33
crooked fronts, 103
crossing over, 34
croup, 21, 30, 31, 37
crowded teeth, 64
curly, 10

dam, 120
D'Aosta, [37]
dark mask, 7, 162
deaf, 111
deep snow, 4
deeply pendant, 7, 66, 68
Dein Hard's, [160], [161]
Denoncourt's, [42]
dentition, 63
depth of flew, 68
depth of muzzle, 59, 61, 68
desire to breed, 108
deviant behavior, 44
dewclaws, 9, 11, 101, 102, 123
dewlap, 8, 11, 30
discipline, 108
dish-faced, 14
distemper, 123
divergent, 62
doggy bitches, 140
dog-pound fodder, 138
dominant, 127
double coated, 32
down-faced, 14, 62
drafting, [166]
dry, 26
dry animal, 46
dry dogs, 45
dry mouth, 68

ear/ears, 8, 26, 54, 71, 79, 81, 82, 84
ear color, 27
ear set, 69, 82
ear shape and texture, 27
ear size, 28
easy keepers, 141
easy steps, 144
eating dangerous objects, 103
Elation, [44]
elbow dysplasia, 46
elbows, 30, 31
elegance, 5
elephant legs, 1
eliminating faults, 134
Elkeef, [114], [158]
Engler's, [50]
entire dog, 131, 138, 140
entire head, 148
entropion, 77
essence of the breed, 159, 164
even bite, 7, 11, 112
exaggerated, 5
exaggeration/exaggerations, 1, 5, 155, 167
Excalibur's, [4], [165]
excess, 1
excess skin, 45, 47
excessive growth, 103
excessive shedding, 119
excessive weight, 146
excuses, 153
exercise, 104, 105
exhibitors, 150, 151, 152, 155
expectations, 123
experts, 87, 164
expression, 25, 26, 27, 53, 54, 76, 79, 82, 83, 159, 160, 162, 163
extreme, 1
extreme angulation, 161
extremes, 146
eye/eyes, 7, 8, 26, 54, 69, 70, 72, 75, 76, 77, 79, 84, 102, 112
eye color, 27, 75
eye placement, 27
eyelids, 8, 27, 75, 76, 77, 79

facial markings, [103]
facts and fables, 2
fad, 5, 47
fails to gain weight, 98
failure to gain weight, 101
family companion, 165
family pet, 111
famous champion, 140
fanciers, 153
fashion, 5
fashionable, 4, 5
fat, 161
fat dog, 1
fat legs, 1
(fault) aesthetic function, 90
(fault) current function, 90
(fault) difficult, 91
(fault) forbidding, 91
(fault) minor, 91
(fault) past function, 90
(fault) trivial, 91
(fault) very serious, 91
fault/faults, 10, 87, 89, 90, 91, 92, 130
fault judge, 154, 155
fault-free dog, 154
faulty movement, 146
faulty temperament, 146
feature pedigree diagram, 131, 133, 136, 137
feeding, 100
feet, 4, 9, 31, 32
fenced yard, 108
first experience, 142
first glance, 150
first shots, 106
flag/flag tail, 10, 11, 32
flap, 8, 11, 82
flat feet, 103, 113
flatness, 98, 101
fleas, 102
flew/flews, 7, 11, 15, 29, 54, 64, 66, 67, 68, 79, 112, 149
flyer, 141
food, 104
foot, 22, 89
forelegs, 31
forequarters, 31
Forever, [83]
freckles, 85
Fred Anderson, [126]
free-roaming, 108
friendly, 3, 25, 34, 163
friendly dogs, 120
front and rear gaiting, 33

front dewclaws, 31
function, 1, 4, 5, 90
functional Saint Bernard, 165, 168
functional teeth, 64
furrow/furrows, 7, 17, 54, 60, 69, 73, 74, 112, 148

gait, 25, 33
gaiting faults, 33
gene pair, 127
gene pool, 130
general, 7
general appearance, 25, 150
general description, 159
generic dog, 146, 154
genes, 127
genetic inheritance, 127, 139
genetic makeup, 126
genetic recipe, 139
Georgean Ralston, [126]
glossary, 11
golden mean, 1
good family, 141
good home, 95
good homes, 107
good specimens, 164
grace, 4, 160
grading, 112
grading puppies, 110, 115
grading the litter, 111
great bitch, 141
great stud dog, 141
great substance, 145
green needle, 144
gregarious, 3, 120
grooming, 117, 118, 151
gross exaggeration, 165
guarantee, 110, 122, 123
guard dogs, 109
guidelines, 138, 149

hackneyed, 113
hackneyed motion, 34
hairspray, 157
half mask, 33, 84, 85
half-vast methods, 128
hallmark of the breed, 146
hard, firm muscle, 31
harmony of the whole, 151
harness match, [72], [167]
haunches, 9, 11
haw/haws, 11, 75, 76, 77
head, 5, 7, 26, 27, 53, 54, 55, 56, 69, 73
head carriage, 23
head proportions, 58
head quality, 142
head type, 1, 64
head-to-body proportions, 57
health, 121
health check, 109
health record, 109, 123
healthy (puppies), 95, 97
healthy environment, 107
healthy stock, 120
heart problems, 50
Heaven Hi's, [24], [41]
heavy-boned, 4
height, 26
height at shoulder, 9
hepatitis, 123
Herman Peabody, [69]
hernia, 111
high quality, 134
Highpoint, [76]
hindlegs, 9
hindquarters, 9, 10, 11, 20, 31
hip dysplasia, 46, 50
historic task, 3, 158, 165
historical function, 1, 2
hock joint/hocks, 9, 10, 11, 32, 33
hopping, 34
hopping puppy, 114
horizontal axis, 16
hospice, 2, 3, 4, 48
hospice ear, 33, 85
house train, 120
housebroken, 117
how big, 48
hurting each other, 104

ideal dog, 150
ill-natured, 7, 159, 162, 163
immunizations, 106
imposing, 162
impressive, 162
inadequate head, 154
inbreed/inbreeding, 125, 128, 129, 139
incisors, 63, 64
indiscriminate outcross, 139
infections, 102
informed decisions, 131
inoculated, 111
inoculations, 117, 123, 124
insanity, 43
intelligence, 5, 27, 116, 121, 165
intelligent, 25, 27, 163
intelligent expression, 7
interfering, 33

Japan Kennel Club, [85]
jawbone/jawbones, 64, 65
judge/judges, 150, 153, 164
judge's eye, 157
judge's job, 154, 158
judge's placements, 154
judge's purpose, 151
judging, 145, 159
judging assignment, 150
judging gone awry, 153

Keepsake, [5], [166]
Kennebank, [78]
kennel blind, 140
kennel blindness, 153
kennel cough, 123
kindly, 27
knowledgeable judges, 164
Koolandra, [144]

La Casa, [110], [112], [114], [166]
labor, 96
lachrymal glands, 8, 11, 27
lack of ethics, 153
lack of soundness, 154
lack of substance, 145
lack of virtue, 139
lack of virtues, 151
Laurence Powell, [75]
layback, 112
laying on of hands, 145
learning process, 138
legs, 20
length of stride, 33
length of the muzzle, 60
leptospirosis, 123
less experienced breeder, 138
lifelong commitment, 134
light-boned, 4
like beget like, 126
limited registration, 109
linebred, 130
linebreeding, 128, 139
lip/lips, 8, 29, 54, 64, 66, 67, 68
listlessness, 101
litter, 112
locomotion, 161
loin/loin section, 9, 11, 13, 19, 26, 30, 36, 112, 145
Lone Ranger, 102
long axis, 7, 11, 69, 70
long back, 10
longhaired, 10, 32, 118, 119, 127
Lontanpark, [158]
loose skin, 25
loose stools, 102
lot of lip, 68
love for your dogs, 138
Lovecraft's, [viii], [121]
lower leg, 9
lumbering, 33
Lynchcreek's, [6], [44], [97], [117], [143], [156]

making excuses, 43
mandibles, 64
man-made heads, 149
mantle/mantle coat, 9, 12, 33, 86
markings, 27, 32, 33, 62, 83, 84, 85, 86, 149
mask, 9, 12, 27, 32, 33, 83, 84
mass of muscle, 145
massive, 4, 25, 26, 31, 36, 145, 157, 160, 162
massive skull, 7
massiveness, 51, 142, 148, 161
mastitis, 101
mating, 139
mating of extremes, 140
mats, 118, 119
Matterhorn's, [74]
medical history, 123
medical record, 122
mediocre animals, 139
mediocre bitch, 141
mediocre dog, 154
membrana nictitans, 77
mental dog, 158
mental picture, 138
Mia, [147]
Mill Creek's, [25]
mismarked, 115
Mistihil, [45], [147]
moderate, 4, 9, 36, 168
moderate angulation, 146
moderately, 9, 22
moderately angulated, 36
moderation, 1, 5
molars, 63, 64
monks, 3
monk's cap, 33, 85
monocle mask, 84, 85
Mont Blanc's, [91]
morosity, 7
Morris', [29]
mountain rescue dog, 2, 3
Mountain Shadow's, [124]
mouth, 29, 63
movement, 35, 37, 113, 114, 150
moving close behind, 34
muschel, 12
muscle, 25, 32, 45, 113
muscle development, 145
muscle mass, 25
muscle tissue, 1
muscle tone, 157
muscular, 8, 9, 20, 30, 31, 159, 160
muzzle, 7, 11, 14, 17, 26, 28, 33, 54, 58, 60, 61, 62, 64, 65, 66, 70, 71, 74, 76, 84, 112
muzzle furrow, 59

nail clipping, 117
nape, 8, 12, 30, 33
National Specialty, x
National Specialty Show, 142
neck, 8, 30, 36
need to be touched, 106
neutered, 118, 119, 123
neutering, 117
never make excuses, 44
newborn puppies, 106
newly born, 98
nipple, 100
noncomplimentary types, 139
normal legs, 1
nose, 8, 29, 54, 62, 66
noseband, 9, 12
nostrils, 8
novice exhibitor, 153
nursing, 98, 99, 101, 104, 105
nursing surface, 105

obedience, [166]
obedience class, 107
obedience trials, 90
obvious faults, 139
obviously rectangular, 146
occiput, 7, 12, 69
OFA, 142
older years, 141
opportunities, 142
optimum, 5
optimum development, 116
original purpose, 2, 48
original task, 34
orphaned puppies, 100
Osage's, [65]
out at elbows, 10, 12
out at the elbows, 33
outcross, 125, 130
outcrossing, 139
overall beauty, 55
overall dog, 159
overall quality, 131, 155
overall silhouette, 150
overangulated, [2], 4, [88]
overreaching, 33
overshot, 7, 12, 30, 65, 112
owner/breeder, 120

paddling, 33
painted face, 84, 85
pale-colored, 115
parainfluenza, 123
parasites, 119
parvovirus, 123
pasterns, 12, 31, 113
pedigree, 122, 131, 139
pendulous, 15
pendulous flew, 47
people-oriented, 3
perfect dog, 140
permanent teeth, 63
persevere, 144
personality, 160, 162
pet quality, 119
pet shops, 119
phenotype, 128
physical character, 159
physical soundness, 116
pick of the litter, 115
picking puppies, 111
pictogram, 133
pig rail, 96
pink on lips, 68
pitfalls, 138
placenta, 96
plan a breeding, 140
planes, 29
point of shoulder, 31
poor proportions, 154
poor quality, 134
poor-moving, 154
postweaning stage, 103
potential, 116
pounding, 34
Powell's, [75]
powerful, 7, 9, 19, 25, 26, 28, 30, 31, 36, 37, 62, 69, 145, 159, 160, 161, 162
powerful build, 145
powerful head, 7, 160, 162
Prairieaire, [v]
premolars, 63, 64
prepotent sires or dams, 126
presentation skills, 151
press on, 144
principles, 138
progress in breeding, 155
proper breed type, 146
proper head, 145, 148
proper judgment, 151
proper proportion, 146
properly socialized, 95
proportionately tall, 7, 13, 25, [34], 35, 146, 159, 161, 162
proportions, 4, 26, 56, 112, 113
pseudo-experts, 138
puppies, 95, 97, 98, 101, 102, 104, 107, 111, 113, 115
puppies' environment, 99
puppies' nails, 105
puppies' stool, 103
puppy, 100, 102, 106, 114, 116, 117, 119, 124
puppy brokers, 119
puppy chow, 103
puppy formula, 100
puppy mills, 121
puppy play, 106

puppy producers, 108

quality, 119, 131, 138, 142, 163
quality of life, 120
quantity, 138

rabies shots, 106
reach and drive, 146, 165
realities of competition, 142
rear angulation, 31, 113
rear dewclaws, 32
rear legs, 31
rear pastern, 32
recessive, 127
recessive characteristics, 130
rectangular proportions, [89]
registration application, 122
registration form, 122
registration papers, 123, 163
reputable breeders, 121
rescue, 4
rescue dog, 5
Rescue's, [v]
rescuing people, 2
respect, 144
responsible breeder, 124
retaining virtues, 134
retarded development, 105
return policy, 121
Revilo's, [10], [54], [63], [147], [160]
rib cage, 30
ribs, 30, 36
rise to the skull, 59
rolling, 34
rolling gait, 33
Roman nose, 29
root of muzzle, 12
rough coat, 118
rump, 9, 12, 21

safe environment, 107
safe place, 107
Saint Bernard fanciers, 142
Saint Woods, [7]
saintly disposition, 167
saintly temperament, 142
sales agreement, 109, 122, 123
sales contract, 109
San Subira, [8]
Sanctuary Woods, [iv], [vi], [vii], [ix], [8], [26], [56], [69], [81], [86], [126], [132], 153, [157]
sanitary, 120
sanitary environment, 98
sanitation, 101
Santa Gertrudis cattle, 129
SBCA, [6]
scaling tools, 65
scapula, 18
schwamm, 8, 12
scissors/scissors bite, 7, 12, 29, 127
sculptured, 165
search-and-rescue, 90
Sebring's, [48]
second best, 142
selection, 129, 134, 139
selection criteria, 131
self-colored, 84, 85
self-feeding program, 104
self-imposed duty, 43
seller responsibilities, 121
serious, 163
serious breeder, 131
serious faults, 139
Serpentina, [38]
Shagg Bark, [42], [46], [60]
shaggy, 10, 32
shallow furrow, 62
sharply cut (flews), 15, 66, 67
sheep's head, 33, 85
short coupled, 146
short legs, 4
short neck, 145
shortcomings, 167
short-coupled, 36, 168
shorthaired, 7, 9, 10, 32, 118, 119, 127
short-legged, 13
shoulder blade, 31, 112
shoulders, 9, 18, 31
show animal, 111
show dogs, 115
show quality, 110, 115, 119
showmanship, 151, 165
shyness, 39, 40, 146
sick (puppy), 98
sickle hocks, 37, 113
side gait, 33, 165
Siegfried's, [8]
signs of a bad home, 108
single people, 108
single tracking, 33
sire, 120
size, 1, 4, 5, 25, 48, 49, 50, 51, 52, 54
size and substance, 154
skin, 45, 47, 113
skin problems, 119
skull, 7, 26, 28, 54, 57, 58, 69, 70, 71, 72, 76, 112
Skycroft, [9]
Skycroft's, [168]
Slaton's, [27], [73], [164]
slightly broken, 61
slightly overhanging, 66, 68
slipped mask, 33, 84, 85
slope, 7, 12, 16
sloping, 36
small deviations, 146
small teeth, 65
small-bucket judge, 154, 155
smooth coat, 118
snow, 4
snow trial, 2, [3], [92]
Snowsage, [88]
socialization, 103, 106, 107, 116, 124
socialized, 117
soft tissue, 161
solid foods, 102, 103
sound, 167
sound body, 145, 146, 165
sound dogs, 142
sound mind, 145, 146, 165
soundness, 25, 35, 121, 142, 152, 154, 157, 160
soundness of mind, 25
splash coat, 33, 86
splash-coated, 9, 12
stages of development, 102
standard, 24, 25, 35, 37
Starlight, [85]
static balance, 146
status symbol, 109
staying dry, 99
staying warm, 98, 99
steep terrain, 4
step-on puppy, 101
stern, 7, 162, 163
sternum, 30
stifle, 36
Stiniyasu, [80], [144]
Stoan/Stoan's, vii, x, [3], [6], [36], [40], [49], [53], [55], [72], [86], [88], [89], [103], [132], [133], [147], [148], [152], [163]
stockhaarig, 12
stomach torsion, 46
stop, 12, 57, 73
stoplight chart, 131, 135
strength, 4, 25, 160
stride length, 36
strong, 9, 30, 145, 159, 160
strong and muscular, 7
strong back, 165
stud dog, 133, 140, 141
Stud Dog of the Year, [156]
style, 152
style of judging, 155
substance, 1, 25, 26, 47, 112
substantial, 145
successful breeder, 125, 138
supplement, 102
supplemental feeding, 99
supra-orbital, 7, 12, 16, 69, 70, 71, 72, 73, 76
swayback, 10, 12
Sweden, [160], [161], [162]
Sweetholm's, [55], [77]
Swissong's, [51]

swollen belly, 102
swollen limbs, 102

tail, 9, 11, 31, 32
tail position, 79
talking to puppies, 106
tall proportions, 146
Tasmania, [46], [66], [114]
teat, 101
teeth, 7, 30, 63, 65, 102
temperament, 3, 34, 39, 40, 41, 43, 44, 116, 121, 157, 160, 162, 165
temperature, 96
tender, 12
test breeding, 142
testicles, 111
Therapy Dog, [38]
third eyelid, 77
three varieties, 164, 168
ticking, 85
too long back, 4
too much, 1
toothbrushes, 65
top line, 30
torn mantle, 12, 33, 86
total dog, 154, 155, 157, 158
total dog judge, 155
tooth cleaning, 117
touch test, 145
toxic material, 103
toys, 105
training, 116
Tremel, [46]
true beauty, 1
trustworthy, 34
tube feeding, 99, 100
Twin Oaks, [2], [35]
type, 5, 25, 54, 65, 152

umbilical cord, 96, 100, 102
unbalanced, 154
underangulated, 4
undershot (bite), 7, 12, 29, 30, 65, 112, 127
uniformity, 130, 153
uniqueness of the head, 160, 162
unpleasant odor, 119
unsanitary conditions, 100
unsound dogs, 142
unsuccessful breeders, 138
untrue to type, 140
upper arm, 9, 31, 112
upper thigh, 32, 113
useless bulk, 4

Valinta, [49]
van Rijn, [34]
Vanity's, [vi]
vicious, 43
viciousness, 40
virtue/virtues, 87, 130, 139, 153, 155, 158
von Mallen, [149]

warning signs, 101
wavy, 10
weak (puppy), 99
weak pasterns, 10, 103, 113
weaned, 101, 102, 103
weaving, 34
weighing schedule, 98
weight pull, [72], [91], [167]
Weight Puller Superior, [48]
weight pulling, [36], 90
welfare of the breed, 138
well angulated, 4
well muscled, 1
wet dog/wet dogs, 25, 45, 46, 165
wetness, 142, 145
whelping, 95, 99, 100
whelping box, 95, 96, 100
whelping problems, 141
when the best dog wins, 155
white face, 33, 84, 85
whole dog, 158
whole dog concept, 156
wide chest, 4
width of muzzle, 59, 61
wild outcrossing, 130
winging, 33
winning, 168
withers, 9, 12, 19, 30
Working Dog, [4]
Working Dog Champion, [36]
worm control, 105
worm treatment, 124
wormed, 111
worming, 105, 109
worms, 123
wrinkles, 7, 27, 47, 79
written instructions, 109
wrong motives, 108
wry mouth, 12, 156

X-ray, 142

zygomatic arch, 76

Your Comments are Invited

If you enjoyed *Saint Bernards from the Stoan Perspective* or found it especially helpful, we want to hear from you. If you would like to comment on any aspect of the book, write:

Editorial Office
Alpine Publications, Inc.
225 S. Madison Avenue
Loveland, Colorado 80537

For a Free Catalog

or for information on other Alpine Blue Ribbon titles, please write to our Customer Service Department, P. O. Box 7027, Loveland, CO 80537, or call toll free 1-800-777-7257.

We invite you to visit our web site at ***www.alpinepub.com*** for new releases, special offers, breeder referral program information, contests, and more.

Additional Titles of Interest:

How to Raise a Puppy You Can Live With
Clarice Rutherford and David H. Neil, MRCVS
A "must" for every breeder, as well as for new puppy owners, this highly recommended book covers puppy development and socialization from birth to one year of age. First, the breeder's responsibility; then the new owner's part in shaping a dog that's a joy to live with.

Your Saint Bernard
Marian J. Sharp
Now a collector's item, this small book published in 1978 by Denlinger's Publishing contains a history of the breed and the SBCA, information for pet owners, and photos of early Saint Bernards.

Canine Reproduction: The Breeder's Guide
Phyllis A. Holst, DVM
The most thorough, most accurate, and most widely recommended handbook on breeding and whelping available for serious dog breeders. The author is a well-known breeder/exhibitor, researcher and veterinarian.

Owner's Guide to Better Behavior in Dogs
William E. Campbell
Understanding your dog goes a long way toward preventing behavioral problems; knowing how to communicate effectively with your pet is a major requirement for correcting behavior. This book tells you how to do both, and a whole lot more with kind, logical, easy-to-use methods.